Bata

Bata

SHOEMAKER TO THE WORLD

THOMAS J. BATA
WITH SONJA SINCLAIR

Stoddart

Published by
Stoddart Publishing Co. Limited
34 Lesmill Road
Toronto, Canada
M3B 2T6

CANADIAN CATALOGUING IN PUBLICATION DATA

Bata, Thomas J. (Thomas John), 1914–
    Bata

ISBN 0-7737-2416-8

1. Bata, Thomas J. (Thomas John), 1914–
2. Bata Industries Ltd.   3. Shoe industry – Biography.   4. Czechs – Canada – Biography.   I. Sinclair, Sonja.   II. Title.

HD9787.C32B38 1990   338.7'68531'0092   C90-094402-1

Typesetting: Tony Gordon Ltd.
Printed in Canada

To my children, Tom, Christine,
Monica and Rosemarie,
and their children

CONTENTS

P R E F A C E

An autobiography is, by definition, a subjective piece of writing. It is based on the author's own recollections of events, his feelings or opinions. In the process, one risks creating the impression that one's own life was somehow distinct from the lives of others, that it occupied center stage in a drama with few if any supporting actors.

That, of course, isn't true, certainly not in my case. I am by nature a gregarious guy. I love being with people from all walks of life, and though I was my parents' only child, I was seldom alone. All my life I have been surrounded by friends, fellow workers, colleagues, customers and members of my family.

It is impossible, in a book such as this, to enumerate all the individuals who have stood by me and who, in many instances, have initiated or created the projects for which I appear to take credit. As chief executive of a global enterprise, I may have appeared to be making decisions on my own. In fact, those decisions were invariably the product of consultations with advisers and associates whose views often prevailed over my own.

Almost every time I say "I," I should by rights be saying "we," and I hereby beg the forgiveness of hundreds of wonderful people whose input hasn't been sufficiently emphasized or whose names, somehow, haven't found their way into these memoirs. They are the people who have enabled me to live a happy, exciting, productive life. Without their friendship, loyalty, enthusiasm and guidance, there would have been nothing to write about.

THE LEGACY

It was like a beautiful dream. There I stood on a balcony over-looking the town square of Zlin, the hometown I had left almost fifty years ago in anticipation of the Nazi invasion. After the war, ever since the Communists seized power in Czechoslovakia, my family had been reviled as unrepentant capitalists, our assets confiscated, my father's memory besmirched. Yet on this drizzly December afternoon in 1989, every inch of the square was packed with thousands of people, seemingly oblivious to the cold, out to welcome me and my wife. There were flags everywhere, along with pictures of my father, the late founder of the Bata shoe organization. "Right on, right on," they responded as I told them how much the world admired their heroic fight for democracy. I managed to say a few more words. "Long live Bata," they chanted. "Give us back our chief."

In my seventy-five years I have been greeted by many people, ranging from factory workers to heads of state. But there had never been anything to compare with this particular welcome. It was an experience I shall never forget, all the more so since I know that, in the eyes of those people, I wasn't so much a person as a symbol. Many of them probably didn't know and, if they knew, didn't care that I was the chairman of a global shoe manufacturing and retailing organization that employs 70,000 people in seventy-three countries. Their cheers were for the embodiment of a proud tradition that decades of Communist rule had failed to eradicate, for a return to the innovative spirit and the search for excellence that had been the hallmark of Zlin in days gone by.

For anyone not familiar with pre-World War II Czechoslovakia, it may be difficult or impossible to appreciate not only the economic importance of the Bata shoe organization, but its psychological impact on a young country still struggling for recognition as a model democracy. At the time of my father's death in 1932, the business he had founded on a shoestring around the turn of the century was annually producing thirty-six million pairs of shoes and exporting a third of them to countries throughout Europe, North America and Asia. To the people of Czechoslovakia, Bata was proof that they could take on the world and win. The growth of the enterprise had transformed Zlin from little more than a hamlet at the turn of the century into an industrial center renowned all over the world for its productivity, its standard of living and the quality of its work force. It had become, said the *New York Times*, "the Detroit of Czechoslovakia." At the time, that was a compliment.

Two reasons for the organization's success were its pricing policy and its emphasis on customer service. Thanks to advanced technology and mass production methods, Bata shoes were so inexpensive that even the poorest of the world's people could afford to buy them. In spite of the ravages of the Great Depression, Czechoslovaks were buying in the 1930s an average of three and a half pairs of shoes a year, thereby displacing Americans as the best shod nation in the world. At the same time, millions of Bata shoes sold on export markets were providing Czechoslovakia with a valuable source of foreign exchange.

But to me, the most remarkable attribute of the organization was the spirit of its employees, the real pride they took in being part of a modern success story. Most of them were sons and daughters of nearby farmers or artisans, young people who, having emerged from the public school system with only the most basic education, would in the normal course of events have ended up in low-paying humdrum jobs. At the Bata School of Young Men and, later, Women, students spent three years working in the factory on weekdays and attending classes at night and on Saturdays in subjects such as science, technology, mathematics and design. They were paid like full-time workers, and an important part of their schooling consisted of practical economics in areas such as budgeting and management of their own money.

It was a tough grind and quite a few of the students fell by the wayside. But those who persevered emerged from the school not only with a good education, but also with fairly substantial savings. Most of them advanced quickly to positions of responsibility within the organization. They were the pioneers, many of whom went to India, Indonesia or Latin America. They became managers in their early twenties and, in many cases, ended up as regional coordinators with responsibility for dozens of factories, hundreds of stores and thousands of employees.

Critics claimed that the school system imposed a quasi-military discipline on the students, that it invaded their privacy and deprived them of freedom of action. No doubt in the latter part of the twentieth century, some of the regime's aspects would be unacceptable to the "me" generation. But in its time, and considering that the recruits were young teenagers transplanted from farms and small villages into a fast-growing industrial environment, tight discipline wasn't inappropriate. In any case, the students themselves didn't seem to object. Though the schools' annual intake grew to 1,000 a year, thousands of applicants had to be turned away for lack of space. As far back as I can remember, being a "Bataman" was a badge of distinction, proof that a person had what it took to belong to the most demanding, most dynamic enterprise in the country. But, then, I wasn't around during the early days when Zlin was a tiny dot on the map and Father's fledgling shoe business was teetering on the verge of extinction.

He was an apprentice in his father's shoemaking workshop when, at age eighteen, he persuaded his elder brother and sister to take the modest amount of money bequeathed to them by their mother, the equivalent of about $350, and launch with him a business of their own. Within less than a year their capital was gone and they were deep in debt. Bankruptcy seemed inevitable, but Father, who had emerged as the dominant member of the trio, refused to give in. With sheer willpower and round-the-clock work, he weathered the storm. Six years later he was employing 120 people, a considerable achievement for a village boy with virtually no formal education and nothing but his wits to rely on.

But he knew all along that there had to be a better way of making shoes than by the primitive, mostly manual methods that prevailed in Zlin and, indeed, in most of Europe. In 1904 he crossed the Atlantic and spent six months working on the assembly line in a New England shoe factory, where he learned firsthand what American machinery and management techniques could do to modernize shoemaking. Back in Zlin he began implementing what he had learned and, in the process, laying the groundwork for an organizational culture that was, in most respects, way ahead of its time.

Unheard of concepts such as profit sharing, an internal communications network and autonomous profit centers were in place in Zlin by the end of the 1920s. So was a five-day work week, introduced so that employees could attend classes or study on Saturdays. Wages were among the highest in the country, and employees earned ten percent on that part of their profit-sharing bonus that they deposited with the company. At a time when social benefits, let alone a home of their own, were, for most industrial workers, an impossible dream, Bata employees lived in low-rent modern houses, had free access to medical care, shopped in low-cost grocery stores and competed in company-owned sports facilities. At a time when commercial airlines were in their infancy, the Bata organization had a fleet of aircraft that reduced to a minimum the time managers spent traveling between various parts of the fast-growing enterprise.

While the vertically integrated organization manufactured everything from shoe boxes to machinery to building supplies, every department had to compete for business with outside suppliers. The son of a textile manufacturer recalls visiting Zlin to negotiate a sale of high-quality sewing yarn — an important item in an enterprise that produced tens of millions of shoes a year. After quoting a price, the visitor watched the Bata executive on the far side of the desk pick up the telephone and dial the appropriate department. "How much would you charge for the yarn?" he asked. The young man waited with bated breath, convinced that he was about to lose the sale. "I have a supplier in my office who is prepared to let us have it for less," he finally heard the man across the desk say, and they shook hands on the deal.

On the other hand, suppliers who didn't play fair got short shrift with Bata. Shortly after World War I, fire destroyed a warehouse full of raw materials that were, at that time, irreplaceable. When the insurance company tried to settle the claim with worthless prewar Austrian currency, Father was so incensed that he canceled the policy and went, for a number of years, without insurance. Eventually it occurred to him that he could have the best of both worlds by founding an insurance company of his own, which is exactly what he did.

Being the only son of a legendary father can be a mixed blessing.

On the minus side there is an enormous weight of expectations, along with a sometimes frustrating struggle to acquire one's own identity, away from the parent's shadow. When the son is successful, he is perceived as a chip off the old block; when he makes a mistake, he has failed to measure up to the father's standards. Fortunately, in my case, these liabilities have always been far outweighed by pride in my father's accomplishments and by my determination to enhance, to the best of my ability, the tradition he created.

In line with that tradition I have tried to roll with the punches and to embrace change as a challenge rather than a disaster. The postwar decolonization of Africa is a case in point. Unlike many Europeans who pulled up stakes and headed for home, my associates and I believed that the Bata Shoe Company should do business in newly independent countries, whether the people in power happened to be white, black or yellow; and with few exceptions, events have proved us right. I have never pretended that my prime motive was to "do good," to help the underprivileged of the world. I consider myself a businessman, not a philanthropist. Yet few things have given me more satisfaction than seeing hopelessly poor, unskilled individuals transformed into successful managers or independent entrepreneurs, and knowing that the Bata organization could claim part of the credit.

On the other side of the ledger, I have had to come to terms with many traumatic events: the subjugation of my homeland first by Nazi Germany and then by a Communist regime, the loss by expropriation of everything Father had created in Czechoslovakia and other "socialist" countries, the injustice and humiliation inflicted on some of our most loyal employees, a painful family rift, the political and economic roller coaster the organization has ridden in various parts of the world. Adjusting to these changes wasn't easy. But adjust we did, which is one of the reasons why the enterprise that my son heads today is vastly different from the one my father left behind in 1932.

Instead of being based in Czechoslovakia, it has its headquarters in Canada. Rather than being highly centralized, it is a commonwealth of semiautonomous units. Rather than exclusively selling footwear produced in Bata factories, it offers consumers a vast choice of brands. Yet, in many important respects, our organizational culture, what has come to be known as the Bata system of management, hasn't changed. We still believe that the customer is king, that service to the community is the essence of private enterprise, that talent has nothing to do with color of skin.

Which goes to show that there is at least some truth to the saying that "the more things change, the more they remain the same." One of the most difficult challenges faced by chief executives is knowing when and how to respond to genuine changes in the business environment while ignoring fads that are temporary and therefore inconsequential. My life story is essentially an account of how I tried to face that challenge.

1

GROOMING AN HEIR APPARENT

W HEN I WAS FOUR YEARS OLD, my parents gave me a miniature shoemaker's bench for Christmas. It was a perfect replica of the real thing: a table with compartments for nails, tacks and other shoemaking paraphernalia, along with a little stool for me to sit on and a leather strap that helped shoemakers hold the shoes they were working on between their knees. In the past, I am told, the strap also served as a tool for administering punishment to the backsides of recalcitrant apprentices.

Surprising though it may appear, I was thrilled with my present. Most little boys, it seems, plan to become firemen or railroad engineers or astronauts. But during my childhood — I was born on September 17, 1914, a month after the outbreak of World War I — astronauts were still the stuff of science fiction. As for other career options, I don't recall a time when I considered becoming anything other than a shoemaker. It wasn't just that the Batas had been in the shoemaking business for nine generations or that, in Europe, it was considered a matter of course that a son, particularly an only son, would follow in his father's footsteps. More than that it was my father's energy, his enthusiasm, his sense of mission that made me look up to him as a role model. Throughout my childhood and adolescence, my main ambition was to live up to his standards and to grow up to be like him.

He was a tough, no-nonsense type of person, the product of a lifetime of struggles against odds that a lesser man might have found overwhelming. Having lost his beloved mother at the age of nine and his brother in his early twenties, he had guided his fledgling enterprise through World War I, the disintegration of the Austro-Hungarian Empire and a postwar economic crisis that brought many businesses to their knees. But, as Father used to say, "Fighting is the essence of life. If you don't fight, you can't win." Once, when I was a schoolboy, I became involved in a battle royal with my cousin Fred Mencik. He was smaller than I and, when he found he was losing, he resorted to biting and hair pulling. I screamed murder, but Father said, "A fight's a fight," and refused to intervene.

The winter when I got my shoemaker's bench we took off on a family holiday in an Austrian resort called Semmering. In 1918 skiing was yet to become a popular winter sport, but I had a great time sleigh riding with my father until he developed a violent pain in his leg. At first he thought he had strained a muscle, but back home the doctors diagnosed his condition as phlebitis. In those days that was an extremely serious verdict; indeed the odds for his survival were considered no better than fifty-fifty. Even at the age of four, I was aware of the danger and I was terrified that he might die.

For a man with Father's temperament, being bedridden for weeks on end was an excruciating experience. At one point during his illness he summoned to his bedside a prominent medical specialist, who proceeded to assure him, with a soothing tone of voice and his best bedside manner, not to worry, that everything was going to be all right. "Now listen to me, Professor," Father said, "I asked you to come because I wanted your professional opinion about my blood clot. Had I been looking for someone to comfort me, I would have asked for a priest." The professor wasn't pleased.

It was one of many occasions when Mother felt compelled to step in and smooth ruffled feathers. Unlike Father, she was a tremendously gentle, compassionate person, fondly remembered by some of the old-timers for turning up late at night in the factory during some crisis, feeding everybody lemonade and sandwiches and telling Father that it was time to let people go home.

As the daughter of the custodian of the emperor's library in Vienna, Mother had been brought up in a manner considered suitable for young ladies in the pre-World War I capital of the Austro-Hungarian Empire. She spoke several languages, was well read and played the piano, in addition to being an accomplished homemaker. I understand that, at the time of my parents' court-ship, Mother's socially prominent Czech family was considered a cut or two above the upstart Batas, and that her parents made extensive inquiries about my father's background and morals before consenting to the match.

After her marriage in 1912, Mother worked briefly in the factory in order to find out what shoemaking was all about; but from the outset, she was more interested in the welfare of the employees than in the ins and outs of manufacturing. When medical problems following my birth prevented her from having further children, she made up for her disappointment by virtually adopting the work force as her extended family. Mother loved people, regardless of their station in life, and they in turn loved her. She always knew who'd had a baby or whose child was down with whooping cough, and people came to her for all sorts of personal advice. Nowadays that sort of thing would be frowned upon as paternalism. But at a time when there was no Medicare or government-sponsored welfare services, she performed a vital role in the community.

At home Mother's favorite pastime was cooking. Though she always had household help, she spent a great deal of time in the kitchen, supervising the preparation of meals. Most of her Viennese recipes were delicious but rich, and since she kept making sure everything tasted right, she soon put on a lot of weight. I never knew her as the slim, blue-eyed beauty my father married, nor did I care about her corpulence. Indeed, I suspect that I inherited her love of good food, though, fortunately, not her weight problem.

My early childhood differed from that of other little boys only insofar as I saw less of my parents. Father left home every morning in time to punch the clock at the factory a few minutes before seven. One of the self-imposed precepts by which he lived was that bosses should abide by the same rules as subordinates. Since workers had to be at the factory at seven, so did the managers. There were no exceptions. The same rule applied to smoking. In many parts of the factory, particularly where gasoline was being used to soften rubber, there was an acute danger of fire, so smoking was, of course, strictly forbidden. Accordingly Father decreed that since some workers weren't allowed to smoke, nobody would smoke.

In the evening Father was seldom home before my bedtime. Besides, he and Mother did a fair bit of traveling, so that I was frequently left in the care of a governess, a young woman called Miss Aida. Fortunately I liked her, and while I looked forward eagerly to my parents' return, I don't recall ever feeling deprived because of their absence. Since one of Miss Aida's responsibilities was to teach me German, that was the only language she spoke to me. This total immersion method was so effective that I soon spoke German as well as my native Czech, at which point she switched to English and never uttered another word in German. The result was that by the time I started school, I spoke three languages. With the benefit of hindsight, I'd say that my parents couldn't have done me a greater favor.

Though both my parents came from large families, we didn't see much of our assorted relatives. Of my four grandparents, the only one still alive when I was born was my maternal grandmother, an impressive-looking lady whom Mother and I visited from time to time in Vienna until she died shortly after World War I. Of all my cousins on Mother's side of the family, the only one I knew at all well was Fred, the son of the youngest of my mother's three brothers. But the Menciks lived in Trebic, a Moravian district capital some 150 kilometers from Zlin, and, given the state of country roads, Fred and I didn't see each other more than three or four times a year.

On the paternal side of the family, Grandfather Bata was, by all accounts, an imaginative but mercurial character whose modest shoemaking business went through repeated ups and downs. One day, while minding his stall at the marketplace and waiting in vain for customers, he was taunted by his fellow cobblers about his grandiose ideas that never seemed to materialize. Clearly irritated, he pointed to the tall chimneys of the local sugar refinery. "I may not be a successful businessman," he conceded, "but one of these days my sons will have a factory with a chimney just as high as the ones over there." In later years my father, who was an apprentice at the time, used to recall how mortified he was by this seemingly preposterous boast.

Widowed twice and married three times, Grandfather Bata ended up presiding over a brood of twelve offspring, including several by his wives' previous marriages. It was a complicated and not exactly close-knit household. My father, the youngest of three children born to my grandfather by his second wife, lost his brother Antonin to tuberculosis long before I was born. His sister Anna was married to the manager of an aristocrat's estate not far from Zlin, and we visited back and forth occasionally. But their children were quite a bit older than I and we didn't seem to have much in common. Among the offspring of the third marriage, the most impressive was Uncle Jan, who, in appearance, bore a striking resemblance to my father. Jan's wife was the daughter of our family physician, Dr. Gerbec, and the sister of my closest friend, so that was the branch of the family to which I felt closest.

Our house in Zlin was substantial, though far from palatial. Topped by a roof turret, its most distinctive features were two pergolas that jutted out from the ground floor into the large garden. The furnishings were traditional, with lots of wood paneling in the living and dining rooms and in my father's ground-floor study. A grand piano in the living room served mainly decorative purposes. Though my parents had wanted me to take piano lessons, I refused on the grounds that piano playing was a girlish pastime — a misconception I have regretted ever since.

My formal education began at the age of six. It took me fifteen minutes to walk along a dusty road to the primary school in Zlin and, except in the winter, I went barefoot. I guess my parents weren't overly happy whenever I came home with a bloody toe, but all the other boys went barefoot and there was no way I was going to be different. Actually, I don't believe children at that age are aware of social distinctions, though the thirty-five of us certainly came from vastly different home environments. One of my classmates lived with his parents and half a dozen brothers and sisters, plus an unspecified number of dogs and goats, in a one-room house in the woods. At the opposite end of the economic scale was the son of the railroad station superintendent, whose house was roughly the same size as ours. Most of the other boys were the sons of local tradesmen, shopkeepers and factory workers. After school some of them usually joined me in our garden to play cowboys and Indians or cops and robbers. When we got a little older, we switched to soccer, which, like most outdoor sports, appealed to me tremendously. From my earliest childhood I have enjoyed any activity that involves speed and competition, be it soccer, hockey, skiing, flying or car racing. Golf, as far as I am concerned, is too slow and time-consuming.

Most of our weekends were spent at our country home in Loucka (literally "little meadow"), formerly the estate of a minor Austrian squire about half an hour's drive from Zlin. In addition to a glorified farmhouse, the estate included fields and forests as well as a farmyard populated with chickens, cattle and pigs. During those weekends, I often accompanied my father on long walks through the countryside. There was never any idle chitchat: all our conversations had to have a purpose, preferably some educational content. One day, while walking through the woods, Father stopped and said, "What do you think the cubic content of this tree is?" I proceeded to apply the mathematical formulae I had learned at school, but it took me several minutes to come up with an answer. "That's correct," he said, "but I could have given you an approximate figure in thirty seconds." All I had to do, he explained, was take the square of the diameter at the bottom of the tree, reduce it by twenty percent (because the trunk was round rather than square) and multiply the result by half the height of the tree. While the result wouldn't be perfectly accurate, it would be good enough for most practical purposes. The object of the exercise was to teach me how to differentiate between issues where it is essential to have accurate information and those where a reasonable estimate will do. It's a lesson that has served me well in later years.

Saturday night in Loucka, we invariably sat by the fireplace and listened to my mother read some of our favorite books, mostly adventure stories set in faraway countries. One thing my parents didn't do was play with me. I can't recall either of them helping me run an electric train or unlocking the mysteries of a chemistry set, and I suspect I would have felt embarrassed had they attempted to do so. The American concept of parents as chums or playmates was totally foreign to our Central European variety of family life. I loved my parents for what they were — affectionate and generous, but strict and uncompromising when it came to doing one's duty or telling the truth.

Once, during my early school years, I took advantage of the lunch hour to call on the doctor about a painful rash on my right hand. The doctor was out, but his daughter administered some ointment and covered it up with a large bandage. The class that afternoon was art, which wasn't my favorite subject, and since I had no trouble convincing myself that I couldn't draw with my bandaged hand, I decided to skip school. My absence was duly reported to my parents, and the following morning at breakfast-time they demanded to know where I had been and why. Apparently my explanation was less than convincing. "Had you shown your hand to the teacher," Father said, "you probably would have been sent home, but it was your duty to turn up at school." Whereupon he went to the cupboard and extracted from it a feather duster attached to a bamboo cane. With a penknife he cut off the feathers, after which he put me over his knee and administered a number of rather painful whacks.

To the best of my recollection that was the only time I ever got a caning, and I knew I deserved it. By searching my conscience hard enough, I had to admit to myself that I might have been able to draw, bandage and all. But by way of compensation the incident turned me temporarily into the center of attention at school. In an apparent attempt to discourage other would-be truants, the teacher that morning informed the class that he understood adequate disciplinary measure had been taken. At break time my classmates clustered around me and insisted on examining my backside to see how it had responded to the ordeal.

Though both of my parents were Roman Catholics, they weren't regular churchgoers, and my own exposure to the scriptures was considerably less focused than the rest of my education. The public school curriculum included two hours a week of religious instruction, and one year, much to my delight, the priest recruited me to serve as altar boy in our church. In a small town like Zlin there were no organized after-school activities for children, so this was a welcome change. My duties, such as waving the censer during mass, were far from onerous. The part I enjoyed most was ringing the church bells at five o'clock every afternoon. That meant climbing up the church steeple, grabbing the rope attached to one of the three bells and swinging back and forth with it. That I thought was great fun.

In planning my education and upbringing, my parents were agreed on a number of fundamental principles. First, since I was an only child and the son of the number one employer in town, a special effort would have to be made to ensure that I was neither spoiled nor conceited. Even in my early childhood I was expected to keep my room tidy, perform minor household chores and keep track of the way I spent my modest pocket money. While I never had any doubt that my future career lay within my father's company, I also understood that I would have to prove myself in order to qualify for a responsible position, let alone as heir apparent. "I have a thousand sons," my father wrote in a widely quoted magazine article, "though only one of them bears my name; and the best one of them all will inherit my violin." It was a clear warning that there was to be nothing automatic about the succession.

My parents' second objective was that I should develop a sense of self-reliance and responsibility. At the age of six, while driving with my parents in an open convertible to Brno, the Moravian capital, I failed to hold on to my hat, in the true sense of the term. Twice it blew off, and each time my father ordered the chauffeur to stop the car so that I could retrieve the hat. But the second time he warned me that I'd better not let the same thing happen again. When it did, Father gave me forty Czech crowns (about $1.20) and suggested that I walk to the nearest railroad station and catch a train back to Zlin. I could see Mother wasn't in complete agreement with this disciplinary measure, but she didn't protest. Personally I didn't mind. It was a beautiful summer day, kidnapping or any other violent crime was nonexistent in rural Moravia and I had perfect confidence in my ability to make my way home. Walking in the direction of the station, I met a couple of fellows who asked me what I was up to. When I explained my predicament, they pointed out that my parents' car would have to come back eventually along the same road: why not walk to meet it instead of taking my chances on a train? I followed their advice, and when the car did return, my father was so pleased with my sense of initiative that he allowed me to keep the train fare.

Finally my parents were determined that I should be exposed at an early age to foreign cultures and languages. Since, by the time I was eight, I had forgotten most of the German and English that Miss Aida had taught me, they decided I should spend my holidays at a summer school on the Frisian Islands off the North Sea coast of Germany. This was to all intents and purposes my first exposure to girls, and while I thought that, on the whole, they were a nuisance, I did enjoy tugging at the long, hefty pigtails that hung from the heads of the little German Fräuleins. A slight problem arose when the time came for me to return home. My mother had deposited me at the school, but, as part of my training in emancipation, Father decreed that I'd have to make my own

way back. All summer long I had insisted to the school propri-
etress that I was nine years old because nine-year-olds were
allowed to stay up an extra hour in the evening. But when I learned
that children under the age of nine could travel in Germany at
half fare, I announced that I was really only eight. Frau Busch gave
me a murderous look, but I stuck to my guns. Fortunately, by the
end of the summer, my German was reasonably fluent, because
my journey was far from simple. I had to take a boat to the
mainland and a train to Leipzig, transfer to a train that took me
as far as Dresden and transfer again to go to Prague, where I
caught a train to Zlin. I was home in time for my ninth birthday.

As a further step in my linguistic training and, I suspect, as an
antidote to the only-child syndrome, I was enrolled at age eleven
in an English prep school called the Golden Parsonage, on the
outskirts of London. The school consisted of a brick country
house, presumably a parsonage in days gone by, where we slept in
dormitories and had our meals. Attached to this building were five
corrugated iron structures that served as classrooms. While the
classrooms were equipped with kerosene heaters, no such luxury
was available in the dormitories. In the morning we washed with
cold water poured into washstands, though hot water was available
at night for our baths. These ablutions were supervised by a
formidable matron with a scrub brush, which she applied with
vigor to any part of our anatomy that, in her opinion, hadn't
received sufficient attention.

The school was run by two retired Royal Flying Corps officers,
both veterans of World War I. Under their leadership students
were divided into three teams that competed with one another for
special treats awarded on the basis of scholastic achievement and
good behavior. A team earned a plus if a boy had done all his
homework ("prep") or solved a math problem; talking in class or
spilling milk at mealtime would be penalized with a minus. Every

two weeks the pluses and minuses were added up and the winning team earned some special honor such as heading the procession in church. To me it was a lasting lesson in the power of group incentives and rewards.

According to the rules, every boy had to hand over all his cash to the matron at the beginning of each term and use a specially designed checkbook to withdraw funds for sweets or other "tuck" purchases. The only catch was that you were expected to keep accounts and show exactly how much you had paid for what. This was a field in which I was a star pupil because, ever since my earliest childhood, I had had to account for the way I spent my few cents of pocket money. Years later in Canada I tried to inculcate the same practice in my own children, with middling success.

Once again my mother accompanied me on my first trip to England, but when the time came to spend holidays at home, or to return to England at the end of my holidays, I traveled alone across Germany, across the English Channel and by train to school. At the end of the first four-week Christmas holidays, Father made up a budget, including the school fees and all my travel expenses, for the two years I was going to be at school in England. Then he opened a credit account at the London branch of the Guaranty Trust Company of New York and told me what to do once I got back to London.

In true British fashion the accountant at Guaranty Trust pretended there was nothing unusual about an eleven-year-old demanding money and a checkbook. He listened politely to my request and gave me what I had asked for, upon which I went to the headmaster of my school and wrote out a check for the following term's fees. The "old" gentleman (he must have been all of thirty-five) was clearly taken aback, to the extent where he wrote to my father and suggested that his concept of independence training might be going a little too far. Apparently he was concerned that, since I was paying my own school fees, I might feel entitled to special privileges. Of course, it never entered my mind that transmitting my father's money would in any way affect my status as a pupil. Indeed, had any such thought occurred to me, I have no doubt Father would have driven it out with a good paddling. Though corporal punishment was administered in our family only on rare occasions, this certainly would have been one of them.

What with holidays at Christmas and Easter as well as in the summer, I became a pretty experienced traveler during my school years in England. Each time I went home or back to school my ticket consisted of a book of coupons for the various legs of the journey, and at each stage the conductor would tear out the appropriate coupon. Ever conscious of opportunities to teach me a practical lesson, Father suggested that, instead of getting the whole package, and presumably letting a travel agent make a profit, I might save money by buying the individual tickets as I went along. That turned out to be easier said than done. Sometimes the train stopped for only two or three minutes at the place where the previous segment ended and the new one began; sometimes it was the middle of the night; and, of course, I had to make sure I always had the appropriate currency. I never splurged on a sleeping car or on dining-car meals, though my budget was generous enough to allow for such luxuries. The understanding was that any money I saved was my own, and I took full advantage of this aspect of the deal. It wasn't that I had any particular need for the money; to the best of my recollection most of it ended up in my savings account. I guess I looked upon the whole exercise as just another competitive sport, a way of proving to myself and to my parents how well I could manage my financial resources.

Naturally enough I was homesick during my first few days at

school — I believe I even shed a few tears — and leaving home at the end of my holidays or saying goodbye to my mother after her occasional visits was always an emotional wrench. But, on balance, my years in England were a thoroughly happy experience. I loved the school's competitive atmosphere, its team spirit and its emphasis on sports. Though I was the only foreigner among some fifty boys, they never made me feel like an outsider. In that particular school, being called by a nickname was tantamount to a badge of approval, and when the boys christened me "Czecho," I knew I had been accepted as one of the gang.

After a year at home, I was off once more, this time to a French boarding school in Switzerland. The 150 students in Lausanne represented some thirty nationalities from all over the world, and though French was the compulsory language of communication in class and in the dining room, the place was like a Tower of Babel at all other times. So, while the school helped me to develop an appreciation for different cultures, it contributed only marginally to my fluency in French. From my point of view, a welcome bonus was the opportunity to improve my hockey game. Indeed our team won the interschool championship, and though I was merely an extra who wasn't called upon to play, I proudly qualified for a silver pin that said *Champion Suisse*. One boy who did play and who was a mainstay of the team was a Canadian by the name of Allan Burton, whom I met again years later after he had become chairman of Simpsons, one of Canada's leading department stores.

Another classmate, a Jewish boy from Germany, asked me one day in the shower if I knew anything about Hitler. I said I didn't and he replied, "You'd better find out about him, because both of us, I as a Jew and you as a Czech, are going to have trouble with that character." With some soap on his hairbrush he drew a swastika on the mirror and added, "You're going to see a great deal of this emblem." The year was 1929, four years before Hitler came to power, and I didn't have the faintest idea what he was talking about. But he was so intense that I've never forgotten that incident.

When my parents came to visit me shortly after Christmas, they were dismayed to discover that, while I had made excellent progress in such social graces as inviting a young lady to a tea dance at the Beaurivage Hotel, where girls filed in two by two with a chaperon for every group of ten, my French was decidedly unimpressive. So instead of letting me come home, my parents made arrangements for me to spend my Easter holidays with a Swiss family in Geneva. Hearing and speaking nothing but French for four weeks had the desired effect.

The year in Switzerland marked the end of my formal schooling and the beginning of my training as a shoemaker. According to Czechoslovak law, any operator of a shoe manufacturing business had to serve a three-year apprenticeship and pass an examination set by the Guild Masters in order to obtain a certificate of competence. Finally, to be fully qualified, the candidate had to have two years' experience as a "journeyman." Because my father had left his father's workshop and struck out on his own before completing the journeyman portion of his training, his competitors accused him of operating his business illegally. He was determined that no such charges could ever be leveled against me.

When I returned home shortly before my fifteenth birthday, Father devised for me an intensive training program that combined apprenticeship in the factory with classes at night and on weekends in subjects such as chemistry, marketing and technology. Each course lasted two to four months and was taught by an outstanding expert in the field. The idea was that I should know enough about each subject so that I could assess the qualifications and performance of people working under me. Years later, in wartime, I mentally thanked Father for enabling me to manage, with a reasonable amount of technical know-how, the engineering division of the fledgling Canadian enterprise. When we switched from manufacturing shoes to armament production, I knew enough to discuss such basics as gauges and tolerances with government representatives and subcontractors.

Since Father didn't believe I should have a private tutor, he selected from the Bata College a group of students my age to attend classes with me. Many of these young men, and others with whom I worked in the factory, were the cream of the crop, people with obvious potential who went on to become the backbone of the organization all over the world. By getting to know literally hundreds of them, I was unwittingly laying the groundwork for a personnel pool that would prove invaluable in years to come.

Busy though I was with my work and studies, I did find time to have fun. Shortly after my return home, Sir Sefton Branker, who was then director of civil aviation in Great Britain, and a pilot by the name of Ted Buckingham came to Zlin to stage a demonstration of the latest De Havilland product, a three-seater monoplane. It was beautifully engineered and equipped with leather upholstery and wings that could be folded back so that the aircraft would fit into a standard garage. Father was so impressed that he bought two of them on the spot, and two more later on. I, too, was impressed to the extent where, at age fifteen and a half, I persuaded my parents to let me take flying lessons. Unfortunately, about the same time, Father bought an outboard motorboat, probably the first of its kind in Czechoslovakia. While chasing around in that boat, my friends and I occasionally had close encounters with hidden objects in the shallow water of the Morava River. Worse still, one day while cleaning the engine I lost one of the screws that held the spark plug cable in place. As bad luck would have it, Father came by at that very moment and saw my predicament as well as the telltale scars on the engine. "I'm afraid," he said, "we'll have to suspend your flying lessons until you prove to me that you're mature enough to do a proper maintenance job on a piece of mechanical equipment."

Though I persuaded him within a year to let me resume my lessons, I was dismayed to learn that, in Czechoslovakia, I'd have to wait until I was nineteen to qualify for a pilot's license. Fortunately I discovered that pilots could be licensed at age seventeen in England. By then I had done a great deal of traveling, both with my parents and on my own, so England didn't seem that far away. I enlisted in the De Havilland Flying School in Hatfield and got my license the day after my seventeenth birthday.

The timing was fortuitous. Within three months Father was to set out on a fact-finding flight to the Middle East and India in order to explore markets for Bata shoes. I had been entrusted with the responsibility of planning his trip, which meant finding a pilot familiar with that part of the world — no mean feat in 1931. But in England, which was then the world center of aviation, it didn't take me long to find a suitably qualified pilot as well as the required maps and charts. That sort of thing was unobtainable in Czechoslovakia or, for that matter, anywhere else in continental Europe.

Having successfully discharged my responsibilities, I was secretly hoping that Father might take me along to India. But he didn't, possibly because Mother dissuaded him from exposing me to what, in those days, was a decidedly risky adventure. Radio communications, weather forecasting and navigational aids were all in their infancy, and it took a pioneering spirit like Father's to take off in a private airplane and brave the dangers of such a trip. Certainly no other industrialist, let alone any shoe manufacturer, would have dreamed of flying to those distant places, which was one of the reasons young people were attracted to the Bata organization. In this, as in many other respects, Father was simply decades ahead of his time.

Which is not to say we saw eye to eye on all issues; it may be that, had he not died so young, we would have had some serious disagreements. As it was, the closest I ever came to actually rebelling against his authority was when we had an argument — I forget what about. On the spur of the moment I drafted a telegram to Endicott Johnson, our friendly competitors in the United States, asking them if they would give me a job. Fortunately or otherwise, I was sloppy enough to mislay the sheet of paper and I proceeded to forget all about it. But I understand that when my mother found the draft and showed it to Father, he was delighted at my display of independence. If I had sent the cable and received a favorable reply, I believe he would have encouraged me to go.

Another conflict arose when four of us boys wanted to spend our summer holidays canoeing in France. Father objected partly, I suspect, because he considered the scheme frivolous. He was extremely concerned, in those days, that I might want to become part of what was known as *jeunesse dorée* — the offspring of wealthy parents who knew more about spending money than about earning it. This was the age of the likes of Tommy Manville, when newspapers were full of stories about rich young Americans becoming involved in multiple divorces and extramarital affairs. On one occasion Father got quite incensed when a young employee, a bit of a playboy who had a summer job in Zlin, drove all the way to Prague to see a performance by Josephine Baker, the world-renowned American striptease dancer who was widely considered a pioneer in that particular art form. Spending time and money in pursuit of such entertainment seemed to him unconscionable.

As for the canoe trip, Father's main objection was that one of my three friends was considered too much of a ladies' man and therefore morally objectionable. The problem was resolved when Dr. Wettstein, our Swiss lawyer and Father's confidant, came up with a substitute canoeist, an upright young Swiss student whose morals were above reproach.

Toward the end of my apprenticeship, Father conceived the idea that I should find out what it was like to work on the assembly line, performing the same operation not for a limited time and at the leisurely pace of an apprentice, but at full speed for eight hours a day. I must confess I wasn't thrilled by the idea; in fact, I did my best to talk Father out of it. But deep down I knew he was right, so I gave in. When he asked me which job I'd like to do, I selected the sidelasting of men's Goodyear welt shoes. In that operation the leather is wrapped around a foot-shaped block called a last, which determines the shape of the shoe. In those days the operator had to hold the shoe and the wooden last in his hands while a machine drove in twenty tacks per shoe, forty per pair. The last weighed at least half a kilogram, the resistance was considerable and I had to do 500 pairs a day, so it was a tough job that was normally reserved for mature workers at least twenty-one years of age. But it was also the one that was best paid.

Fortunately everybody had two hours off for lunch, and I figured out that if I pedaled my bicycle home at top speed, I could have a quick lunch and a half-hour nap and still be back at the factory at two. After work I used to join my friends in a garden restaurant for a game of chess, but during the first couple of weeks I was so exhausted that I invariably lost. However, both my spirits and my game improved after a while, thanks partly to an attractive young sewing machine operator who began joining the chess players for ice cream and coffee.

In retrospect, there is no doubt in my mind that the ability to perform manual work at full speed has done wonders for my confidence and self-esteem. By the end of my four-week stint, I had developed powerful arm and shoulder muscles as well as a healthy bank balance, all of which pleased me no end. At that point we got a new machine that performed the same operation with staples rather than tacks, so that the operator was no longer subjected to the shock treatment that I had endured for four weeks. I couldn't believe what a difference that made; I'd say the physical effort was reduced by more than half. For me it was a valuable lesson in the virtues of technology.

Another lesson I learned, albeit somewhat reluctantly, was the true meaning of customer service. Throughout my apprenticeship I had summer jobs during my holidays. That may seem perfectly normal in Canada or the United States, but in Central Europe in the 1920s, it was a radical departure from the customary pursuits of the offspring of well-to-do parents. One summer I was given the job of selling shoes outside the factory gates in a store patronized mostly by young people from nearby farms. Since early childhood I had had it drummed into me that the main purpose of our organization was to provide service to the public, that in the words of the company slogan, "the customer is king." But mouthing a slogan is one thing; living by it is another. At first I did have a bit of difficulty waiting with due deference on some of these decidedly unsophisticated boys and girls. But, by the end of the third day, I had overcome my reluctance and from then on enjoyed the job thoroughly.

After finishing my apprenticeship, I began working in the company's export department. By then Father had opened, in half a dozen foreign countries, retail outlets for Bata shoes made in Czechoslovakia. In Switzerland, for instance, we had a chain of about twenty-five stores whose merchandising statements arrived in Zlin at 6:00 a.m. every Monday, which meant the three of us in the Swiss export department had to be at work at six. Our job was to scan the sales of each article in each store, make any desirable adjustments and send the orders one floor down to the distribution department. Around five o'clock that same afternoon a freight car with merchandise for the Swiss stores left Zlin, accompanied by a Bata employee who made sure that, in Vienna, the car was switched to a fast train bound for Switzerland. In those days we could ship merchandise by freight on Monday afternoon and know that it would be delivered in Switzerland by Tuesday noon.

But in other respects, our exports were running into severe problems. For some time Dr. Wettstein had been warning my father that, if he continued expanding his export operations like a whirlwind and selling shoes at prices well below those charged by local manufacturers, he would find himself faced with import restrictions. But Father refused to believe that any government would dare penalize a business that was providing consumers with quality and economy. Unfortunately Dr. Wettstein was right and Father was wrong.

What Father failed to appreciate was the difference between bucking the powers that be in his own country and trying to do it abroad. Sure, he had political opponents in Czechoslovakia, particularly within the powerful party of small artisans who claimed that his mass production methods were driving them out of business. But there the public did protect him because he was the native son who had made good and whose fame was spreading throughout the world. In Switzerland he was a bloody foreigner and a convenient scapegoat for the country's high unemployment. Where job opportunities are at stake, xenophobia strips foreigners of public support.

In those days Switzerland was riddled with cartels that kept prices artificially high, and the last thing its members wanted was a competitor who sold inexpensive merchandise. So the Swiss shoe manufacturers banded together and persuaded the government to impose severe import quotas along with other draconian restrictions. Switzerland, incidentally, was by no means the only protectionist country in the 1930s. Much the same thing was happening throughout Western Europe and in the United States, where the Hawley-Smoot Tariff Act was only one of several pieces of legislation designed to make life difficult for the likes of us. There were even restrictions on interstate retailing to the extent where, in some states, no one organization was allowed to have more than four stores.

Because of these developments Father found himself faced with two alternatives: either abandon the foreign marketplace and the magnificent distribution network he had built up, or take up the challenge and start manufacturing outside Czechoslovakia. For a born fighter the decision was obvious. The first of the new factories to be built in Western Europe was in a place called Möhlin, on the Swiss side of the Rhine. And so in June 1932, the three of us in the Swiss export department, along with a number of technicians, left for Möhlin. We spent about a week unloading machinery and putting it in place, after which word came that Father was coming on Tuesday to throw the switch at the official plant opening.

About seven o'clock on Tuesday morning I got a phone call from my friend Karel Englis, the son of Czechoslovakia's minister of finance, who was working in Zlin that summer. "Your father has had a serious accident," I heard him say. "You'd better come home." A little while later Dr. Wettstein rang to say that he was sending his car to pick me up. The car arrived, I was driven to Zurich and there, in Dr. Wettstein's office, I was told that my father had been killed in an aircraft crash. Apparently the pilot, who had just completed a course in instrument flying, had taken off in spite of heavy fog. Within a minute the single-engine Junkers aircraft had dived into the ground and broken into pieces. The date was July 12, 1932.

I caught the day's only flight to Vienna, where one of our small aircraft was waiting to fly me the rest of the way to Zlin. It was a sad homecoming. When I arrived, I found Mother, Uncle Jan and other senior executives gathered around the dining room table, drafting a statement about the company's future. It was important to respond to nasty rumors that were trying to link Father's death to the Depression and speculating that, far from dying accidentally, he might in fact have committed suicide rather than watch his enterprise go down the drain. Actually, the business was in great shape, without a cent of bank debt, so we were able to reassure both the employees and the public that there was nothing to worry about. Our communiqué also announced that, in accordance with my father's wishes, Jan was taking over as chief executive.

The following morning I went to the hospital where my father's body lay. The coffin had been soldered shut, but the hospital director ordered it to be reopened and went on to explain proudly how much plastic surgery had been done to restore the corpse's shattered face. All I wanted to do was to say a quiet goodbye to my father and, in a sense, to my childhood. I thought of the eulogy written by the well-known journalist H. R. Knickerbocker. "Every nation," he said, "has its heroes; the Czech nation's hero was a shoemaker." He was certainly my hero, and without him, my life was never going to be the same again.

Among the papers found in Father's safe was what has become known as his "moral testament." In essence, it said that the business he had created was to be considered not as a source of personal profit, but rather as a public trust. As he put it, "We were motivated by the knowledge that our enterprise was providing an entire region with new, previously unknown advantages, that its growth was contributing to the wealth and the education of the nation." And he warned that any successor of his who failed to abide by that philosophy would prove unworthy of his legacy. Two days later, as I watched Father's casket being lowered into his grave, I said, "I promise."

2

GATHERING STORM

PART FROM ITS EMOTIONAL IMPACT, my father's premature death didn't mark a dramatic turning point in my life. By tacit agreement, responsibility for my continuing education and training was assumed jointly by Mother, Uncle Jan and Dominik Cipera, my father's trusted deputy and the company's general manager. Early in his career, Cipera had been an accountant in a bank branch in the Polish city of Lvov, where a distant cousin of ours, Bozenka Klausova, was manager of the local Bata shoe store. They met and fell in love, and when they decided to get married, he accompanied Bozenka to Zlin to meet the family. My father was so impressed with the young man that he offered him a job, and, as usual, his intuition served him right: Cipera's intellect, managerial ability and unconditional integrity remained the backbone of the organization both during and after my father's lifetime.

The trio concluded that my training to date had left two gaps to be filled. First, I needed additional education over and above what was available in Zlin, something that would broaden my horizons and, incidentally, provide me with a recognized certificate or degree. Accordingly I enrolled, in September 1932, as a part-time student at the commercial academy in the nearby town of Uherske Hradiste.

The second gap to be filled was my lack of managerial experience. Though I had handled various jobs and assignments within the organization, I had always worked under somebody else's supervision. It was time I tried to run my own show. So my three mentors decided that, in addition to my studies, I should spend a few months managing one of the company's stores in Germany. Ideally it should be large enough to provide me with plenty of experience, yet not so big as to overwhelm a young fellow barely eighteen years of age.

The store they chose was on the main street of Hindenburg, a sooty coal mining town in Upper Silesia within easy walking distance of the Polish border. There I learned a great deal, not only about the merchandising of shoes, but also about poverty and the ugly fanaticism generated by political extremists. During the fall of 1932, about one-third of the city's inhabitants were unemployed, and I remember people scrounging the slag heaps for bits of coal they could use as fuel for cooking. Political demonstrations were the order of the day, with violent clashes between Hitler's National Socialists on the one hand and Communists on the other. Most of the time the police were unable or unwilling to intervene. In the four months I was there I saw four people clubbed to death.

Had my superiors in Zlin known the full extent of what was going on, I suspect I would have been recalled posthaste. But they didn't know, and while the scenes I was witnessing filled me with disgust and foreboding about the future, I didn't go out of my way to provide people back home with the gory details. At the same time, there was no point in taking chances. Whenever the disturbances erupted, I promptly closed the store and watched the mayhem from behind the protection of metal shutters.

At night I thought it best to go straight to my hotel and go to bed. Not that there was much else to do. Hindenburg was a uniquely bleak place from the point of view of social life, and going to the movies was the most exciting form of entertainment.

I returned to Zlin in January 1933, a week or two before Hitler and his cohorts came to power in Germany. A couple of years later I went back to Hindenburg to see if it had changed. Though the town was still far from beautiful, I sensed a palpable improvement in the atmosphere: unemployment was a thing of the past and people were clearly enthusiastic about the Nazi regime. They didn't know or possibly didn't care that their labor was producing guns rather than consumer goods, or that they had purchased their newfound prosperity at the cost of their democratic freedoms. Certainly none of them seemed to suspect that they were careening toward a world war that would cost millions of lives, cause terrible suffering and ruin their country.

At home I buckled down to studying for my final examinations at the commercial academy — a kind of hybrid between a European lycée and an undergraduate business school. Most of the curriculum seemed easy after the intensive schooling I'd had in Zlin and the languages I had learned abroad. But subjects such as commercial law, banking and finance were new to me, and since the standards were remarkably high, I had to work hard to pass my examinations. Another subject to which I'd had only limited exposure was Czech history; it was taught by the principal, who dictated his lectures to me and insisted that I memorize every word. No doubt such learning by rote would send shudders down the spines of modern pedagogues, but in my case it worked.

After graduation in June, I headed once again for Switzerland and my new job as manager of the Bata store in Zurich. At my age — I was yet to turn nineteen — being in charge of one of the largest stores within the organization was a major challenge. I was free to hire staff, decide how much they should be paid, redesign the store, plan what and when to advertise. All in all an excellent and, to me, thoroughly enjoyable entrepreneurial experience.

In order to familiarize myself with both the merchandise and the clientele, I made a special effort during the first few weeks to wait personally on as many customers as possible. At the same time I asked the cashier, a "mature" lady approximately thirty-five years of age, to let me know anytime a customer had anything to say about my service. One day a heavyset man with the looks of a prosperous farmer came into the store and asked for lace-up boots of a style that was popular at the time. They were made of cowhide and sold, as I recall, for twenty-nine Swiss francs. I fitted him with a pair and when I saw how much he liked them, I pointed out that, for ten extra francs, the identical boots were also available in fine box calf with a leather lining. He agreed to try them on and, much to my delight, decided to buy both pairs.

I was pretty pleased with myself until the evening when the cashier reported to me a conversation she'd had with that particular customer. Apparently he told her that he had been well served by a young man who seemed to know his business. However, he couldn't help noticing that the salesman didn't speak the distinctive Swiss brand of German. Given the high unemployment that prevailed in Switzerland at the time, he felt the store should be hiring local staff rather than blankety-blank Germans. I took the hint and promptly began taking lessons in *Switzerdeutsch*. It wasn't easy, but by the end of my stay I believe I could have passed myself off as a resident of some remote Swiss canton. I have made a point of keeping it up ever since, to the amusement of my wife and our Swiss friends.

Possibly the most difficult challenge I had to face occurred when an employee whom I had let go took me to labor court, where both the plaintiff and the defendant had to plead their own case without the assistance of lawyers. Here I was, a teenage foreigner in a country notorious for its distrust of outsiders, defending myself against the accusations of a Swiss national. Had I been a little older I might have been scared. As it was, I simply explained that the man's performance had been unsatisfactory and disrupting to the work of other employees. I thought I detected a slight smile on the lips of the three "assessors" as they questioned me; I don't suppose they had ever had as young a chap appear before them. But I must have been convincing because I won the case.

After little more than a year in Zurich, I embarked on yet another stage in my apprenticeship when Cipera appointed me manager of the Bata department store in Zlin. The store had been built at a time when the company was attracting thousands of new employees, and my father had been concerned, with good reason, that local merchants and tradesmen might take advantage of this influx to jack up their prices. But apart from keeping a lid on prices, the department store also provided the citizens of Zlin with the opportunity to purchase modern appliances, fashionable clothing and fresh produce, all of which weren't normally available in small towns. We even had a self-service supermarket that Father had seen in the United States and proceeded to copy at a time when nothing like it existed anywhere in Europe.

Once again mine was a self-contained project that covered every conceivable function — purchasing, selling, finance, personnel, display, you name it. It was like running an independent business. I had the authority to implement my own ideas, and I loved every minute of it. At that time the company was expanding rapidly abroad and people were frantically trying to learn foreign languages. I managed to capitalize on this trend by obtaining exclusive distribution rights to Linguaphone records, and they sold like hotcakes. Then I scored another "coup" by securing the local representation for Skoda cars and negotiating advantageous financing for Bata employees.

Every spring, just before the May 1 Labor Day festivities, the company awarded a prize to the department that posted the best results for the previous year. This was a big event and the competition was fierce. In 1935, when the department store's financial statements showed that our sales and profits had doubled, we were declared the winners. At that point Cipera, apparently satisfied that I had mastered that particular job, said to me, "Tom, I guess it's time for you to move on."

Accordingly I was assigned to the cost and production control of men's shoes. Two other young men of approximately my vintage were responsible for ladies' and children's shoes respectively, and the three of us competed with one another in trying to achieve or surpass profit targets. To do this we would think up ways of lowering costs or improving quality by, for instance, stimulating the research and development department to come up with new ideas, or suggesting the use of new materials to the purchasing department. Ours was an area that combined manufacturing, marketing and product development, so it gave us a tremendous insight into the three main facets of the company's operations.

My final job in Zlin was as manager of the company's model coal mine. Its existence as part of the Bata organization was due entirely to Father's determination to fight the cartels that discriminated against domestic customers by charging inflated prices at home but not abroad. Ours was decidedly the cleanest and most modern coal mine in Czechoslovakia, if not in Europe, with exemplary working conditions. But it wasn't operating at all efficiently, and I doubt that the three months I spent at the helm improved that situation to an appreciable extent.

By the time I left Zlin to take up my new appointment in the head office of our British company in East Tilbury, just outside London, the buildup of Germany's armed forces was becoming increasingly menacing. Whenever I traveled through Germany on my way to and from England or Switzerland, I recalled my father's warning just a couple of days before he died. On his return from a business trip in July 1932, he summoned a Sunday meeting of the company's top executives to sum up his impressions. He predicted that if Hitler came to power, which he considered highly probable, there was going to be serious trouble in Europe. To prepare for that eventuality, he decided that reserves of low-priced overseas commodities such as rubber (it was selling for something like one cent a pound) should be substantially increased, and that the company's expansion program in Western Europe and over-seas should be accelerated. Talk about strategic planning!

At that time our corporate counsel in Germany, a Jew by the name of Kurt Calmon, introduced us to a friend of his named Stuart. Regardless of his Scottish name, Stuart was a bred-in-the-bone German, a former cabinet minister in the Weimar Republic and an active member of a World War I ex-officers' association called Stahlhelm. Stuart was invited to join the board of the German company and by 1934 had become its chairman. One Sunday afternoon he and Calmon were playing tennis in Berlin, when someone warned them that the Gestapo had arrived at the club and were looking for them. Under the circumstances it seemed best to assume the worst. The two friends climbed the fence at the far side of the club premises and disappeared.

When I heard what had happened, I flew to Switzerland in the hope of organizing a rescue mission. By then Calmon had turned up in Holland, but Stuart was still missing, though Calmon thought he knew where he was. So I hired a Swiss pilot to fly me to Stuart's hiding place as soon as we received confirmation that he was indeed there. My intention was to airlift him out of Germany. Since radar was yet to be invented, it seemed reasonable to assume that our aircraft might remain undetected. But in the end Stuart, too, managed to escape to Holland, so the mission was aborted.

Calmon later became our agent in England, and his son came to work for us in Zlin until just before the war when he joined his father in England. As for Stuart, he and I met again during my prewar stay in England when both of us were appointed members of the Rubber Industry Wage Board. This was a body set up by the British Ministry of Labour to help set minimum wage standards within the industry; at twenty-three, I was at least ten years younger than any of its other members. Later, during the war, Stuart turned up in Batawa, the site of our Canadian company. He was accompanied by another German and three senior Canadian officers, all of whom were extremely friendly but uncommunicative about the purpose of their visit. That was the last time I saw him; I wouldn't be surprised if he died on some secret mission.

From the corporate point of view the 1930s was a time of disengagement between the home base in Zlin and Bata holdings in the rest of the world. As Hitler's rhetoric and actions became increasingly belligerent, we had to face the possibility of seeing Czechoslovakia and, with it, Zlin destroyed or overrun by the Germans. Already we had all but lost our substantial manufacturing and retail operation in Germany, complete with its large modern plant and some 250 stores. Soon after they came to power the Nazis indicated they didn't consider it appropriate for racially inferior Czechoslovaks to control such a large part of Germany's shoe industry. In an attempt to avoid outright expropriation, we had placed our holdings in the hands of a Norwegian consortium whose Teutonic ancestry was presumably more acceptable to the Hitler regime. But although Bata Germany remained technically our property, we had ceased by the mid-thirties to exercise any control over it. Even the name had been changed.

Whatever might happen to Zlin, we were determined to prevent the Germans from grabbing control of the rest of the organization and using it as a springboard for spreading the Nazi gospel. So Dr. Wettstein, in his capacity as chairman of our Swiss holding company, set out to cut or camouflage all corporate ties between Zlin and the rest of the organization. To cover up the tracks he created a number of subholding companies in various parts of the world, including Newfoundland, which, of course, was not part of Canada at the time. He also made sure that the gold bars my father had begun accumulating in his lifetime and that constituted an important part of our foreign assets were stashed away safely in bank vaults in Canada, India and South Africa. It was that gold that later kept us alive during the war.

The closest I ever came to experiencing personally the less than tender mercies of the Third Reich was around 1937. By then I had spent five years in increasingly responsible management positions, but in each case I was reporting to someone higher up in the organization. Now I felt the time had come for me to run a show of my own. Uncle Jan agreed and jointly we decided that I would launch a shoe manufacturing and marketing operation in Belgium. For the sake of mutual support I intended to locate the new plant as close as possible to our Dutch factory near Eindhoven, within a few kilometers of the German frontier. Which is why I had detailed maps of the border area in my briefcase one day when I was flying from Zlin to Milan.

In those days there was a rule that an aircraft had to touch down in every country it overflew, so we decided to land in Munich. "What have you got in that briefcase?" asked an elderly German customs officer, clearly a relic from the previous regime. I replied that I was on my way to Italy and was carrying some business documents. "Let's take a look," the man said. When he saw the maps, his eyes almost popped. "Put them away quickly," he said. "I believe you're telling the truth about the plant you're planning to build in Belgium. Just the same, you're lucky that it was I who saw those maps and not one of the young chaps." I don't scare easily, but I felt my knees shaking as I climbed back into the plane. I'd had a narrow escape.

In Belgium, as in other countries, we planned to have a suitable retail organization to market the shoes we were going to manufacture, so I began looking for retail outlets we might add to the small number of stores we already owned in the country. I soon found exactly what I was looking for: a chain of stores called Chaulux, which dovetailed with ours perfectly. The question was how to sound out the owners, a family by the name of Sangster, and negotiate a deal. Given the fact that the Bata name was anathema to many of our competitors, a direct approach didn't seem advisable.

At a party in London I had met a man named Edward Bach, a direct though by then thoroughly anglicized descendant of the illustrious German composer Johann Sebastian Bach. He was working for the Prague Credit Bank in London, dabbling in the wine trade and writing weekly articles about economic and banking issues for *Die Wirtschaft*, the German language equivalent of the British *Economist*. Right away I was enormously impressed with the man, and after consulting some of my associates, I asked him to go to Brussels and sound out Monsieur Sangster on behalf of a potential purchaser. Bach was a financial expert rather than a shoeman, and when he advised me that the French owner seemed receptive to his advances, I arranged to have him joined by one of our managers. Bentley was a shrewd Englishman who looked as though he had stepped out of a John Bull cartoon, so I was confident no one would suspect him of having Bata connections.

Negotiations proceeded satisfactorily until Bentley decided to take a few notes, at which point the Frenchman looked at him in horror. "That's a standard Bata notebook you have!" he exclaimed. For a moment our two emissaries thought their cover had been blown. But Bentley quickly recovered and explained that he had acquired the notebook during a shoe-buying visit to Zlin.

In due course the contract was signed, and at a celebration champagne dinner Monsieur Sangster proposed a toast. He was particularly happy, he said, that the deal had been consummated, because otherwise he might have been compelled to sell to "those abominable Batas." In reply Bach surprised his host by drinking to a long and happy association between the Chaulux and Bata organizations. Once the Frenchman got over the shock, everybody had a good laugh and, eventually, we became good friends with the Sangster family.

Soon after Germany's annexation of Austria in September 1938, it became painfully obvious that Hitler had singled out Czechoslovakia as his next victim. I was convinced there was going to be a war; it never occurred to me, nor, as far as I know, to any of my compatriots, that our allies would desert us. Since I was traveling back and forth between England and Zlin about once a month, I took advantage of one of my visits to call on Dr. Albert, head of the Zlin hospital, and ask him to remove my appendix. I explained that it had been acting up on me off and on, and though it was behaving itself at that particular time, I wanted to make sure I wouldn't be laid low with appendicitis in the midst of some major battle. He wasn't exactly enthusiastic about my suggestion, but after performing the operation, he agreed that it had been a wise precaution.

During that winter of 1937 and spring of 1938, I spent much of my spare time in London with Jan Masaryk, Czechoslovakia's ambassador to the Court of St. James and son of the late president, Thomas Masaryk. Our families had known each other for many years. I remember when I was a little boy being invited with my parents to dinner at the Masaryks' summer residence and eating, for the first time in my life, corn on the cob. I assume the president's American wife must have introduced this exotic dish to the household. Later my mother and the Masaryks' daughter Alice saw a great deal of each other because of their common interest and leadership in the Red Cross; and whenever Mother came to visit me in England, we always spent at least one evening with Jan.

Though he must have been worried sick about Hitler's designs on our country, he never lost his legendary sense of humor nor his ability to put on a brave face. During the Easter weekend in 1938, he invited me to dinner along with two of my closest friends and contemporaries, Vladimir Cerny and Honza Stransky. Cerny, the son of Czechoslovakia's minister of the interior, was managing the London branch of the Anglo-Czechoslovak Bank; Stransky, whose father was to become minister of justice, was the London correspondent of a major Czech newspaper.

Inevitably the conversation at Masaryk's dinner party revolved around the international situation, and by the time the evening was over, we had agreed that, if Hitler were to swallow Czechoslovakia, the four of us would join forces and open a restaurant in London. Masaryk, who, in addition to all his other talents, was a gourmet cook, was the unanimous choice for chef. I was going to be the business manager, Cerny the maître d' and Stransky the wine waiter. For the moment, at least, we became so engrossed in our imaginary venture that we forgot about the real world closing in on us.

Masaryk was also a frequent guest at the country estate of the Schichts, a family of Sudeten German soap and margarine manufacturers who had settled in England and whose company had become one of the components of the worldwide Unilever empire. Unlike most Sudeten German industrialists or, for that matter, unlike many members of the British aristocracy, the Schichts were violently opposed to the Nazi regime, to the extent where they turned their home into a meeting place for like-minded politicians, diplomats and business executives. Outwardly these gatherings took the form of typical English house parties, complete with a staff of servants who might have stepped out of the *Upstairs Downstairs* television series. Whenever I was invited I was one of about twenty guests who had their luggage unpacked, their baths drawn, their dinner clothes laid out for the evening meal. In the daytime there was riding, golf or croquet for those who felt so inclined. But with the deepening international crisis, these parties became increasingly an opportunity for Masaryk to meet informally with his supporters and discuss the political situation with them.

Later that spring and summer, my Czech friends and I decided we had to do something tangible to counteract Germany's hate propaganda. In those days London had a number of movie theaters that screened nothing but newsreels. So we organized a group of young people to attend as many of these theaters as possible. Whenever there was an item that was favorable to Czechoslovakia, they clapped and cheered wildly; and, of course, they booed at every mention of Hitler or Nazi Germany. Some-what to our own surprise, we found that five or six vocal people could sway an entire audience one way or the other.

Around that time I got a call from a prominent British business-man whom I had last seen at the age of twelve when we had been pupils at the same prep school. He came to see me because, he explained, he was convinced that peace must be preserved at all costs. Since I was a Czechoslovak who had gone to school in England and who had traveled in Germany, the man believed I was the ideal person to go and see Hitler and explain to him that he needn't worry, that he wasn't really being encircled by hostile nations. Somehow I resisted the urge to throw him physically out of the room. Instead I just told him to get the hell out.

Meanwhile the crisis kept escalating, and in September Prime Minister Chamberlain, who apparently shared my schoolmate's naive illusions about Hitler, embarked on his shuttle flights to Germany. By then I was on the phone to Prague every day, giving a synopsis of British editorial opinion to Hugo Vavrecka, a distinguished ex-diplomat and lifelong friend of my father's who had joined our company in Czechoslovakia as executive director a few weeks before Father died, and who had subsequently been appointed minister of information in President Benes's government. At the time he had a little grandson by the name of Vaclav Havel, who was destined to make headlines around the world fifty years later as a brilliant playwright, a courageous defender of human rights and, eventually, as president of a newly reborn democratic Czechoslovakia.

Mother was visiting me in London when Chamberlain returned from his abortive peace mission to Bad Godesberg, where Hitler had confronted Britain's prime minister with his new, outrageous demands. From the windows of our rooms at the Savoy Hotel, we watched antiaircraft guns being positioned on the embankment. Good, I thought, the British aren't going to let Hitler get away with it after all. Just to be on the safe side, my friends and I decided we'd better resume our efforts to publicize our cause. When we heard that two French cabinet ministers were coming to London for consultations, it occurred to us that the only thing that might conceivably stop Hitler would be a convincing display of solidarity between the two western allies. Given the success of our claques in the newsreel movie houses, we hoped against hope that some spectacular gesture on our part might have the desired effect on public opinion.

So we raided our stockroom in East Tilbury for textiles and made up a giant banner that read We Welcome Our French Allies. When some twenty or thirty of us carried this banner, along with British, French and Czechoslovak flags, to the roof of Croydon airport, the police tried to stop us. But when we showed them the banner and explained what we intended to do with it, they said, "That's great. Go right ahead." Fortunately the news photographers were out in force, and so the following day a number of British newspapers carried on their front pages pictures of our flags and our banner, which we unfurled just as the French ministers were landing.

But for all the publicity our gesture proved futile. Chamberlain proceeded to make his infamous speech about how incredible it was to be digging trenches "because of a quarrel in a faraway country between people of whom we know nothing," and later that month Czechoslovakia was sacrificed in Munich on the altar of appeasement. When Chamberlain returned home, he claimed he had secured peace with honor, but Winston Churchill was a much better prophet. As he told the prime minister in the House of Commons, "You were given a choice between war and dishonor. You chose dishonor and you will have war."

During the balance of 1938, I spent a great deal of time traveling back and forth between England and Zlin, where I participated in conferences about the company's future. During one of these trips, Dominik Cipera, who had been appointed minister of public works in the post-Munich cabinet, offered to have his chauffeur drive me from Prague to Zlin in his ministerial Packard. We arrived safely even though all the way I could hear the ominous sound of bearings going "clickety-click." So before he left me I said to the driver, "Be sure to get those bearings fixed." He promised he would.

I was back in Zlin for yet another conference on March 12,

1939, when I got a long-distance call from Jiri Udrzal, the head of our tire production operations. Being the son of a former prime minister, he had his ear pretty close to the ground. "Tom," he said, "I know the weather is filthy, but could you possibly send a plane to Prague to fly me to Zlin? And try to get hold of Jan and all the other top people, because I have some important news for you." We were in the midst of a terrible snowstorm, but the plane did manage to take off. Meanwhile I made sure there was a spare tank of fuel in the back of our old Lincoln.

It was getting dark when Udrzal arrived in Zlin and told us what his news was all about. Apparently the provincial government of Slovakia had decided to announce the following day that it was seceding from Czechoslovakia and allying itself with Germany. The news wasn't altogether unexpected. Ever since the founding of Czechoslovakia following World War I, there had been tensions between the highly industrialized, relatively affluent Czechs and the essentially agrarian Slovaks. The two parts of the country had different histories, different cultures and slightly different languages. While the majority of people in the western provinces of Bohemia and Moravia were nominally Roman Catholic, there was a strong Protestant tradition and an equally strong strain of agnosticism. Most Slovaks, on the other hand, were devout Roman Catholics.

After the Munich fiasco, Slovakia had formed an autonomous provincial government whose fascist, strongly anti-Semitic orientation mimicked its German model. On several occasions the premier and his followers traveled secretly to Germany to visit Hitler and Göring and plan Slovakia's "liberation" with them. Apparently the central government had finally got wind of these plans and decided to forestall them.

Accordingly Czechoslovakia's minister of national defense was on his way to Bratislava, the capital of Slovakia, where he was going to charge the Slovak government with treason and have them arrested. Several army divisions would be there to assist him in case he encountered any resistance. The central government in Prague assumed that Hitler, when faced with this gesture of defiance, would invade Czechoslovakia. But since that was clearly what he intended to do sooner or later anyway, the Czechs decided they might as well show the world where they stood.

We decided we'd better get out of the country as quickly as possible. Jan had a Polish visa, so he said he'd take his wife and children to Poland. Udrzal and I got into the car and headed for Switzerland via Austria, or rather what by then was the eastern tip of Germany.

After being held up at the border for what seemed like an eternity but was probably no more than a quarter hour, I began driving toward Vienna. The snow was coming down harder than ever and I could hardly see where I was going, when suddenly, in the middle of the road, there stood a man in a brown Nazi uniform signaling, us to stop. I had no choice but to obey. "Could you please give me a lift as far as Linz?" the stranger asked. We were only too happy to oblige; having him aboard provided us with an appearance of legitimacy and, therefore, a certain amount of protection.

Our passenger left us when we reached Linz around 2:00 a.m., but we decided to push on toward Salzburg. That, it turned out, was a mistake. Before long we came to a hill with trucks and cars stuck all over the place, trying in vain to negotiate the slippery slope. It was a hopeless mess, so we asked the driver of a snowplow if there was any other way of getting to Salzburg. "If you fellows want to walk across the hills through the forest," he said, "about three kilometers ahead there is a railway line and a passenger train will be along in an hour or so. If you get a move on, you may catch it. Chances are it will be late in this weather, anyway." So that was what we did. We arrived in Salzburg about 5:30 in the morning, only to find that all trains to Switzerland had been canceled because of a shortage of coal.

So we ordered coffee and waited for the six o'clock news to see if Hitler was on the march. But there was no news about a German invasion of Czechoslovakia at six, or at eight. By then it had stopped snowing and we thought the roads might be passable, so we hired a taxi and drove back to the place where we had abandoned our car. Sure enough the German army had cleared the road, so we got back into the car and drove all the way to Munich where we boarded a train for Switzerland.

Seeing there was still no word about trouble in Czechoslovakia, I phoned Prague to find out what was happening. And guess what? The chauffeur who had driven me to Zlin had failed to replace the faulty bearings in the ministerial Packard, and so the car had broken down while the minister of national defense was on his way to Bratislava. As a result, the separatist government hadn't been arrested, Slovakia did announce its secession and Hitler didn't have an excuse to march on Prague. Not that he needed a pretext. A couple of days later, on the morning of March 15, I was on the train from Basle to Brussels when I got the news that the German army had crossed the border of Czechoslovakia and was approaching Prague.

After lengthy discussions and assurances by the German authorities that no harm would come to us, Jan decided to return to Zlin, at least for the time being. Personally I had no wish to live under a Nazi regime, temporarily or otherwise. On April 1, 1939, barely two weeks after Hitler's rape of Czechoslovakia, I boarded the *Queen Mary* in Southampton and set out for my new life in Canada.

3

TO CANADA BY CHOICE

WHY CANADA? I guess it was a combination of circumstances. Ever since my early childhood, when Father and I had listened to Mother read aloud romantic tales about the Wild West and about northern explorers, I had a mental image of Canada as a glamorous, exciting place to be. That impression was reinforced in the 1930s during my stay in England when I saw a film that pictured Canada as a land of opportunity. I liked the film so much that I phoned the producers to tell them how much I had enjoyed it, upon which they invited me to dinner. My hosts turned out to be four young members of the Moral Rearmament movement who told me about their plan to create harmony between employers and employees throughout the world. It all sounded most commendable until, being the blunt kind of guy I am, I asked, "Where do you get your money?" They said, "We get it from God." If they were hoping for a new recruit, they lost me then and there.

Still, I continued to think of Canada as the best of two worlds, a blend of British traditions with the progressiveness and dynamism of the United States. Then, in the summer of 1938, with war looming on the European horizon, Jan and I decided that I should abandon my plan to start a Bata enterprise in Belgium and go overseas instead. For a young man of twenty-four anxious to flex his entrepreneurial muscles, Canada seemed like a more appropriate environment than the huge, highly industrialized United States. And so, given my lifelong fascination with the country, Canada emerged as an ideal place to prove to myself, and to others, that I had what it takes to start up and manage an independent Bata company. The assumption, of course, was that the Canadian enterprise would continue to enjoy access to and support from the enormous resources of Zlin.

My illusions suffered a slight setback early in December when the immigration officer at Canada House in London, a chap by the name of Little, informed me that only farmers were being admitted to Canada. Since I wasn't a farmer I wasn't eligible, and that was that. However, I knew the local manager of the Royal Bank, so I went to see him and asked for his advice. He phoned Mr. Little, and whatever he said must have been persuasive, because a few days later I got a call to say that the high commissioner wanted to see me. Together with Little I was ushered into a huge office that looked like something out of the movies, and there, at the end of the room, sat the diminutive figure of High Commissioner Vincent Massey. He asked me a number of questions, after which Little explained to me that the only way I could be admitted to Canada as a permanent resident was by an order in council. However, he asked, had I by any chance brought my passport along? When I said I had, Little produced a pen and wrote in my Czechoslovakian passport: "Admit the bearer as a visitor," or words to that effect. "Signed, Little." No official stamp, no further formalities. I was elated and enormously impressed by the speed with which the matter was settled. Somewhat naively I assumed that I had just witnessed a typical example of the efficient way in which Canada's bureaucracy operates, and I congratulated myself on having elected to make my new home in such a progressive country.

The original idea was that I would build in Canada a modest-sized factory to produce the same type of utilitarian women's walking shoes and nurses' oxfords that we had previously sold to department stores and wholesalers through our one-man import office in Toronto. But later that month, during my Christmas visit to Zlin, the plan underwent a fundamental reappraisal. At a strategic planning meeting with Uncle Jan and several other senior executives, we concluded that Czechoslovakia in its post-Munich state wasn't likely to survive. After being forced to give up a huge part of its territory to the Germans, the country had been attacked by Hungary and Poland, each of whom took advantage of the situation to extract their pound of flesh. What was left of Czechoslovakia was nothing but a helpless rump, which Hitler could swallow whenever he felt so inclined. Reluctantly we had to envisage a Bata Shoe Company without Zlin.

As a result, it was decided that the Canadian enterprise was to be upgraded to an important technological development center, a possible alternative to Zlin as a producer of shoe machinery. In addition, the shoe manufacturing operation was to be expanded to the extent where, in the event of war and German conquests in Western Europe, Canada could become the supplier of Bata retail stores in other parts of the world. I had a violent argument with John Hoza, a manager who had lived in the United States during World War I and had hung on to his U.S. citizenship ever since. Having been chosen to head up a prospective manufacturing operation in the United States, Hoza wanted the technological center to be located within his jurisdiction. But Jan sided with me, and so Canada won.

This meant that, instead of the handful of people I had planned to take with me, I had to find in Zlin some 250 managers, technicians, designers, tradesmen and skilled workmen willing to transplant themselves and their families to a country about which, by and large, they knew nothing. The man I had chosen to become maintenance manager told me to count him out because, he explained, he didn't want to live in a tropical country. As it turned out, he arrived in Trenton, Ontario, in June in the midst of a stifling heat wave.

In addition to a first-class team of people, I had to extract from Zlin more than 1,000 machines, complete with electric motors and connecting equipment, and have them prepared for shipment along with modern machine tools and all the materials required to produce the first 100,000 pairs of shoes. There were even the molds for a standard five-story Bata factory building, along with a specially designed crane and a man to operate it.

As far as financing the project, the company had an agreement with the government, according to which we were allowed to ship capital goods out of the country on three years' credit and trading goods on six months' credit. The rest of the capital, to the tune of $300,000, would have to come out of the Swiss holding company. Though that was a huge amount of money in 1939, it wasn't going to last forever, so it was essential that the Canadian venture should begin earning income as soon as possible. I finished my recruiting campaign around mid-January, and my target was to start manu-facturing both shoes and machines in August. It took the self-confidence of a twenty-four-year-old to embark on such a project without apprehension.

I decided to go via New York mainly so that I could sail on the *Queen Mary*, at that time one of the world's fastest and most luxurious ocean liners. The moment I stepped on board ship I felt as though an enormous burden had been lifted off my shoulders. During the past few months, I had traveled back and forth across

Europe at least half a dozen times, participated in important decisions concerning the future of the company, planned every detail of the Canadian venture and seen my homeland wiped off the map. Five days of enforced leisure on the high seas, and the prospect of a new beginning in the promised land, seemed just what the doctor had ordered. The presence on board ship of a number of attractive young American ladies on their way home from Europe was an unexpected bonus.

Another fellow passenger was Ted Buckingham, the pilot who had come to Zlin in 1930 to demonstrate and, as it turned out, sell to my father De Havilland's monoplane with its fold-back wings. I was able to bring him up to date on the developments triggered by that sale nine years ago. In the 1930s commercial aviation was still in its infancy and since, for an international organization such as ours, the availability of fast, dependable transport was a vital necessity, the two aircraft my father had bought from De Havilland became the first step toward the buildup of a substantial corporate fleet, including the Junker3 F-13 in which Father was ultimately killed. We even began manufacturing sports planes called "Zlin," which won a number of championships and the descendants of which continue to collect prizes to this day. When the Nazis marched in, they carted all the aircraft off to Germany. The only exception was one of two beautiful eight-passenger Lockheed Electras, which succeeded in taking off literally under the noses of the Wehrmacht. During the war, it became the first modern executive transport aircraft owned by the Royal Canadian Air Force.

At the end of a thoroughly enjoyable and uneventful voyage, I was greeted in New York by the Czechoslovakian consul, an old friend of mine by the name of Janecek. He informed me that, unfortunately, I'd have to go to Ellis Island. The United States

government, he explained, had canceled all visas issued to people who couldn't be deported without being endangered. This new regulation applied to all citizens of Czechoslovakia, including those who were already in the United States.

Janecek telephoned Washington and persuaded the authorities to release me in his custody, on the understanding that I would report to Ellis Island first thing the following morning. When I boarded the ferry at 7:00 a.m., I was told that the governor of Ellis Island wanted to see me up on the bridge. "So you're the young man who didn't want to come to Ellis Island," Mr. Rayner, a man of about fifty with brown mustachios, said. "Yes, sir," I replied. "Well," he said, "I have a ranch in Arizona and I don't want all these people filling up the country. When I pack my sleeping bag, I want to be sure there isn't another soul for miles around." I wondered if I was one of the people he didn't want to see in Arizona or anywhere else in the United States.

When the ferry reached Ellis Island, Mr. Rayner took me to see a man with rimless glasses and neatly brushed hair whom he introduced as the director of immigration. He explained to me that he was deeply worried about the new regulations that compelled him to quarantine, so to speak, people with perfectly valid visas and travel documents. Ellis Island was already playing host to some 300 Czechoslovaks, and more would undoubtedly be rounded up. The immigration people's appeals to Washington to bend the rules and allow these people to stay in the U.S. had run up against a wall of bureaucratic silence.

Now there had been a fair amount of publicity about my arrival in the country and about my predicament. Just who leaked the news I have no idea, though I wouldn't put it past the immigration authorities, who may have thought that the confinement on Ellis Island of the "shoe king," as the American news media described

me, might galvanize the government into some sort of decision. Anyway, the director of immigration informed me that I would have to submit to a special board of inquiry, which would decide whether or not I could stay in the United States.

I pointed out that I had no intention of remaining in the United States, that I was on my way to Canada, where I had important business to transact. But the director of immigration explained that I could help him by agreeing to submit to the inquiry, though he warned me the result was a foregone conclusion. Under the existing rules I was bound to be "excluded" from entering the United States. However, I could then appeal to "Ma" Perkins, the secretary of labor who was responsible for immigration, at which point I would be released on parole for an indefinite period. It seemed like a strange charade, but since they were all so friendly and since, frankly, I didn't seem to have any choice in the matter, I agreed to cooperate.

The board of inquiry consisted of five uniformed immigration officers, who asked a number of questions about conditions in Czechoslovakia and about the danger people might face if they were sent back. After I had told them what they obviously wanted to hear, the chairman announced that they were going to have "a little consultation." Right there in front of me they went into a huddle, after which the chairman stood up and said, "The Board of Special Inquiry has concluded that you have to be excluded from entering the United States." And then, nodding emphatically to make sure I gave the right answer, he continued, "Do you wish to appeal to the secretary of labor?" I said I did, and having been warned that a decision concerning my appeal might take four weeks, I was allowed to leave Ellis Island. That evening I got a call from Consul Janecek. "You will be pleased to know," he said, "that all Czechoslovaks are being released from Ellis Island, and that

those with valid documents will be allowed to stay in the United States." So apparently the game I had been persuaded to play had served its desired purpose.

The train ride from New York via Fort Erie to Toronto was a bit of an eye-opener. It was a dreary April day, the snow beside the tracks was gray with soot deposited by passing locomotives, the farmhouses and adjoining barns looked shabby and dilapidated. Somehow I had imagined southern Canada to be another Holland, immaculate and tidy, and for the moment at least, I felt let down.

I arrived in Toronto with a letter of introduction to a lady named Ione Gibson, so I called her and she invited me to Sunday dinner. I was to be in the lobby of the Royal York Hotel at half past eleven so that her daughter could call for me in her car after church. "Clara May will wear a navy blue suit with a white collar and a blue straw hat," she explained, "so you can't miss her." Already I knew that this was a new world. Nothing like it had ever happened to me in the more formal environment of England, let alone in Czechoslovakia.

After welcoming me like a long-lost friend, my ebullient hostess introduced me to the rest of the family, including her father, George Heintzman, the head of Canada's famous piano manufacturing company. At the end of a thoroughly enjoyable meal, Mr. Heintzman turned to me and said, "Tom, you'll make a good Canadian." Those few words made a deep impression on me. In all the years I'd spent in England, no one had ever suggested I might become an Englishman, good or otherwise. Over there I would remain a foreigner, no matter how long I stayed or what I did.

As though to reinforce the message, the Heintzmans proceeded to tell me that every Sunday evening their family assembled at their home for an early supper after which they all listened to

Charlie McCarthy. Would I like to join them? I had never heard of Charlie McCarthy, a ventriloquist's puppet whose gift of precocious repartee entranced millions of North American radio listeners in that pretelevision era. But I went anyway and loved every minute of it. By the end of that day I knew I was going to feel at home in Canada.

On a more mundane plane, my main concern was to get permission for 250 Czechoslovakian families to join me in Canada. Up until then, the only Bata representative in Canada had been Karel Herz, a lawyer by training who had formerly been in charge of our exports from Zlin to North America. C.K., as he was generally called, managed in Canada one of many trading and shoe importing companies we had established around the world. Most of them operated under the name Kotva (Czech for "Anchor"), but in Canada the Kotva name had been registered by someone else, so we called it Canadian Commercial Enterprises.

In the late 1930s, as the situation in Czechoslovakia became increasingly critical, this network of offices in New York, Brazil, South Africa, Australia and Western Europe provided an opportunity for Jews and other endangered individuals to leave the country and obtain employment abroad. By 1939 I would estimate that two-thirds of the Kotva managers and employees were, in effect, refugees.

One of C.K.'s many invaluable contributions to the Bata cause was the relationship he established with a distinguished Toronto lawyer by the name of Wilfred Parry. I cannot begin to assess the debt I owe to Wilf for his professional excellence, his wisdom, his candor and, above all, his friendship. To the extent that the Canadian venture has been successful and we managed to resolve the horrendous problems that lay ahead, much of the credit belongs to him.

As soon as I arrived in Toronto, Wilf, C.K. and I got on the train to Ottawa to see what could be done about visas for our 250 Czech families. On that cold April day, with snow still on the ground, Ottawa looked more like a dirty provincial town than a national capital. In the former school building that housed the Department of Immigration, we were shown into the office of the director, F. C. Blair. He was a handsome, gray-haired man who looked serious but surprisingly benign considering what we'd been led to expect. After I had put my request to him, he leaned back in his chair for a few seconds, then said, "Mr. Bata, we will admit them." Wilf Parry almost fainted with surprise. The reason for Blair's reputation as an ogre, I was later told, was that he was a rabid anti-Semite and therefore determined to prevent Jews from entering Canada.

As it was he insisted that the three of us go with him to see the minister of mines and resources, who, for some strange reason, was responsible for immigration. So we put on our galoshes and trudged through the snow to Parliament Hill, where the minister, a big hearty fellow named Tom Crerar, received us in his office. He seemed intrigued with our plans and even insisted on seeing the shoe samples I had brought along in a bag. By the time we left, all our immigration problems appeared to be settled.

My next problem was choosing a site for the Canadian venture. The Canadian Pacific Industrial Commission had recommended a location south of Trois-Rivières in the province of Quebec, and its recommendation was reinforced by a luncheon invitation and a powerful sales pitch from Maurice Duplessis, the province's premier. He was at his most ingratiating and persuasive best, but he couldn't do anything about the climate. It was darn cold when I toured the suggested area toward the end of April, the river was still frozen over and the highway to Montreal and Quebec was blocked by snow. Traveling by horse-drawn sleigh may be romantic, but it isn't my idea of efficient transportation.

Language was another problem. I was about to bring to Canada people whose mother tongue was Czech and whose second language, to the extent they had one, was German. Yet in Quebec they would have to learn French to communicate with the work force and with most of their customers, as well as English in order to operate in other parts of the country. Compelling them to learn two languages, in addition to all the other challenges of adjusting to a new country, seemed like a serious obstacle. The final straw was a kind of government-approved collective agreement, a thick document that legislated every aspect of every operation in the footwear industry and, as far as I was concerned, enshrined every old-fashioned work practice. As soon as I'd read it, I headed for the Ontario border.

The whole of western Ontario, including Toronto, had to be ruled out because it had twenty-five-cycle power, while our equipment from Europe had a fifty-cycle power base. A converter, apart from being exorbitantly expensive, couldn't be delivered for at least nine months or a year. We didn't have time to wait nine months to start production; we would have been broke by then. So I decided to hire a small airplane and fly from Toronto up the shore of Lake Ontario, along the St. Lawrence Valley to the Quebec border and then inland to see if I could find a suitable site. I wanted a location with pleasant surroundings and plenty of vacant land we could buy so that we wouldn't have to pay inflated prices once we began to build houses for our employees. Good transportation facilities and the availability of a labor force were additional requirements.

The Trenton area, halfway between Toronto and Kingston, seemed to fit all the specifications. There was a railroad, a waterway and a military airport just outside of town. The countryside was beautiful, the Trent River offered excellent fishing and recreational facilities, there was plenty of land and a good power supply.

Above all, the town was amazingly hospitable. Among the people who rolled out the welcome mat for us, none did more to help us get established than the local Member of Parliament, Bill Fraser. Almost dwarfishly short, shabbily dressed and with a protruding stomach, Bill didn't look like a knight in shining armor, yet to me that was what he turned out to be. He was a brilliant, honest, patriotic Canadian who worked very hard to pave the way for us. Also tremendously helpful were Trenton's mayor, Ken Couch, and a lawyer named Howard Graham, who was to rejoin the army during the war and become chief of the general staff.

In addition to all our other requirements, the site we chose had to have a building that could be adapted to manufacturing. With people about to arrive from Czechoslovakia and mounting costs, we had to start producing something for sale and begin paying our way. The modern factory we planned to build would have to wait. In a village called Frankford some ten miles north of Trenton, a long-abandoned, decrepit old paper mill was offered to us for rent. Adjoining it was a large area of open land that, we were told, was almost useless for agricultural purposes and therefore, presumably, could be bought cheap.

On a Saturday afternoon we sat down with the city fathers, unfolded a map and drew a line around some 1,500 acres that we wanted to buy. They, in turn, allocated to themselves one or two farmers each to deal with. Led by Ken Couch and Howard Graham, they fanned out the following Sunday after church, and before the day was over twenty-five farmers had agreed to sell.

With the purchase of land, our presence in Canada became public knowledge, and before we knew what had hit us, all hell broke loose. There were dozens of shoe manufacturers in the country, all struggling to compete with imports from the United States and, to a lesser extent, from Japan. While Canadians were ahead of their competitors in waterproof winter footwear, they were in no mood to share their limited market with a brash newcomer. In fact, we were told not to apply for membership in the Shoe Manufacturers' Association because it would be embarrassing for them to have to turn us down. Later the shoe manufacturers came to see that we weren't about to eat them alive, and eventually Lorne Savage, owner of the Savage Shoe Company in Galt and the head of the association, invited us to join, which we promptly did.

The shoe manufacturers, by the way, weren't our only opponents back in 1939. In their anti-Bata campaign they found staunch if unlikely allies in union leaders as well as the United Shoe Machinery Corporation, the powerful American company whose management resented us for not being their customers. Deputations journeyed to Ottawa to lobby the government, and letters to the editor accused us of every conceivable sin, from union bashing to dumping to antisocial behavior.

In the midst of the controversy the Ottawa representative of the Czechoslovakian government-in-exile, a man by the name of Frantisek Pavlasek, wrote and mailed two letters. One, written in English and addressed to Mr. Euler, minister of trade and commerce, extolled the virtues of the Bata organization and the tremendous benefits it would bestow on the country. The other epistle, written in Czech and addressed to me, painted a decidedly unflattering picture of Mr. Euler. The minister, Pavlasek explained, was the Member of Parliament for Kitchener-Waterloo, an important shoe manufacturing center. Being a typical politician, Mr. Euler was using all kinds of pretexts to persuade his cabinet colleagues that the Bata organization should be kept out of Canada.

Somehow the envelopes for the two letters got switched. By the time Pavlasek realized his mistake and phoned the minister's office to ask if he could have his letter back, Euler's executive assistant,

Finlay Sim, had sent it to the Royal Canadian Mounted Police to be translated. Sim promptly phoned the RCMP and said not to bother, but they replied the letter had already been translated and that they thought the minister would be interested in its contents. As it turned out, the translated letter ended up in Sim's wastebasket, so Mr. Euler never did get to see it. As Sim later told a friend, "There are times when an executive assistant has to decide what his boss should or should not know."

But in spite of Sim's efforts on our behalf, the director of immigration, F. C. Blair, telephoned from Ottawa a few days later to say that, given the political implications, his previous approval for Bata employees to come to Canada was being suspended. This was a stunning blow. Our machinery was being loaded in Europe, our people were getting ready to leave, we had bought land in Canada and now, all of a sudden, everything had to grind to a halt.

Eventually Prime Minister Mackenzie King defused the controversy by appointing a cabinet subcommittee to look into the matter. During the next couple of months, I spent most of my time in Ottawa, talking to influential people to whom I was being introduced by Bill Fraser. In retrospect, I'd say he was subjecting me to a crash course in lobbying. As a veteran Member of Parliament and a former whip of the Liberal Party, Bill enjoyed open access to the corridors of power, and he used his privileges unsparingly on my behalf.

The same can be said about Wilf Parry. Being a Conservative by persuasion didn't prevent him from making sure I met everybody who was anybody in the Liberal government of the day. His strategy consisted of taking me to lunch two or three times a week at the Rideau Club across the street from Parliament Hill. In those days there were no good restaurants in Ottawa, so the Rideau Club was the one place where VIPs could be sure of getting a decent meal. As cabinet ministers passed our table on their way in or out of the dining room, Wilf would introduce me and we would exchange a few words. Having been initiated into the club's unwritten rules, I knew that it was taboo to take advantage of such casual encounters to talk business or ask for an appointment. But at least the ministers, including the three members of the cabinet subcommittee, could form an impression, which, I hoped, was more favorable than the draconian picture painted by my opponents.

Around the middle of June F. C. Blair called again and presented me with a typically Canadian compromise: could I make do with 100 Czechoslovaks instead of 250? I asked, "Can we take it for granted that 100 will be allowed to come?" He replied, "Yes, that is my mandate from the cabinet subcommittee." It took me about five seconds to make up my mind. "Fine," I said. "Let's get going."

As soon as our people began arriving, they set to work cleaning up the old paper mill. It took them a month to dismantle the antique paper machinery, tear out the wiring, repair the roof and floorboards and remove layers of dust and cobwebs. In what had once been an office they found a dried-out ink pot and an unfinished letter dated 1927. When at last the job was done and we began installing our own machines, we hit another snag. Because our Czechoslovakian motors and equipment hadn't been approved by Ontario Hydro, then known as the Hydroelectric Power Commission, they couldn't be installed or used. To complicate matters further, all our equipment had five-point plugs, which enabled us to move every machine wherever it was most urgently needed on the assembly line. Unfortunately five-point plugs were unheard of in Canada at the time, so it took quite a bit of time and persuasion to have the inspection team set up by Ontario Hydro come to terms with them.

An equally serious problem cropped up in the form of the duty and sales tax that Canada levied on imported machinery. Far from getting the exemption we had asked for, we were informed that the valuation for duty purposes was being increased because, the customs people argued, the machines were invoiced by an affiliated organization and therefore presumably underpriced. The finance minister, Mr. Dunning, tried hard to be helpful, but apparently even he couldn't prevail against the customs bureaucracy. In my experience all over the world that is the one institution that no one can budge.

So the valuation on the machines imported from Czechoslovakia was upped by twenty percent, which meant we were stuck with a substantial duty that took a hefty bite out of our liquid resources. We were told that wasn't such a serious blow because we could take advantage of an accelerated depreciation scheme that was intended to encourage industrialization. The problem was that in order for depreciation to do us any good we would have had to be making a profit. It took us a long time to recover from that setback, but somehow we squeaked through.

Even before the arrival of the Czechoslovakian contingent, I had hired half a dozen Canadians to act as understudies for our managers, and a number of workmen to apprentice under our production people. But until the training program got under way, the highly skilled instructors we had imported manned the machines. As a result, the shoes we produced during those first few weeks were the best we ever made. What is even more remarkable is that those first shoes rolled off the assembly line before the end of August, barely two months after our people had first set foot in Canada.

As soon as we had any merchandise, I joined our sales people on the road, and I managed to land a contract for nurses' oxfords from the owner of a small chain of stores in Peterborough, a medium-sized city some 260 kilometers southwest of Ottawa. I had the first sixty pairs delivered to him by a chauffeur-driven car so that he could see the quality and the styling. That was one of the best things I ever did. For the rest of his life — and he lived for another twenty-five years — he proclaimed to anyone willing to listen that he was my first Canadian customer, and that the shoes he'd ordered from me had been delivered to him in my private car. It was the kind of publicity money couldn't buy.

Even so, it soon became clear that selling shoes in Canada wasn't going to be easy. As in most other countries, our plan was to establish our own retail organization. But as we had previously learned in England, wholesalers and other important customers who had previously sold Bata shoes imported from Czechoslovakia were in no mood to market the same footwear that was being sold in our own stores. A few days after we had opened a couple of stores in southern Ontario our main wholesale customer came to see me. "Tom," he said, "you'll have to make up your mind. Are you going to sell to us or through your retail stores?" There was nothing for it but to capitulate, at least for the time being. But we did launch a retail chain in northern Ontario, places like Sudbury and North Bay. They operated under the name Falcon, and while I'm sure the name didn't fool the shoe trade, nobody objected as long as the stores were away from the mainstream.

All that summer I was living in the caretaker's cottage outside the former paper mill, and when my mother arrived early in August she moved in with me. We had a living and dining room, one small and one tiny bedroom and a single bathroom plus, of course, a kitchen. Our lawyer's wife, Dorothy Parry, took us to a wholesale warehouse and helped us choose some furniture. Come fall our cleaning lady, Mrs. Patrick, put up storm windows, which, as my mother was quick to notice, didn't open except for three thumb-sized holes covered by a wooden slide. When she protested that they didn't allow for enough fresh air, Mrs. Patrick proceeded to enlighten her about Canadian winters. "It may not look like much today," she explained, "but by the middle of December you'll find it quite sufficient." She was absolutely right.

Toward the end of that ominous summer of 1939 I had no doubt that we were heading toward another world war. Hitler was screaming daily about the "provocations" committed by the Poles, and then sealed their fate by negotiating his infamous pact with Stalin.

On the last day of August many of the most valuable machines we had ordered from Czechoslovakia were on board a German ship due to dock in Montreal the following day. Steaming up the St. Lawrence River, the SS *Königsberg* had passed Quebec City and tied up in Sorel for the night. Later that night I got a telephone call informing me that the ship had slipped out of Sorel under cover of darkness and was heading downstream toward the open sea. I immediately called Bill Fraser, who in turn contacted some of his influential friends. Whether or not as a result of these calls, an RCMP boat intercepted the *Königsberg* and ordered her back to Quebec City, where she was told to unload the finest machinery available at the time anywhere in Canada.

The following day, September 1, 1939, Hitler's troops invaded Poland.

C H A P T E R

4

WARTIME PURSUITS

O N SEPTEMBER 10, 1939, the day Canada declared war, all Czechoslovaks living in Canada became "enemy aliens." As citizens of a country occupied by Germany, we had to register, be fingerprinted and report regularly to the RCMP. Fortunately this state of affairs didn't last long. As a result of the controversy that had erupted shortly after my arrival in Canada and the appointment of the cabinet subcommittee, we had been investigated more thoroughly than any immigrants before or, I suspect, since. By the time war broke out the police had voluminous files about the Bata organization and knew all there was to know about us, including the fact that we were every bit as anti-Nazi as the most patriotic Canadian citizen. Within a matter of weeks we were upgraded to "neutral" and eventually "friendly aliens."

Meanwhile I was anxious to find some way we could contribute to the war effort. As usual, I enjoyed the full support of Bill Fraser, the Member of Parliament for that part of southeastern Ontario where Frankford is located. Two or three times a week Bill traveled with me to Ottawa, where we presented the powers that be with an offer I thought they couldn't refuse. In essence, what I told them was: "We have excellent engineering equipment that we brought over from Czechoslovakia. It was intended to make shoe machinery, but you're welcome to use it for whatever purposes you wish." I can't pretend that I got a rousing welcome. Here I was announcing that we could make shoes for the military, we could make machines, we could make precision instruments; but it was hard to find anyone who was even remotely interested.

Having witnessed, a year earlier, Czechoslovakia's mobilization and determination to fight Hitler's evil empire, I was taken aback by the business-as-usual atmosphere I encountered in Canada. There were no military bands, no newspaper headlines about events on the front, no sense of impending crisis. At one point a few of us decided to drive to Petawawa, one of Canada's major military bases north of Ottawa. There were no barbed wire fences, no one to demand identification from our group of recently arrived foreigners. To our amazement we watched soldiers in the true north parading around in helmets designed as a shield against the tropical sun. Nevertheless my lobbying efforts did bear some fruit. Apparently the military were having trouble obtaining equipment for the automatic inspection of small arms ammunition, so the officials at the Department of Munitions and Supply asked me if we could make it. We most certainly could, though we were a bit surprised to find that the prototype was of 1915 vintage, while the drawings dated back to 1912. But at least we felt we had begun participating in the war effort.

A couple of weeks later a British technical mission arrived in Frankford. After touring the corrugated iron shed that housed our engineering division, one of the commission members, a man by the name of Crone, said to me, "Mr. Bata, you've got marvelous machinery, but where are the fitters?" I wasn't familiar with the term, but once he explained to me what it meant, I was able to introduce him to twenty skilled technicians, every one of them thoroughly experienced and qualified to operate the machinery.

After interviewing them, Mr. Crone was so impressed he urged me to make sure our "fitters" didn't do anything foolish such as joining the army. Later that fall a man who had been our agent in Holland and Britain turned up in Frankford and placed an order for lathes on behalf of the British Ministry of Aircraft Production. That was our first export order, and an important step in the engineering division's conversion to wartime production.

By then our standard five-story factory building was under construction and the municipality that was to become Batawa was beginning to take shape. It was high time. During their first few weeks in Canada, our Czechoslovakian employees had been staying in one or, if they had families, two rooms in the homes of Frankford citizens. Once they got over the shock of being invaded by so many foreigners, the villagers were remarkably hospitable, even to the extent of organizing parties in the local church, while I did my best to provide some entertainment by way of weekend picnics and sing-songs with accompaniments on my accordion. But none of this was a substitute for suitable housing.

Early in the fall we began to build 100 two- and three-bedroom houses that were to be ready for occupancy by the end of the year. At that point we still didn't have a name for our new community. Then one evening, while a group of buyers were sitting around with me in my Frankford cottage, the man from Eaton's department store said, "Why not combine the Bata name with the last syllable of Ottawa? Batawa has a nice native sound." So Batawa it became. The houses were completed on schedule, except for one detail. We had waited too long to lay sewers and water pipes, and once winter set in our primitive blasting and digging equipment was useless against the frozen ground. So that first winter we joked about the "Outhouse Lane" that graced the back of all those otherwise attractive new homes.

But lack of plumbing was a minor problem compared to the

sense of gloom that descended on our community when war broke out. While hoping fervently that, in the long run, war would lead to the defeat of Hitler and the liberation of their homeland, people were painfully aware of their isolation from family and friends. They had left home thinking they would be back in a year or two, at least for a visit. Now suddenly they found themselves completely cut off, unable to communicate even by mail, wondering if or when they might be reunited with elderly parents, sweethearts, brothers and sisters.

A tragic incident early that winter dealt a further blow to the community's morale. Our chief designer, Gerry Janecka, took his little daughter and a friend of hers on a sleigh ride across the frozen Trent Canal. Being a newcomer he didn't realize that the ice under the bridge would be thinner than elsewhere. The sleigh broke through the ice, and though Janecka succeeded in pulling both little girls out of the water, his daughter died, possibly from shock. I shall never forget the mother's cries of anguish, or the way she blamed Canada for her misfortune. The Janeckas later had a son who grew into an attractive young man and, eventually, the family became the mainstay of the community. But it took them and their neighbors a long time to recover from their grief and the notion that Canada had somehow let them down.

In those early months of the war it wasn't only individuals who felt isolated. The separation from the home base was equally traumatic for the business. It was as if the umbilical cord had been cut between the weak Canadian embryo that was about to be born and the protective parent whose resources were supposed to sustain it. At first my associates and I were naive enough to think that, since the United States was still neutral, we could keep in touch with Zlin via New York. We were promptly disabused of that notion by our lawyer, Wilf Parry, who explained to me that it was strictly illegal for Canadian residents to maintain any kind of contact with enemy-occupied territory. The prohibition applied even if we happened to be visiting south of the border.

Personally I didn't experience the full impact of the severance from Zlin until the end of the year when my mother decided to return home. The reason, quite simply, was to try to save the company's home base from being taken over by the Germans and used for the production of armaments. During the first few months after the German occupation, there had been no attempt to interfere with the company's operations. The only concession to the new order had been the appointment to the board of a German shoe manufacturer by the name of Miesbach, who turned out to be a decent and helpful chap. In my experience, not all Germans were bloodthirsty monsters. Even so, knowing what had happened to our large business in Germany, which was four times the size of Batawa, we had no illusions about the long-term future of Zlin. In the meantime, however, we thought we might enjoy a bit of a respite.

But the outbreak of war triggered new German regulations concerning property whose owners or shareholders were living abroad. Our faithful Czech director, Hugo Vavrecka, took advantage of a business trip to Italy to phone Uncle Jan in New York and warn him that, unless a member of the family returned to Zlin, all Bata assets within the "Protectorate" would be considered abandoned and confiscated by the German government. Jan phoned my mother in Batawa and suggested that she might help us resolve the problem. As Father's widow, she was entitled to twenty-five percent of his estate, so there could be no doubt about her being a major shareholder. If she were to return home and if, in addition, four Zlin executives were each to receive seven percent of the bearer shares that technically belonged to Jan, then fifty-three percent would be held by residents and a takeover might be averted.

It took an awful lot of soul-searching: would or should she go back as a representative of the family? In the end she was the one who said, "I believe it's my duty to go." What was at stake was not the preservation of personal property. She knew she was taking a hell of a risk and that, if she ever changed her mind, she would have no hope of getting the Gestapo permit that was required to leave the country. But she was willing to gamble that she could keep Zlin out of German hands and, as it turned out, she was right. Letting her go or, rather, failing to dissuade her from going was one of the hardest decisions I've ever had to make.

She sailed from New York in December 1939, stopped in Italy long enough to have lunch with our lawyer, Dr. Wettstein, who came to Milan to meet her, and then disappeared behind Hitler's iron curtain. John Taylor, the British consul in Baltimore, told me he had made arrangements for me to keep in touch with her via one of the neutral countries, in the hope that her letters might provide useful tidbits of information for Allied intelligence. But I was afraid of endangering her, and so, apart from a couple of brief messages sent to me by Swedish diplomats, I had no news of her for the next four and a half years.

Mother's decision raises a fundamental question: when a country is occupied by its enemy, should freedom-loving citizens try to escape or stay put? In my own opinion, people who are in acute danger for religious, racial or political reasons should make a run for it, and the same goes for anyone whose special talents or know-how may help defeat the enemy. As for the others, it may be better for them to stay and do whatever they can to frustrate the invader rather than abandon ship. In the case of Zlin, staying on the job enabled our people to shelter, within the work force, a number of individuals who otherwise might have ended up as concentration camp inmates or slave laborers in Germany. By no stretch of the imagination could they be accused of collaborating.

In at least one instance our general manager, Dominik Cipera, and his counterpart in Yugoslavia paved the way for the escape to England of a former Czech cabinet minister, Ladislav Feierabend. Had those same managers run away or tried their hand at sabotage, the two rather benign Germans who represented their government's interests in Zlin — the shoe manufacturer Miesbach and a Wehrmacht officer by the name of Colonel Rustenholz — would undoubtedly have been replaced by more militant specimens of the master race. Before long I imagine the Bata Shoe Company, suitably renamed Hermann Göring Werke, would have been producing munitions instead of footwear. It's hard to see how such developments would have benefited the Allied cause.

As for Mother, I didn't find out until after the war how bravely she had played her difficult role. Not only did she, as resident representative of the Bata family, help forestall a takeover by the Germans. According to a letter from my friend Frantisek Schwarzenberg, scion of one of the oldest and most distinguished aristocratic families in Central Europe, Mother also acted as conduit for money that was being channeled to the resistance movement. Apparently she was one of the few people who could withdraw large sums of money for supposedly legitimate purposes without attracting the attention of the Gestapo.

During those wartime years, she consolidated her friendship with General Elias, head of the Czech "puppet" government in Prague, and more particularly with his wife. In order to remain in office and play his part as a secret agent of Czechoslovakia's government-in-exile, Elias had to pretend he was a collaborator. Eventually, however, he was arrested by the Germans, convicted in a secret trial and hanged. After the war, when his widow visited us in London, I was impressed with the way she could fix our radio when it refused to work. It wasn't the kind of skill she was likely to have acquired at finishing school.

Toward the end of the war Mother was questioned by the Gestapo, not about her financial transactions or her social contacts, but about a Canadian army captain by the name of Thomas J. Bata, whose photograph, flanked by a platoon of soldiers, the ever thorough Germans had somehow got hold of. "Is this your son?" they wanted to know. Fortunately she was able to claim, quite truthfully, that she knew nothing about my activities, and by 1944 the Germans were too busy losing the war to spend much time worrying about a lowly Canadian captain.

Not that I considered my rank lowly. As a matter of fact, I was pretty proud of it when I finally got it, in 1943. But during the early stages of the war I was a foreigner and therefore not eligible to join the armed forces. However, Canadian citizenship was not a prerequisite for membership in the Legion of Frontiersmen, a kind of militia that had been at one time affiliated with the RCMP. While that association had faded, the Frontiersmen still wore uniforms that were identical to the Mounties' except that their coats were blue rather than red. So I joined and, from then on, I spent two evenings a week as well as weekends marching around the Trenton coal shed, which was being used as an armory. There were quite a few of us who had joined, people from all walks of life. The chap who drilled us was the personnel manager I had hired a few weeks earlier.

By the spring of 1940 the Bata organization was becoming acclimatized to the severance from Zlin and to that strange interlude between war and peace generally known as the phony war. There was nothing phony about it for the poor Poles or the citizens of the Baltic states, whose countries had been overrun by hostile armies and divided up between Hitler and Stalin. But from the corporate point of view, apart from the loss of our substantial Polish business, the international organization didn't suffer during those early months of the war. Our British and French companies were going great guns, we were doing well in Switzerland and in Holland, Yugoslavia was still free and profitable.

But we were in for a rude awakening. In May 1940 we were working in the newly completed Batawa factory, when news came that Germany had invaded Belgium and unleashed a savage bombing attack against Holland. Within weeks most of Western Europe up to the Spanish border was under German domination, the Allies had lost thousands of men and priceless equipment at Dunkirk and the Battle of Britain was about to begin. At last Ottawa seemed to have awakened to the fact that Canada was at war and that what was still referred to as "the mother country" was in mortal danger. Nine months of bureaucratic inertia were replaced by a full-scale commitment to the war effort.

One day, while visiting a shoe show in Boston, I got a telephone call from Batawa to say that there had been no mail for two days. At first I assumed there had been some foul-up at the post office, but instead it turned out that our mail was being intercepted on orders from the custodian of enemy property, a position recently reactivated after lying dormant since World War I. Upon arriving back home, I met for the first time a brilliant young lawyer who was to play an important part in my life. In his capacity of counsel to the custodian, Glen McPherson explained to me that, according to regulations enacted under the War Measures Act, the custodian was empowered to investigate all enterprises that were directly or indirectly owned by persons in enemy territory, or that were suspected of trading with the enemy.

Apparently Britain's Ministry of Economic Warfare and, by extension, the Canadian government took a dim view of the fact that, during the early months of the war, Bata companies in neutral countries such as Holland, Belgium, Switzerland and Yugoslavia continued to trade with Zlin. I pointed out to McPherson that while, secretly, our managers in these neutral countries were every bit as anti-Nazi as the rest of us, they couldn't be seen to take sides in a war that, technically, was of no concern to their host countries. Indeed, by doing so they would be committing a criminal offense for which they could conceivably be jailed.

Eventually the custodian of enemy property, in the person of the secretary of state, decided to set up a supervisory committee for our operations in Batawa. I didn't like it and I expressed my views in no uncertain terms. But it wasn't long before I realized that the appointment of the committee marked a happy turning point in the fortunes of our Canadian company. Up until then the powers that be in Ottawa had viewed us with a certain amount of reserve. We were, after all, total strangers, and while the RCMP had given us a clean bill of health, there was an understandable reluctance to entrust us with major war contracts. The appointment of highly respected committee members changed all that. Far from being hostile, their supervision turned out to be friendly and helpful. As McPherson later told me, Canada's formidable minister of munitions and supply, C. D. Howe, whom I had met a number of times during my lunches with Wilf Parry at the Rideau Club, made it clear that he didn't want the committee to upset our employees or interfere with the company's war work.

The net result was that, from then on, I was received in Ottawa as a member of the team rather than an outsider. While we had been switching gradually from footwear to defense production, I had had to badger the authorities to let us participate in the war effort. Now, suddenly, unsolicited orders came flooding in. Before long our production facilities were converted almost entirely from footwear to gun mounts and precision instruments. One of our more interesting contracts was for the manufacture of gyroscopes, which govern the course of torpedoes. Only two other companies on the Allied side, one in Scotland and the other in the United States, had the expertise and the equipment to make these delicate instruments.

As soon as the time I'd spent in England and Canada added up to the mandatory five years, I applied for citizenship, and early in 1942, by special order in council, I became a Canadian citizen. Now that I was no longer a foreigner I was technically free to join the armed forces. But active service was out of the question considering my responsibilities in Batawa and C. D. Howe's express orders that I was to devote my energies to managing the business. So I decided to become a foot soldier in the Hastings and Prince Edward Regiment of the Canadian reserve army. By then many of the young men who had come with me from Czechoslovakia had joined the Allied forces in Britain or the Czechoslovakian squadrons of the Royal Air Force. But a number of those who couldn't be spared had followed me into the reserve army, where I got permission for them to form a special platoon and wear Czechoslovakia badges below the Canadian ones. According to an article in *The Trentonian*, the Czechoslovaks, who had had a minimum of two years of compulsory military service in their native country, "completely overshadowed the raw Canadian recruits."

In the summer of 1942 the Czechoslovakian platoon decided to hold a United Nations Day in Batawa. Though the United Nations Organization didn't officially come into being until the last year of the war, the term had already become part of our vocabulary. Under the leadership of Tony Daicar, a Bata veteran who had joined the company in 1928, our people organized a celebration of international solidarity that was attended by 10,000 visitors, including two Canadian cabinet ministers and representatives of every Allied country. There was a military band, a march past before the assembled dignitaries and a gymnastic display by members of both the Canadian and the U.S. Bata organizations. Tom Crerar, the cabinet minister who had approved my application for 100 Bata people and their families to come to Canada, used the occasion to present me with my commission. I believe it was the first and only time that a freshly minted second lieutenant had his first pip pinned on by a Canadian cabinet minister. My later promotions, to first lieutenant and finally captain, were more conventional in nature.

The success of the United Nations Day was a sorely needed morale booster at a time of invariably bad news from just about every war front. True, the United States was now officially our ally. But the crippling of the American fleet at Pearl Harbor had been followed by equally devastating losses of personnel, equipment and territory in Southeast Asia. Two of Britain's largest battleships were at the bottom of the Pacific, enemy U-boats were ravaging Allied convoys in the Atlantic and Germany's seemingly invincible Field Marshal Rommel was sweeping across North Africa. Nevertheless, most of us were convinced that, in the end, we were going to win the war. But we would have been hard put to explain how.

Quite apart from their military implications, events in the Far East had dealt traumatic blows to the Bata organization. Our substantial businesses in Burma, Singapore, Malaya and the Dutch East Indies had all fallen to the enemy, and the Japanese were bombing Calcutta, presumably in anticipation of a push into India. At age twenty-seven I was too much of an optimist to think that the organization might not survive, but there were times when I couldn't help wondering how much of it was going to be left. As far as I could see, the healthiest parts were the British and the Indian companies, both under the superb management of two dedicated Bata pioneers. In North America, on the other hand, the Canadian operation was still in its infancy, while the equally young U.S. company was experiencing serious financial difficulties. As for the bits and pieces we had launched in Africa and Latin America, their only asset in most cases was a group of exceptionally resourceful individuals whose ingenuity had to make up for the lack of material resources.

For many of them, just reaching their destinations had been a major challenge. Take Joseph Volf, who had joined the company in 1930 as an apprentice in the Bata School of Young Men in Zlin. Nine years later, with war looming on the horizon, he was told that he would be going either to Nigeria or Kenya, depending on which visa came through first. Nigeria won and with forty-eight hours' notice he left Zlin on August 13, 1939, bound for Prague, Hamburg and Lagos.

The German ship on which he sailed got only as far as the Canary Islands when news came that the war had begun. The captain promptly changed course and headed for the Spanish port of Vigo, where all the crew and most of the passengers disembarked in response to Germany's call to arms. Left to fend for themselves, Volf and two fellow passengers from Zlin made their way to Tangier in North Africa and eventually to Lisbon, where they boarded a ship bound for Angola. But to get from Angola to Nigeria they had to pass through the Belgian Congo, and the Congolese authorities refused to let them in without entry visas. They were, however, allowed to phone Mr. Kohn, our representative in Leopoldville, who agreed to send a car to Angola to smuggle them across the border. "The three of us were lying on the floor of the car," Volf recalled later, "with our people from Leopoldville sitting on top of us." Fortunately it was nighttime and the immigration officer didn't have a light. In Leopoldville Mr. Kohn made arrangements for our travelers to take a French ship to Cotonu, the capital of Togo, from where they proceeded without further mishap to Nigeria. They arrived in Lagos on January 17, almost exactly five months after leaving Zlin.

But getting there was a minor inconvenience compared to the enormous problems that faced our people in most of these distant countries. Egypt was a case in point. Slavo Blazek was a senior accountant in our Singapore operation, who, in the summer of 1939, had qualified for home leave. He was passing through the Suez Canal, when he got a cable asking him to stop off in Egypt for a few weeks. Little did he suspect, when he got off the ship, that he would be in Egypt for the next twenty-five years. Until then our Egyptian company had been essentially a retail organization that sold shoes imported from Zlin. As in many other countries, the government favored industrialization only to the extent that it didn't drive out of business the small workshops that provided a living for thousands of cobblers. Even after we finally got permission in 1938 to manufacture rubber and canvas footwear, the old cigarette factory we rented was no more than an assembly operation for made-in-Zlin shoe parts and rubber compounds.

Then the war came and suddenly there were no shoes from Zlin, no raw materials, no spare parts for the machinery, no money. Yet under Blazek, who rose to become manager of the operation, the Egyptian company survived. To produce shoes, Blazek and his team organized hundreds of cobblers into production teams whose handmade shoes they bought for resale in our stores. They used old sacks to replace unobtainable textiles and extracted cement from discarded crepe-soled shoes. They engaged local garage workers to make spare parts, literally by hand. To save money all the expatriates lived together in one house and settled for living allowances instead of salaries. "Anyone in our place would have done the same," Blazek later said.

While that may be an overstatement, it is a fact that many other

Bata managers displayed amazing initiative in the face of monumental difficulties. In Kenya, which had plenty of hides but no chemicals to tan them, a chiropodist on our staff discovered, by studying books about tanning, that the bark of mimosa trees yielded an acceptable substitute. In the Belgian Congo the retail sales manager moved shoe repair machines from the shops to a central location and had them converted for manufacturing. In Nigeria Joseph Volf and his colleagues alleviated their cash flow problems by buying indigenous products such as ebony heads and lizard skins from inland traders, and selling them at a profit to visiting sailors. By the end of the war Bata Nigeria, which at the time of Volf's arrival seemed about to die of malnutrition, was in reasonably good health.

In a number of countries, the economic and financial problems were compounded by the appointment of a "custodian of enemy property." Fortunately in Egypt, the British custodian eventually reached the conclusion that far from being enemies, our people were valuable allies and that the company should be handed back to its rightful management. Unfortunately, at that point, it wasn't at all clear who that might be. The prewar general manager had died and no one was legally empowered to take his place. Undeterred by such a minor difficulty, the authorities appointed an Anglo-Czech Military Committee to take over the company, with Blazek as one of the committee members and company manager. The chairman of the committee was the commander in chief of the Egyptian armed forces, a British general known as Spinks Pasha. He was a short man, not impressive to look at but very able and tremendously influential. More than anyone else he enabled our company to keep on functioning in the Middle East throughout the war.

Blazek pointed out to him that the Egyptian company's branches in other Middle Eastern countries were mostly small and in need of expert advice; yet, as a civilian, he had no hope of obtaining the required travel permits. "No problem," said Spinks Pasha. "You are hereby appointed a lieutenant in the Allied forces. Go get yourself a uniform, and whenever you need to travel, just ask for a military movement order." So, for the rest of the war, Blazek would go to the airport in civilian clothes, change into uniform in the men's room and report to military travel control. Once he arrived at his destination, he reversed the procedure. On many occasions, when he was sitting in a Dakota transport, wedged between senior officers, he was scared to death that he might be asked about the identity of his military unit or his battle experiences. Fortunately this never happened, not even during the Big Three meeting in Teheran when all air traffic was grounded and he had to spend four days on a military base in Iraq.

A major problem during the latter years of the war, for the Allied forces as well as the Bata organization, was the acute shortage of rubber. Japan controlled all the sources of supply in Southeast Asia and synthetic, insofar as it was available, often had to be used in combination with natural rubber. The resiliency of natural rubber was, for instance, essential for the production of airplane tires.

What little natural rubber there was in India, Africa and Latin America had to be made available for war production. In Peru, where our company owned a piece of jungle on the banks of the Amazon, we engaged people to tap any rubber trees they could find and to cart bales of smoked rubber in trucks across the Andes. It was an outrageously expensive and laborious operation, but the shortage was so desperate that it was considered worthwhile.

Inevitably we had to stop manufacturing rubber footwear both in England and in Canada, though, thanks to the ingenuity and dedication of our people, we managed to keep producing small amounts in a few African outposts. In Kenya, for instance, bales of rubber from torpedoed cargo ships were occasionally washed up on the beaches. After floating for weeks or even months in saltwater, such rubber had deteriorated beyond the point where it could be used for the manufacture of tires, but it was good enough for rubber heels or soles. In Egypt Blazek and his team bought old tires and tubes and boiled them for hours in barrels of oil. Though the tide of war had finally turned in our favor, the shortage of rubber was as critical as ever. I believe that, at one point, the Allies' stock was down to two weeks' supply.

In the summer of 1944, as Allied armies were sweeping across France and up the Italian peninsula, Jan Masaryk asked me to come to London and help the Czechoslovakian government-in-exile with its plans for postwar reconstruction. Fortunately my military status entitled me to travel, and though my priority as a captain was low compared to that of all the instant colonels and generals I kept encountering, I managed to get a seat on a flight to Britain.

I was busy looking into the availability of various materials that would be needed to revive the industry of Czechoslovakia and other war-damaged countries, when I was asked to present myself at the British Ministry of Production. There an official informed me that His Majesty's government wanted me to go to India and see if I could persuade the local authorities to provide more natural rubber for the Allied war effort. I accepted on the understanding that I would take advantage of my stay in India to contact potential suppliers of hides for the reconstruction of Czechoslovakia's shoe industry.

"Can you go tomorrow?" the official asked as he handed me my movement orders. When I asked what on earth was the "ghost train" by which I was supposed to leave London, he explained that this was a train I would find at Euston Station, even though, officially, it didn't exist. "Don't bother asking anyone when or where it's going," he warned. "They'll think that you're crazy."

So I packed my belongings, found the "ghost train" and went to sleep in a comfortable compartment. The next morning in Liverpool all the passengers were driven to the docks, where I boarded a ship that was due to sail the following day to Bombay. Unfortunately a storm blew up and our departure was delayed for a full week. Nevertheless, we had to assemble every day on deck for lifeboat drill. On day four or five I decided to skip the drill and go instead to the medical office to see if I could get a laxative. There was a long lineup, so it was quite a while before I could see the doctor and get some pills to remedy my complaint. When I returned to my boat station, there was blood all over the place. Apparently the crew of a frigate that was anchored beside us had accidentally fired an antiaircraft gun and killed a number of the people with whom I should have been drilling. So I may owe my life to being constipated on that particular day.

Finally our convoy sailed, and we had a slow though blessedly uneventful journey across the Bay of Biscay, through the straits of Gibraltar and past Algiers and Malta. There must have been about 4,000 of us on board a ship that had been built for 600 passengers, but, given the Mediterranean sunshine and the exotic scenery, a little congestion seemed a small price to pay. The idyll was shattered in Port Said, where a police launch pulled up alongside our ship, and the next thing I knew the loudspeaker was summoning Captain Bata to report to the security officer. I am sure my fellow passengers must have thought I was a spy who was being taken off to jail.

Upon responding to the summons, I was surprised to find not a police escort, but "Lieutenant" Slavo Blazek. The schedules of naval convoys were, of course, a closely guarded military secret. But thanks to his excellent contacts, Blazek knew not only when and on what ship I was arriving, but also where I was going. He informed me that he had arranged for me to stop off in Egypt, tour the local Bata works and then continue my trip to India by air. All the paperwork had been done, and he even had a Middle East identity card waiting for me. So I left the ship and spent four or five days in Egypt, after which I took off in an RAF transport on the first leg to India.

One of my fellow passengers was the maharajah of Kashmir, and when we landed in the United Arab Emirates, he was greeted by a guard of honor, a parade of camel-mounted infantry and a display of horsemanship by soldiers charging each other with sabers drawn. After another couple of stops and more guards of honor, we arrived in Delhi, the final destination of most of my fellow passengers, while I flew on to Calcutta. There wasn't a soul to meet me at the blacked-out airport, so I hitched a ride with an army truck, which deposited me with my luggage in a downtown hut that served as the airport terminal. As I looked around, I saw two figures emerge from the dark, and I recognized, to my relief, John Bartos, the general manager of the Indian company, and the chairman of the board, M. L. Khaitan. They explained that they hadn't been able to meet me because civilians weren't allowed near the airport in wartime. Before long I was relaxing in a beautiful guest house beside our factory in Batanagar.

After a few days in Calcutta, I embarked on a circuitous journey to Delhi. In contrast to the Spartan travel conditions that most Westerners considered normal in wartime, I found myself and three or four of my Bata colleagues traversing India in a luxurious private car attached to the rear of an express train. A "bogie," as these cars are called, has several bedrooms, a dining room and a staff to attend to the passengers' wishes. It was a far cry from the night train I used to take from Bonar Law to Ottawa. On our way to Delhi we visited a number of tanneries and hide-collecting centers and negotiated substantial purchases with them. This was, of course, several years before partition, and though Hindus consider cows sacred and forbid their slaughter, that prohibition didn't apply to what was then India's large Muslim population.

In New Delhi I did my best to persuade the authorities to provide more natural rubber for the Allied war effort and to use synthetic rubber for domestic needs. I am sure a dozen other people must have been carrying the same message, so I have no idea to what extent I may have been successful. I did manage to collect samples of rubber, which I was going to take back with me to London so that British experts could analyze them and suggest ways of improving both quality and yield. But at the airport the government people took them away from me and sent them by what they considered a more secure route. Clearly my rubber samples enjoyed a higher priority than I did.

After spending Christmas with Blazek and his staff in Cairo, I was diverted from my itinerary for a quick reconnaissance trip to Kenya. During a twenty-four-hour stopover in Khartoum, I met both British and Sudanese officials and discussed with them their plans for the industrialization of their country. I was so impressed with their expertise and their obvious desire to attract foreign investment that I determined to put an independent Sudan high on the list of countries where we might begin manufacturing after the war. There was no way for me to foresee how unfortunate that decision would turn out to be.

Back in Cairo I prepared for my first trip to continental Europe in more than five years. On the eve of my departure I attended a dinner party given by an American general, and the moment word got around that I was going to Paris, every single guest asked would I mind taking "a little something" to a husband or girlfriend. I agreed on condition that the items were small. When I got back to my hotel, I found my room overflowing with parcels of every size and description. I took as much as I could and left the remainder for Blazek and his people to return to the owners.

The old Dakota on which I had managed to secure a bucket seat landed in Algiers, and since we weren't going to take off again until the following morning, I declined an offer to be billeted at the airport and decided to go into town so that I could confer with some of the local Bata managers. At the downtown shack that served as a terminal, I met our regional coordinator, Monsieur Kreuzer, and the local manager, Mr. Mraz, who promptly informed me that the one good hotel in Algiers refused to provide accommodation for anyone below the rank of colonel. So we spent quite a bit of time searching for an alternative and finally settled for a room in the attic of what turned out to be a brothel. It wasn't elegant, but to the best of my recollection, I had a reasonably good night.

At the airport in Algiers I was asked to sign a form to the effect that all my luggage was "equipment required for operations at my destination." I decided that public relations was part of my mission and that coffee for the American general's girlfriend was indeed operational equipment unavailable at the destination, so I signed. The young lady, incidentally, turned out to be a real beauty and had I stayed in Paris for any length of time I might have tried to provide her with more than a package of coffee. As it was I spent four days talking business with the executives who were in charge of our operations in France, all of which had by then been liberated.

My final European stopover was Zurich, where I made the acquaintance of the American consul general, a man by the name of Sam Woods, and his charming Czech wife, Milada. Sam had been commercial counselor at the U.S. embassy in Berlin and, like all American diplomats, had been interned following Pearl Harbor. While waiting to be exchanged for German diplomats interned in the United States, he was contacted by a Roman Catholic priest who identified himself as a member of an anti-Nazi German underground movement. He suggested to Sam that, following his release, he should try to have himself appointed to Switzerland, where the priest or one of his friends would be in touch with him for purposes of further action. Just how Sam managed to get the Zurich posting I have no idea but, according to CIA director Allen Dulles, the priest did turn up and handed over material that Allied intelligence considered rather valuable.

By the time I got back to Canada I had been away for almost five months. Fortunately, while I was gallivanting around the world, a number of first-class people were minding the store back home. Two to whom I feel particularly indebted are C. K. Herz and Antonin Cekota. C.K. was a marketing expert whose low-key management style and ability to make friends proved invaluable both during and after the war. Tony was an ideologue and forward thinker, a brilliant communicator, a great man to have around for strategic planning. Along with our lawyer, Wilf Parry, they were the trio who made it possible for me to serve in the reserve army, act as consultant to the Czechoslovakian government-in-exile and take off on an overseas mission on behalf of the Allies, confident that the business was in good hands.

During my absence, most of Italy had been cleared of German troops, a Free French government had assumed power in France and Allied armies had crossed into Germany from both east and west. At last the end of the war was in sight.

5

PICKING UP THE
PIECES

O N AUGUST 6, 1945, some twenty-five senior Bata executives from all over the world sat around a conference table in England, trying to plan the future of our organization. As yet we had no way of knowing that this was a historic day, that on the other side of the world a city called Hiroshima had just been pulverized by an atomic bomb, or that, within a few days, Japan would surrender. But we did know that the war in Europe was over, and it seemed reasonable to assume that Southeast Asia would be free of Japanese occupation within a year if not before. Clearly the time had come to survey the state of the Bata organization, analyze the wartime damage it had suffered and begin implementing our plans for postwar reconstruction.

Geographically speaking, the brightest part of the picture was Western Europe, particularly Britain. Not only had the British company survived the war almost unscathed, it had also been extremely well managed to the extent where it had succeeded in turning a profit, in spite of heavy excess profit taxes. Once the war was over and the rubber shortage abated, it was faster off the mark than anybody else in producing waterproof footwear for the rain-soaked domestic market. What's more, the company soon became Britain's number one exporter of shoes, not only to the sterling area, but also to Canada and the United States. As a result, it was able to accumulate considerable resources, which enabled us to finance the rehabilitation of other enterprises in Europe and overseas.

On the continent the one company that was undamaged was our relatively small operation in Switzerland. The Dutch factory, on the other hand, had been caught in a type of no-man's-land during the final stages of the war, with British and Canadian guns on one side and German ones on the other. By the time the fighting subsided, the factory was riddled with more than 2,000 shell holes. But through it all its manager, a Czech by the name of Nossek, kept going to his office. Having found out when the British gunners had their tea break, he managed to arrange his schedule so that he could bicycle to and from the factory in relative safety.

In France the Wehrmacht had stripped our main plant in Alsace-Lorraine of its machinery and converted the plant into a military laundry. Fortunately the general manager, a fierce French patriot and wartime resistance leader by the name of Robert Vogt, had evacuated his entire executive team when the Germans invaded France in 1940. On his own initiative Vogt bought a small shoe factory in the Dordogne area, in what was then unoccupied France, where he and his colleagues spent more time working for the Maquis than manufacturing shoes. One of the adventures in which they participated was the escape of General Giraud from a German fortress to northern France so that he could join the Free French forces. Vogt was repeatedly questioned by the Gestapo, but he survived. When the Americans came in 1945, they acknowledged his contribution to the Allied cause by inviting him to ride with them as a liberator back to his native Alsace. They found the machinery from the Hellocourt plant still loaded on a freight train and before long that plant, as well as two smaller, essentially undamaged French Bata plants, were back in business.

Our major problem child in that part of Europe was a Bata plant in Italy. Before the war Italy hadn't been an important shoe manufacturing country, though I had gone to Milan in the 1930s to look into the possibility of building a plant in that part of the country. At that time a business acquaintance suggested to me that the ideal location might be an industrial park about to be created in the city of Ferrara. But our policy had always been to build in small towns with easy access to an attractive countryside and plenty of space for housing and recreational facilities. The moment I saw the huge conglomerate being erected in Ferrara, I knew that was the last place we would want to be. To my surprise and horror I heard, during a wartime visit to Washington, that Ferrara was the place where the Zlin organization had, in fact, built a plant.

At the end of the war the Italian factory had no money and no customers since most of our best retail stores were in the part of the country handed over to Yugoslavia. To make matters worse, the work force was controlled by a Communist trade union whose leaders claimed that we were rich enough to keep on paying them even if they didn't work. In truth we were far from rich; our resources were extremely limited and had to be allocated with great care. After much soul searching we decided that the only thing to do was to split the retail organization from manufacturing and close down the plant. So one weekend Reginald Marshall, our London personnel manager, led a convoy of trucks to the factory, loaded whatever finished shoes were on hand and transported them to a warehouse in Padua, which became the headquarters of our new Italian organization. The plant was closed down, the workers were paid off according to law and that was the end of our manufacturing in Italy. It was the first and, for many years, the only operation I ever closed down, and I felt terrible about it. But it had to be done.

Later, when Italy became an important shoe manufacturing country and the focus of fashionable shoe design, our retail chain developed into a major outlet for Italian-made footwear on both the domestic and export markets. Italy also became the site of our product development center, where some dozen professionals design shoes to be produced by local manufacturers and sold in our stores.

In West Germany Allied bombers had reduced most of the stores we owned to rubble. In retrospect, I wish we had bought some of the prime commercial sites, which, at that time, were available for next to nothing. But in those early postwar days the reconstruction of Germany didn't rank high among our priorities; and by the time I had reconsidered, prices had soared out of sight.

Overseas, the relatively modest operations we had launched before the war in Canada and the United States were healthy enough, though the Canadian engineering division, which employed the largest number of our people, would have to be converted almost entirely from the manufacture of armaments to peacetime production. But in Southeast Asia only the Indian company had escaped the horrors of war and Japanese occupation. Our operations in what was then the Dutch East Indies had been closed down by the Japanese and its managers had spent most of the war in a prison camp. In Malaysia our factory had been burned down early in 1942, in accordance with the scorched earth policy ordered by the Allied command at the time of the Japanese invasion. As a matter of fact, I had sent a cable to the manager shortly after the Japanese landed on the peninsula and ordered him to carry out the instructions of the Allied authorities not only to the letter, but in the spirit of the war effort. At the time, I had no way of knowing whether my cable had reached its destination. Years later, when I visited Malaysia, the manager told me he never got the message. "So what did you do?" I asked. "Did you burn down the factory?" No, he said, he couldn't make himself do that; instead, he and his neighbor agreed that they would set fire to each other's factories.

Before the fire and before being taken prisoner by the advancing Japanese, the Malaysian manager had ordered machines to be dismantled and arranged for as many parts as possible to be taken home by the workers. When the war was over, the workers brought back the parts they had been hiding, the machines were rehabilitated, a few wooden posts were driven into the ground to support a new roof of corrugated iron and in no time at all the plant was back in operation.

As for Africa and South America, whatever production or retailing facilities we had were mostly small nuclei that had survived essentially because of the ingenuity and dedication of their managers, most of them Czechoslovaks sent overseas by the home office shortly before the outbreak of war. The assumption, of course, was that they would continue being supplied with materials, machinery and merchandise by the mother company. When war broke out and contact with Europe was severed, they were left to fend for themselves as best they could.

As a rule these were very small, primitive operations with no resemblance to modern manufacturing enterprises. In a few instances, specifically in Kenya and Rhodesia, they received large orders for military footwear and consequently ended up employing several thousand people. But large or small, by the end of the war, they were all technically bankrupt. To make matters worse, some of the wartime managers who had coped reasonably well in the absence of competition didn't have the ability to adapt to peacetime conditions.

Kenya was a case in point. A year or so after the end of the war I got a call from Vincent Vaisey, the mayor of Nairobi, who was also a director of what was then our East African company. Telephone calls from Africa were highly unusual in those days, so I braced myself for bad news. "Mr. Bata," he said, "things are not going at all well here. Your manager is much too weak to do the job. You'd better do something dramatic or else the enterprise will fold."

The executive team at Bata Development agreed unanimously that Kenya was a country with tremendous potential and that we ought to do whatever we could to save the enterprise. That meant replacing the manager with a highly qualified entrepreneurial executive. It was obvious to me that the best man for the job was Tony Carnecky, who had been running a small operation out of a stable in Baghdad until we transferred him to London as head of personnel for the organization. As much as I hated to part with him, I asked Tony to go to Nairobi and mount a rescue operation. "I'll be glad to go," Tony said, "but not unless I can have some money. Because before I begin to make any changes, the overdue accounts will have to be settled and part of the bank loan will have to be paid off." I knew he was right, but the 50,000 pounds sterling (in 1946 a little over $200,000 Canadian) he figured he needed represented an enormous fortune for us. Fifty thousand pounds to resuscitate the largest industrial enterprise in that part of Africa! That goes to show what has happened to the value of money, and how hard up we were at the time.

However, we did manage to borrow the money from the British company, and within two or three weeks of that ominous telephone call, Tony and his family were on their way to Nairobi. A year later the Kenyan company was one of the most prosperous parts of the organization, and under Tony's leadership most of his previously ineffectual subordinates blossomed into capable managers. For the first but by no means the last time I learned the extent to which one outstanding individual can not only generate economic change, but also bring out the potential of his associates.

Fortunately we did have many such people within the organization, not only among our resourceful and loyal managers, but also among our outside directors. In Britain Jan Masaryk had helped us recruit in the 1930s the chairman of the British company's board of directors, Major General Sir Edward Spears. A Member of Parliament and distinguished veteran of World War I, Spears became Winston Churchill's representative to the French government during World War II. In that capacity he used his personal airplane to fly General de Gaulle out of France in 1940 when the German army was closing in on Bordeaux. Thanks to Spears and other influential directors of the British company, we enjoyed the confidence of government authorities and were able to get approval for travel and other necessities without the usual entanglement in red tape.

In Holland, as in Britain, we had had the good fortune, or good sense, to elect in the late 1930s an exceptionally fine chairman of the board in the person of Professor Verrijn Stuart. After the war, having played an important part in the Dutch resistance movement, Stuart was appointed chairman of both the Amsterdam Bank and the Social and Economic Council of the Netherlands. He was a gentleman in the true sense of the word, a man of terrific integrity and great intellect who contributed a great deal to our postwar planning.

Following the death of Dr. George Wettstein early in 1945, his law partner, Dr. Charles Jucker, had become chairman of the Bata holding company in Switzerland. But in many ways, Dr. Wettstein's legacy was very much with us. It was he who had had the foresight in the 1930s to mastermind a corporate structure consisting of a network of Bata holding companies and foundations in different parts of the world. By effectively divorcing the global organization from its Czechoslovakian roots and carefully covering up the tracks, he succeeded in keeping the Bata assets in most parts of the world beyond the grasp of the German invaders and, as it turned out, their Communist successors.

As for the management team, it consisted essentially of the original Bata disciples, young men who had fanned out from Czechoslovakia in the 1930s and whose ingenuity and loyalty had kept the individual nuclei going throughout the war without the benefit of corporate funds, technological support or sources of raw materials. Many of them were my contemporaries, young men in their twenties or early thirties. We had apprenticed and later worked together in Zlin, attended the same parties, skied together in the winter and canoed in the summer. There was between us a bond of trust and friendship that sustained me during the war and during some of the dark days that lay ahead.

As we sat around that conference table in East Tilbury, we agreed that our immediate priority was to create a structure that would pull together, rehabilitate and, where possible, develop the remnants of the organization. We did have at the time a Bata Limited head office in Batawa, Ontario, under the direction of "Fryda" Meisel, father of political scientist John Meisel, who later became chairman of the Canadian Radio-television and Telecommunications Commission. But given the momentous decisions and problems that lay ahead, we couldn't help but conclude that Canada generally, and Batawa in particular, were too far removed from the focus of international activity.

The British company's financial, technological and human resources clearly made it the pivotal member of that part of the organization that was outside Soviet-occupied Europe. More important, Britain was still the center of a vast empire so that, at a time when most countries were sheltering behind high tariff and nontariff barriers, the British company enjoyed free access to the sterling area in Africa and Southeast Asia. We therefore had no trouble deciding that the new structure should be based in England.

So we set up a kind of advanced headquarters called Bata Development Limited in England. Originally located in our factory just outside London, it was later moved to London's Old Bond Street, where we leased a beautiful old house — formerly the site of a prominent art gallery — and converted it into an attractive though not overly efficient office building. Geographically speaking, BDL's objectives were threefold: first, rehabilitate the European companies; second, rebuild the companies in Southeast Asia that had been occupied by the Japanese; and third, assist and, where appropriate, expand our embryonic enterprises in Africa and Latin America.

I started out by putting together a team, a handful of executives responsible for product development, personnel, manufacturing and technical operations, retailing, marketing, administration, legal matters and, of course, finance. To discharge the latter function I was fortunate enough to enlist the services of Edward Bach, the man who, back in 1937, had negotiated the purchase of the Chaulux retail chain in Belgium on our behalf. During the war, he had joined the army and I had lost sight of him until 1945 when he surfaced as a colonel and controller of central banking in the British zone of Germany. He suggested I might like to meet some of the emerging German bankers and, with this in mind, he invited me for lunch in Hamburg.

At that time we had a company airplane, so I flew to Brussels, the one European capital where you could buy whatever food you wanted, and loaded up with supplies before proceeding to Copenhagen. There I watched Danish customs officials carefully seal up the compartments that contained food, after which I retired for the night. But after arriving in Hamburg the following day, we discovered, to our amazement, that one-third of the food was missing. Someone in Copenhagen, of all places, must have known how to open the containers, remove the contents and reseal them so that there was no trace of tampering.

We took what food was left and made our way through rubble to what had once been one of the finest restaurants in Hamburg. The only item on the menu that was actually available was snails, which turned out to be full of grit, presumably because that was all the nourishment the poor creatures had been able to find. Fortunately we did have our food parcels to fall back on.

Our guests were four senior Reichsbank officials, all considered sufficiently uncontaminated by the Nazi doctrine to be entrusted with important responsibilities in the zone of Germany occupied by the British. One of them was a close associate of Schacht, Hitler's financial wizard, who was in jail at the time. I remember the banker asked and received permission from Bach to testify on Schacht's behalf at the Nuremberg trial, and thereby may have contributed to Schacht's subsequent acquittal. I took advantage of the opportunity to offer Bach a position in our organization, and though his government was courting him with an offer to become British adviser to the newly created Bank Deutscher Länder, he chose to join Bata Development instead.

One of BDL's first tasks was to tackle a morale problem that had developed among our employees of Czechoslovakian origin. Many of them had become citizens of their adoptive countries, had served in the Allied forces and were thoroughly acclimatized to their new domiciles. Still, after six years of complete isolation from their families, their friends and the places where they had grown up they were, to put it in a nutshell, homesick.

Take Marie Reeves, a delightful and highly competent Czech forelady who had come to East Tilbury in 1937 at the age of twenty. She expected to be away from home for a few months, possibly a year, just long enough to train some of the company's English employees. Caught by the war, Marie spent the following six years in England and eventually married an Englishman. When I bumped into her during my stay in Tilbury in 1945, she told me she was expecting a baby and that her one great wish was to see her parents, have them meet her husband and have him see the town where she had grown up.

We had hundreds of people like Marie Reeves, in Canada and all over the world, and something had to be done to help them. I had become aware of the problem during the war and had considered it serious enough to consult a commissioner of the RCMP — a man with a great deal of experience in helping newcomers adjust to Canada. His advice was to find a way, as soon as the war was over, of giving people an opportunity to go home for an extended visit. "You'll find," he said, "that ten percent will decide, for one reason or another, to stay there. But the ninety percent who'll come back will have discovered that the hometown isn't quite as beautiful, the food not quite as delicious and the working conditions not as congenial as they remembered them. After that they'll settle down and become real Canadians."

In the immediate postwar period there were no commercial flights to Prague or anywhere else for that matter, and traveling by train from Western Europe to Czechoslovakia took five days. So we bought an airplane and fitted out a transit house in Paris where people coming from overseas could stay while waiting their turn. Civil aviation resumed on February 1, 1946, and the following day our aircraft took off from Paris with the first group of Bata employees on their way home. We kept those flights up for two years until the Communist takeover of Czechoslovakia in February 1948. The overwhelming majority of our people decided, even before that traumatic event, to come back and settle down in various parts of the world, just as my RCMP friend had predicted.

Another challenge in the human resource area was the recruitment and training of new people to spearhead the organization's rehabilitation and expansion. By 1945 the original Bata pioneers had, admittedly, been joined by a number of nationals from other countries — people who had served their apprenticeship during the war and worked their way up the managerial ladder. We also had a handful of foreign nationals who joined the organization in the 1930s and who, in some instances, became equally if not more imbued with the corporate culture than their Czechoslovakian colleagues. Take Robert Vogt, the Alsatian who joined the French company as a store manager, or Philip Cowell, the British company's export manager. Vogt became general manager of the French company and, following his wartime exploits, the grand old man not only of Bata France, but of the country's shoe industry as a whole. And Cowell, who served in the Royal Air Force during the war, subsequently became a key member of the Bata Development team with responsibility for retailing, marketing and product development throughout the world.

But in spite of a few exceptions the upper echelons were an essentially Czechoslovakian team. In this respect we were no different from other multinational companies created before World War II. It had been standard practice in the 1920s and 1930s to have foreign subsidiaries managed by nationals of the mother country. So just as Philips had sent out Dutchmen and Dupont Americans and Unilever had sent Dutchmen and Englishmen, we sent Czechoslovaks. If anything, the trend was even stronger in our case because the schools and apprenticeship programs founded by my father had created a tight-knit managerial fraternity that was difficult for outsiders to penetrate.

But the world had changed during the war, and in order to rehabilitate and expand our organization we had to find and train vigorous, capable people of various nationalities to assume positions of responsibility throughout the world. To some extent our need was filled by young employees who had left us to join the armed forces. It was remarkable to see people who had previously shown some promise but hardly executive potential come back as seasoned officers with proven leadership qualities and an awareness of the world beyond their own countries.

When it came to new recruits, we were convinced that even though most of them were somewhat older and better educated than the young boys and girls we used to employ in pre-World War II Czechoslovakia, they did need specialized training in such areas as production, design, merchandising and finance. We therefore expanded the company college that had been founded in Britain before the war, reestablished the one in Holland and started a new one in France. While these colleges were much smaller than the one in Zlin, they did become the hatcheries for a future generation of international managers. Many of the recruits were Swiss citizens studying in England, who were interested in joining a global organization such as ours. The Dutch, of course, have always been world travelers, and so were the British. Sad to say, we didn't have much luck in attracting Canadians or Americans, perhaps because descendants of immigrants are less disposed to leave their countries of adoption.

Before long the graduates of the colleges would have to convince the old guard that Czechoslovaks weren't the only people in the world who could run a successful Bata enterprise. The test case came in the early 1950s when a young Dutchman was sent, at age twenty-three, to launch a rubber footwear manufacturing operation in Sri Lanka. His team included five or six expatriates of various origins, but not a single Czechoslovak. It was, I am happy to say, a huge success; so much so that a few years later, when the manager in Sri Lanka needed a good rubber footwear designer and the ideal candidate for the job happened to be a Czech, we sent him there confident that, by then, it had become abundantly clear that competence wasn't a matter of national origin.

Possibly the most important challenge we faced after the war was how to play catch-up with the dramatic changes that had occurred in the shoe industry. For six wartime years customers in Britain and continental Europe had been happy to buy whatever they could get, and with the shortage of raw materials and man-power, there had been no incentive to modernize. But in the meantime enormous improvements in technology, marketing and the utilization of human resources had taken place in the United States. It was obvious to me that, in order to succeed, we had to inculcate that innovative spirit, that American dynamism in the organization we were trying to create in Europe and overseas. To do this we adopted a two-pronged approach. To begin with we selected a number of people who were coming back from the wars and provided them with opportunities to spend extensive periods of time in America, either in our own enterprises or with large marketing organizations. Fortunately we had excellent contacts with such outfits as Sears, Montgomery Ward and Melville Corporation, all of which were generous in welcoming our exchange students and initiating them into their expertise.

The second and more difficult part consisted of converting some of the senior people within the organization to American business practices. These were men of considerable stature, many of whom had managed their respective enterprises under horrendous wartime conditions and, in the process, had saved important parts of the organization. Predictably they were fiercely independent individuals who didn't welcome what they viewed as outside interference. It was up to me to convince them not only that there were new and exciting ways of running a business, but also that the organization needed a certain amount of cohesion, that local autonomy wasn't inconsistent with central guidelines.

That was why in the summer of 1946 I invited the heads of our European companies along with senior executives from the newly created London headquarters to join me for a North American tour. In addition to our own corporate Cessna we chartered two other aircraft and spent three weeks visiting some thirty American and Canadian cities, talking to shoe manufacturers and retailers as well as marketing specialists. These conversations served as an eye-opener for people who had for years been insulated from technological developments, new marketing methods and the need to respond to customer preferences or competition from abroad.

To reinforce the organization's spirit of cohesion, Bata Development executives began traveling around, visiting the individual enterprises, putting on courses, even organizing intercompany soccer matches. Unfortunately these matches had to be discontinued after a couple of years when we found, as others have discovered more recently, that soccer for some reason generates hostility rather than sportsmanship. In England, France and later Germany we began calling on machinery manufacturers whose plants had been badly damaged during the war and advising them about what machinery they should be producing for the shoe industry. I believe this kind of assistance played a considerable part in the reconstruction of the machinery industry in Western Europe.

Particularly heartwarming were the ways in which people in various countries and walks of life displayed their honesty and loyalty to the Bata organization. Take, for example, Alsace-Lorraine, which, unlike the rest of occupied France, was incorporated into the Third Reich following the armistice of 1940. Having expropriated all Bata stores in that part of the country, the

Germans grouped them into a company and handed its shares over to the store managers. Following the liberation of France, the managers returned the shares to us without the slightest hesitation. In about a dozen other cases we had turned operations over to managers or to friendly entrepreneurs on the understanding that we would get them back once the war was over. With one insignificant exception in Guatemala, all these groups and individuals were true to their word. This display of people's fundamental decency and loyalty was an experience I will never forget.

But while the situation in some parts of the world was improving rapidly, the same couldn't be said about Central and Eastern Europe, where most of our prewar assets had been concentrated. There our prospects ranged from uncertain to dismal. Eastern Germany, where we had owned a large plant along with some 250 stores, had been annexed by Poland, whose Communist government proceeded to nationalize both our German and our substantial Polish assets. Also lost to Communist takeover were our holdings in Yugoslavia. But painful though these losses were, my main concern was Czechoslovakia and, specifically, the enterprise in Zlin.

Zlin was more than the site of the largest Bata factories and the homes, schools, hospitals, restaurants and theaters that my father had built for Bata employees and Bata customers. It was the spiritual center of the organization, the mainspring of a corporate philosophy, the home base of a worldwide family. Of all the uncertainties that faced me, the fate of Zlin was by far the most crucial and the most worrisome.

6

CZECHOSLOVAKIA
REVISITED

THE GOVERNMENT THAT ASSUMED power in Czechoslovakia following the defeat of Nazi Germany was a curious hybrid. Theoretically the Communists were only one of four parties in the coalition government under President Benes, and the authorities went to occasionally bizarre lengths to reinforce that image. For instance, in postwar productions at the National Theater of the popular Czech opera *The Bartered Bride* each performance featured a different lead soprano, each associated with a different political party.

But for all the outward trappings of a multiparty democracy, it was painfully obvious as early as the spring of 1945 that real power was concentrated in the hands of the Communists. The conventional wisdom, according to which Marxism was forced down the throat of a reluctant government following the 1948 Communist putsch, is at best an oversimplification. The truth is that ominous signs of subservience to Moscow had become obvious during the last months of the war while the government-in-exile was still domiciled in London.

To me this was all the more disappointing since, up till then, my own relationship with most members of that government had been extremely cordial. Foreign Minister Jan Masaryk and I saw each other whenever he came to North America, and I continued to look to him not only as an old family friend, but as my mentor and role model. As for the other members of the government, most of them seemed genuinely pleased to have me participate in plans for Czechoslovakia's postwar rehabilitation. And while some of them were too cozy for my liking with representatives of the Soviet Union, this could be attributed to the fact that the Soviets were at that time our allies in the struggle against Germany.

Then, in the spring of 1945, the entire government-in-exile packed up and migrated to Moscow, presumably for a concentrated dose of brainwashing. A few weeks later, when the cabinet followed the Red Army into Slovakia and set up a provisional headquarters in the provincial town of Kosice, they announced that in postwar Czechoslovakia all major means of production and all assets would be owned by the state. It sounded ominous, but, being an incorrigible optimist, I kept hoping that their bark might turn out to be more radical than their bite.

Around mid-May I got a message from Sir John Taylor, a career diplomat whom I had first met in the 1930s when he was on the staff of the British legation in Prague. We saw a good deal of each other early in the war when he was serving as British consul general in Baltimore, near our plant in Maryland, and we became close friends. Taylor was subsequently appointed ambassador to Guatemala, a sensitive post given the fact that Latin America was in those days a hotbed of German espionage. Then, in March 1945, I bumped into him in London on my way back from India. "You're the right man at the right time," he said to me. "How long are you staying in London?" I replied that I was due to return to Canada in a converted bomber the following day. "No, you're not," he said, and he asked me to meet him at General Eisenhower's headquarters at ten in the morning. There I learned that I was to be part of a group that would make its way through the Balkans, what Winston Churchill called "Hitler's soft underbelly," into Czechoslovakia. I assumed, though I wasn't told, that the British wanted to make sure Western diplomats got to Prague before the Red Army and its political masters became too firmly ensconced.

The whole plan was rather nebulous and nothing came of it at the time. But before I left for Canada Taylor asked me whether I would be available at short notice for a similar mission. The prospect sounded irresistible and, of course, I said I would. And so, around May 20, I got a message asking me if I would be willing to escort a convoy of Western diplomats on their way to Prague. I accepted without a moment's hesitation, all the more so since the news from Czechoslovakia was becoming increasingly ominous. While sitting in my car in Batawa, Ontario, I heard on the radio that the coalition government had placed all industrial enterprises that employed more than 300 people under a "national administration." That of course included the Bata Shoe Company, and indications were that it was a prelude to wholesale expropriation.

Flying across the Atlantic in those days wasn't the routine affair it is today. But equipped with the required government priority, I managed to get a seat on board one of the flying boats that BOAC was by then flying from Baltimore to Poole in southern England.

Immediately after my arrival in London, Sir John Taylor, by then the British ambassador-designate to Czechoslovakia, presented me with my marching orders. I wish I had kept that impressive document. It said that General Dwight Eisenhower, Supreme Commander of the Allied Forces, was appointing Captain Thomas Bata to be the escort officer for a convoy of diplomatic and military personnel on their way from England across the Channel and Western Europe to their destinations in Pilsen and Prague.

The convoy consisted of six ambassadors, all of whom rated major general status complete with batmen and beautiful Daimlers, each driven by an equally beautiful member of the women's auxiliary army corps. Also traveling with us were some British officers, both male and female, en route to various destinations on the Continent. In addition to the Daimlers we had three less luxurious private cars and about twenty trucks carrying all kinds of furniture and equipment.

The truck that caused me the greatest worry, from the point of view of security, was the one loaded with Scotch and other liquid refreshments destined for the British embassy in Prague. Though we had taken the precaution of letting it be known that it contained ciphering equipment, we thought it best to mount guard with live ammunition around that vehicle every night while passing through the rear echelons of the American zone, where discipline by that time was, shall we say, somewhat lax.

The situation changed drastically once we entered General Patton's operational command area. All of a sudden all military vehicles were clean, the men were immaculately dressed, everyone seemed bristling with energy. My rosy recollections may admittedly be enhanced by the hospitality we enjoyed in Bingen am Rhein in American-occupied Germany. Instead of the somewhat uneven accommodation we had been offered during the early part of our journey, we were directed to a beautiful villa that must have belonged to a local vineyard owner before being taken over by the Americans. There we were served a sumptuous dinner, including strawberries flown in from Spain and vast quantities of excellent local wine.

Our next stop, Frankfurt, was a huge sea of rubble except for one imposing building, formerly the administration headquarters of the chemical conglomerate I. G. Farben. Whether by accident or design, it had survived intact the city's saturation bombings and was serving as headquarters for General Eisenhower and his staff. During our stay in Frankfurt, I went to see what had become of the Mönus factory, the dominant European shoe machinery producer before the war and one of our major suppliers. It had been completely flattened; I don't think the rubble reached above my knees. For me this was a serious problem, since we had no way of obtaining spare parts for hundreds of Moenus machines within our organization. I finally located the manager, who let me have some drawings so that we could manufacture the parts in our own engineering division.

Among the many incidents connected with our journey, there are two that I recall with particular pleasure. One occurred when, having traversed France, we reached the border of Luxembourg. I tore off a movement order issued in the name of General Eisenhower and went to the little box where a lone, cherubic-faced Luxembourgeois customs official was sitting. To my surprise he hardly bothered looking at my impressive document. Instead he threw his arms into the air and exclaimed, *"La guerre est finie."* Frankly I was puzzled. The war in Europe had been over for several weeks, so what was all the belated excitement about? It turned out this was the first time in five years that anyone had bothered stopping at that particular border point, let alone produced papers for this chap's inspection.

The other incident occurred a couple of days later in Nuremberg, where we were scheduled to stop overnight. Though the city had been essentially reduced to rubble, the military authorities had managed to find appropriate accommodation for the ambassadors in our convoy. As for the troops, they were to be billeted in an apartment house in a working-class suburb of the city. To my amazement, I found that this was a beautifully maintained, whitewashed building, about seven stories high and completely undamaged. The German tenants had been ordered to vacate their apartments to make room for the convoy, and when we arrived they were just about ready to move out. But when the British soldiers saw what was happening, they insisted that they didn't want to inconvenience these people, let alone kick them out of their homes. And so a compromise was struck: the Germans stayed in their apartments and our chaps spent the night either in spare rooms or on makeshift beds in the corridors.

I was enormously impressed. True, the war was over, but the British had suffered tremendous losses over the years and no one could have blamed them for feeling bitter toward the Germans. To me it was a remarkable display of their fundamental decency and sense of fair play.

Another Nuremberg building that survived the war was the stadium where the big Nazi rallies used to be held. The Americans had turned it into a fuel supply depot, and so I took our vehicles there to be refueled. As I looked at that huge arena, now, of course, stripped of the Nazi emblems, and as I recalled how the broadcasts of Hitler's prewar ranting at the Nuremberg rallies used to send shivers down my spine, I must admit it gave me a great deal of pleasure to find the stadium finally serving a constructive purpose.

Our next stop was Pilsen, the Czech city in western Bohemia known throughout the world for its excellent beer. Pilsen was in the American zone of Czechoslovakia, which unfortunately was very small, probably no more than 120 kilometers in depth. Stalin had insisted at his meeting with Roosevelt and Churchill in Yalta that the bulk of Czechoslovakia was to be "liberated" by the Soviets.

In Pilsen I went to visit the local Bata store, but the manager was obviously ill at ease when he saw me. I could tell he was wondering how his new bosses would react to my arrival, and whether he would be in trouble for even allowing me to set foot on the premises.

Later that afternoon we left Pilsen and headed for Prague. About fifteen kilometers northeast of Pilsen, we pulled up beside a sentry box, outside which stood an American corporal, spick-and-span in his immaculate uniform and polished helmet. When I showed him my orders, he smiled, saluted smartly and said, "Have a pleasant journey, sir."

We then proceeded to the top of a hill, where a group of Soviet soldiers in dirty, perspiration-stained uniforms pointed machine guns at us and demanded to see our papers. After they had found someone who could read English, we were waved on. As soon as we entered the Soviet zone, we found ourselves passing horse-drawn carts and rickety old trucks, all heading eastward laden with furniture, wash basins, bathtubs and every conceivable piece of equipment, anything they could lay their hands on. And, of course, we heard all kinds of stories about soldiers with ten watches on each arm.

When we reached Prague, we headed for the small square in the city's beautiful medieval quarter where the British embassy is located. Apparently we were the first British military vehicles to arrive in the capital, and the moment we stopped a crowd began assembling around us. I jumped out of the lead truck in which I had been riding, and to my amazement, a number of people came up to me, shook my hand and said, "Welcome home, Mr. Bata." They clearly recognized me, perhaps because of my resemblance to my father, even though I had never lived in Prague and had been away from Czechoslovakia for six years.

While being back on my native soil was an exciting experience, it didn't arouse in me any doubts or feelings of split loyalty. Shortly before I left Ottawa, the Canadian deputy minister of commerce had asked me what I would do if and when Czechoslovakia was liberated and became once again an entrepreneurial type of economy: would I continue to live in Canada and consider it the focal point of my operations, or would I return to my native country and the original base of the Bata organization? I replied that I felt I had both a moral and an economic responsibility to do whatever I could to put the Czechoslovakian company back on its feet and make it once again a prosperous enterprise. Whatever time and effort it might require, that would have to be my top priority immediately after the war. But having said that, I also assured him that I was a Canadian and considered Canada my home, now and in the future.

As soon as I got the diplomats settled, I made my way to the apartment of my mother, whom I hadn't seen for more than five years. Needless to say, we had an emotional reunion. But being a practical woman, she also insisted that I go at once to visit Prague's foremost tailor, with whom she had arranged early during the war to have a suit cut for me and ready for a fitting the moment I arrived. I didn't find out until much later that this suit was a sore point with one of my closest friends, Frantisek Schwarzenberg. Apparently during the war, when suit materials were unobtainable, Frantisek managed to find this one good piece of cloth in the tailor's establishment, only to be informed that he couldn't have it because Mrs. Bata had arranged to have it set aside for her son. "I was furious," he wrote to me good-naturedly forty years later. "As far as I was concerned, you so-and-so were gallivanting all over the world and presumably buying whatever your heart desired, while I had to keep on wearing my old rags."

My mother's large circle of friends included many freedom-loving politicians loyal to the ideals of prewar Czechoslovakia. One of them was the minister of justice, Jaroslav Stransky, father of my friend Honza, with whom Masaryk, Cerny and I had planned to open a London restaurant way back in 1938. At lunch in Mother's apartment the day after my arrival, he was almost in tears while he explained to us that his exalted title didn't mean a thing. Though he was a cabinet minister, he didn't have the power to prevent the unwarranted arrests, beatings and other excesses that were being perpetrated by the Communist-dominated national committees. The Communists controlled all the key ministries, including the ministries of defense and interior, which in turn controlled the army and the police. Whenever Stransky made a decision that didn't suit the national committees, they simply overruled him.

Though my new suit wasn't going to be ready for a day or two, I thought it best to put away my Canadian army uniform and change into civvies before venturing forth to see what if anything could be done to save the Bata enterprises in Czechoslovakia. I had no difficulty getting appointments with Prime Minister Fierlinger, a Social Democrat who had drifted to the far left of his party during his wartime appointment as ambassador to Moscow, or Zapotocky, a Communist who was later to become president. Both were polite though noncommittal. Of course, I also met with Jan Masaryk, whose sad demeanor was more eloquent than his words.

But my most interesting meeting was with the minister of industry, Bohumil Lausman. A few years later Lausman was to die in jail under mysterious circumstances after ending up at the short end of a power struggle within the regime. Rumor had it that he succumbed to an overdose of "truth" drugs. But in 1945 he was a big wheel in the coalition government.

With him at our meeting were two officials of the Bata company in Czechoslovakia: the company administrator, Mr. Holy, and the Communist leader of the trade union, a man named Kyonka. Holy, who had been a virtually unknown journalist in the 1930s, was given a job in Zlin during the war when he appeared to be in danger of being arrested by the Gestapo. The moment the war was over he showed his true colors by accusing the man who had sheltered him from the Gestapo, our general manager Dominik

Cipera, of collaborating with the Germans. The charges were so patently spurious that even the Communist courts were compelled to dismiss them, but not until poor Cipera had spent several agonizing months in jail. As for Kyonka, he was notorious for his strong-arm tactics. Nobody other than he or his cronies was allowed to talk to the workers.

The first question the trio put to me concerned the whereabouts of the shares of those Bata companies that were located outside Czechoslovakia. Evidently the authorities had been sorely disappointed when they opened the safe in the plant in Zlin and discovered that the shares weren't there. I had no doubt that the reason they were so upset was that they had planned to use the international organization to export ideology rather than shoes.

It gave me a great deal of pleasure to explain to them that the shares weren't in Czechoslovakia, that they weren't the property of the Czechoslovakian company and that, consequently, the newly ensconced national administration of the Bata Shoe Company had no way of getting its hands on them. Once this painful truth had sunk in, Lausman came up with what he presumably thought was a brilliant proposition. "How about," he suggested, "transferring that part of the business that is outside Czechoslovakia to the Czech company and, in return, we will appoint you general manager of the whole shooting match?" I tried hard to conceal my amusement and to appear polite while I declined this generous offer.

A day or two after my meeting at the ministry of trade, I got back into uniform, boarded our truck and, along with what was left of our convoy, headed back toward England. Having left behind the elegant Daimlers with their charming chauffeurs, I figured the return trip would seem rather anticlimactic. Instead, it soon became apparent that we were in for excitement of a different kind.

During an overnight stay in Pilsen, Colonel Perkins, the British consul, surprised us with the information that he had with him in hiding relatives of General Sikorski, the former head of the anti-Communist Polish government-in-exile who had been killed in a mysterious aircraft crash near Gibraltar. The pilot, who happened to be one of the pilots we had employed before the war in Czechoslovakia, survived the crash but remembered absolutely nothing about it. As far as he was concerned, there had been a normal takeoff, and the next thing he knew, he was being fished out of the water.

The Sikorskis — the general's brother in a Polish colonel's uniform with his family — had managed to escape from Poland. But the Russians were looking for them and there was a danger, if they were found, that they might be abducted. So Perkins wanted us to spirit them out of Czechoslovakia and out of harm's way, preferably to England. It was a dicey proposition, to say the least. The Sikorskis had no papers and I was afraid that, if the Americans were to discover them at one of the military check-points, they might arrest them and hand them over to the Russians. At that time such regrettable testimonials of friendship between the wartime allies weren't uncommon. In any event, I wasn't about to take any chances, so I made my passengers lie flat under a tarpaulin in the back of the truck whenever we approached a checkpoint. Fortunately that was all it took to get us past the rather casual inspections and we arrived safely in Frankfurt.

There I went to see the deputy supreme commander at SHAEF, explained the situation to him and asked for the required papers to be issued so that the Sikorskis would be allowed into England. Considering who they were and the important role the free Poles had played during the war, I thought that such a formality would be dealt with in a few minutes or a few hours at the most. But I guess bureaucracy had already taken root because I was told that, even if the matter were expedited, it would take a couple of weeks or more for a decision to arrive from London.

This was clearly unacceptable, so I packed up my charges and drove on to the French city of Lille, where I had been told the Polish consulate was still in the hands of the non-Communist Polish government-in-exile. My plan was to leave the Sikorskis in the care of their compatriots and proceed to England, where I hoped to secure entry permits for them. But when we arrived in Lille, I discovered to my horror that the French had just handed over the consulate to representatives of the Communist government in Warsaw. I didn't know what to do. There was no way I could or would try to smuggle them into Britain. Finally it turned out that the French Red Cross in Lille was willing to look after them while I went to England, got in touch with what was left of the free Polish government there and asked them to deal with the formalities. I am sorry to say I never did find out what happened, though I assume the Sikorskis made it safely to England.

In the wake of my visit to Prague, I was more than ever preoccupied with the fate of our enterprise in Czechoslovakia. The future looked bleak, all the more so since the authorities had already launched a barrage of smear propaganda against the Bata family. Their most vitriolic allegations were directed against Uncle Jan, who was accused of collaborating with the Germans as well as antisocial behavior and every other imaginable crime. But the propaganda spinners didn't spare me or the memory of my father, who, they charged, had used "the fruit of the labour of honest Czechoslovakian workers" to put shoes on the feet of black Africans.

Even so, I was nurturing one faint glimmer of hope. There was within Czechoslovakia's Ministry of Industry a controller of the shoe and leather industry — a position actually created by the Germans during the occupation. The incumbent was a Social

Democrat, a reasonable man by the name of Kubelik. While Kubelik had made it clear during my stay in Prague that there was no way of reversing or arresting the process of nationalization, he had suggested that a way might be found to establish commercial and technical links between the Czechoslovakian enterprise and what had become known as the Western Bata Organization.

On the basis of this suggestion, a Czechoslovakian government delegation arrived in London in the summer of 1945. Kubelik, who was a leading member of the delegation, was clearly anxious to arrive at some sort of deal whereby the Czechs might sell us machinery in return for hides and basic essentials, such as sewing machine needles, which were virtually unobtainable in Czechoslovakia.

By early fall the talks had progressed to the point where I felt justified in going back to Prague with a team of our people for further negotiations. In our more optimistic moments we thought that if we could come up with some form of employee ownership that was acceptable to the authorities, the government might postpone nationalization indefinitely once the Soviet troops were out of the country. In this and many other respects we were to be disappointed. The presidential decree that nationalized Bata A.S. (Bata Ltd.) was promulgated October 27, 1945, a few days after my departure from Prague. As for those industrialists whose businesses were too small to be affected by the decree, some of them thought that if they supported the left-wing parties in the coalition government, they would be spared. But it wasn't long before they discovered that they, too, were living on borrowed time. In due course the threshold for nationalization was reduced from 300 employees to thirty, and before long everything went, including mom-and-pop bakeries and barber shops.

During my stay in Czechoslovakia, my mother made sure I didn't spend all my time working. One night she gave a terrific party to which she invited all the eligible young ladies in Prague as well as the British and American ambassadors and their staffs. The apartment beneath Mother's belonged to Rudolf Slansky, a hard-line Communist who had spent the war years in Moscow and had become one of the most ruthless members of the coalition government. The party was a great success, and we were sure Slansky would complain about the deafening noise. To our surprise he didn't, which is probably the only good thing to be said about him.

Six years later Slansky came out at the short end of yet another power struggle within the Communist government and became the number one protagonist, so to speak, in the most sordid show trial ever staged in Czechoslovakia. He ended up being hanged, but, considering his past record, I suspect few people shed any tears for him.

Also during my stay in Prague I renewed my friendship with Charles Katek, an American of Czech parentage whom I had met in 1944 when he was a captain in the U.S. army stationed in London. In Prague Katek was head of the American cultural mission, an outfit whose real purpose I neither knew nor inquired into. What mattered was that the mission's office near the presidential castle was a gathering place for Czech intellectuals, journalists and artists as well as a fascinating array of American officers. Among the people who came and went was the well-known *New Yorker* writer Joe Wechsberg, his boss Patrick Dolan and Eugene Fodor, whose travel guides were soon to become famous throughout the English-speaking world. Another frequent visitor at the center was Julius Firt, the editor of the largest newspaper in Czechoslovakia. After the Communist coup, Firt escaped to West Germany, where he became an important contributor to Radio Free Europe in Munich.

I would have loved to see Zlin. The chief of police in Prague, the son of a former Zlin hardware merchant, offered to take me there and assured me I would be well received. But I was afraid that my visit might trigger anti-Communist demonstrations, which in turn would provide the authorities with an excuse for reprisals. It was the last thing I wanted to inflict on my former fellow citizens. Instead Mother and I invited Charles Katek to join us for a trip to Loucka, where we still owned a country home. To get there we drove through Zlin but, sadly, decided it wouldn't be wise to stop.

At the end of about two months in Prague we signed an agreement in principle with the Czechoslovakian authorities. The gist of it was that they would send us machinery and shoes, while we would provide them with raw materials and other items, such as nails, that were in short supply. To flesh out the agreement, and to act as liaison between us and the Czechoslovakian government, we decided to open in Prague an office under the name of Canadian Commercial Enterprises. The man we chose to take charge of this office was Frank Maltby, one of our English executives who had joined the Bata organization straight out of university in 1936. Having spent a year or so before the war in Zlin, he did speak some Czech, though as it turned out, he found it convenient to pretend that he didn't understand what the government people were saying to one another.

Frank arrived in Prague around midnight late in November 1945. He checked into his hotel and went straight to bed, only to be awakened a couple of hours later by two policemen who wanted to know what the devil he was doing in Czechoslovakia. That was only the beginning of a year of almost continuous harassment. At one point the secret police came to his office, went through all his papers and arrested a member of his staff. Frank himself spent three consecutive days being questioned at the headquarters of State Security, apparently on suspicion of "commercial espionage." It was a totally ridiculous idea: there was nothing to spy on, even if he had been so inclined.

Yet for the first six months Frank Maltby was able to carry on negotiations with the Ministry of Foreign Trade and the Ministry of Industry, whose officials were clearly less radical ideologues than their counterparts in the Ministry of the Interior. In May 1946 a large delegation of these relatively conciliatory functionaries came to London and, after several days of further negotiations, we actually signed a commercial agreement with them. At a luncheon I gave for the delegates several of us made speeches about future cooperation. Two days later our plane took off from London with the first shipment of materials for Czechoslovakia.

But whatever optimism we may have felt soon turned out to be misplaced. For the first but certainly not the last time we found ourselves the meat in the sandwich, squeezed between rival factions of a Communist-dominated regime. The agreement we had signed turned out to be a useless piece of paper: we got neither shoes nor machines and we had a hard time getting paid for the things we had sent. In January 1947, a month before the Communist takeover, Frank Maltby was summoned to the Ministry of Foreign Affairs and told that the weather in Czechoslovakia was injurious to his health. In other words, they kicked him out.

But though Frank's efforts at cooperation with the Czechoslovakian regime failed to bear fruit, he did assist me in a matter that was closer to my heart. Even while I was negotiating in Prague with the government authorities in the fall of 1945, my mother and I had come to the conclusion that she should be in a position to leave the country at a moment's notice. I was afraid that, if the regime's increasingly fragile democratic facade were to collapse, the Communists might be tempted to hold my mother hostage, if not worse.

The problem was that she didn't have a passport, and in spite of Foreign Minister Jan Masaryk's repeated efforts on her behalf, all her applications for a passport failed to produce results. Typically no reason was ever given, nor did anyone dare to criticize her wartime record. As a matter of fact, she was presented with a medal for the way she had assisted the partisans, at considerable danger to herself. But by the end of 1945 a passport would have been a good deal more useful than a medal.

As time went on, I was becoming so anxious that I actually contemplated smuggling her out of the country in the trunk of an automobile. But my mother was a big woman, and such a scheme would have been mighty uncomfortable as well as dangerous. Finally, on July 8, 1946, the passport somehow did materialize. Frankly I don't know to this day whether it was Jan Masaryk's doing, or whether the British or the Americans somehow managed to infiltrate the passport office, or whether it was just a mistake on the part of some government clerk. All I know is that the following day in London I got a call from the Foreign Office to stand by for an important message that was about to be delivered by a dispatch rider. The message informed me, in a prearranged code, that Mother had a passport and that I was to send an airplane immediately to pick her up. Speed was essential because there was a danger that someone in high places or in a rival government faction might find out she was leaving and try to stop her. We knew only too well that, if for any reason she were to be deprived of her passport, she would never get another.

Luckily we had our own plane, so I got hold of a crew right away and they took off for Prague at dawn the following morning. Meanwhile Frank Maltby had warned Mother to be ready by noon and to tell no one where she was going. To make sure her absence wouldn't arouse any suspicions, she telephoned a few acquaintances to say that she was going to her country house and would be back in three or four days. The only friend who was told the truth was Mrs. Eliasova, the widow of the Czech general and wartime prime minister who had been executed by the Nazis for his partisan activities. Mrs. Eliasova enjoyed tremendous prestige in Prague, and Frank accepted gratefully her offer to accompany Mother to the airport.

His immediate problem, though, was ground transportation. There were no taxis, and private cars heading for the airport were apt to be stopped by inquisitive police officers on the lookout for defectors. So Frank got in touch with Charles Katek, head of the American cultural mission in Prague, who loaned him an American staff car. At the airport the customs people seemed slower than usual while examining Mother's passport, but Mrs. Eliasova's presence apparently reassured them.

Our plane was a small six-seater piloted by former Wing Commander Ronnie Knott, who was later to distinguish himself as an organizer of the Berlin airlift. Knowing that my mother was anything but small, Ronnie had taken the precaution of removing the partition between the two back seats so that she could sit in relative comfort. Even so, as she climbed the three rickety steps and tried to squeeze in through the narrow door, Frank Maltby thought it best to push from behind to make sure all of her was on board. At last she was on her way to England. A few days later, I am told, all hell broke loose in Prague when the authorities found out she was gone.

Shortly after the Communists had staged their putsch and imposed their totalitarian regime on Czechoslovakia, I was in Holland talking to the chairman of our Dutch company and a number of other business people. When they asked me why the Czechoslovaks hadn't resisted the coup d'état, I tried to explain that any resistance would have led to bloodshed, which was something the opposition clearly wasn't willing to risk. "Nothing like that could ever happen in Holland," they all said. "We would fight, even at the risk of our lives." Which was exactly what my father had said when he told me about the Communists under Bela Kun seizing power in Hungary in 1919 and pushing into Czechoslovakia. At that time my father and his friends took their shotguns and went out to face the invaders and defend the country if necessary.

But in 1948 the opposition in Czechoslovakia had been emasculated by years of collaboration and compromise. A year or so later, when there was a danger of a similar Communist takeover in Italy, the American ambassador Clare Boothe Luce made a speech in which she emphasized the dangers of slow, step-by-step penetration. By way of illustration, she described an experiment whereby a frog was dropped into a jar filled with water that had been heated almost to the boiling point; the moment the frog felt the scalding temperature, it jumped right out of the jar. But then a frog was placed into cold water, which was heated slowly to the same high temperature; this time the frog swam around happily inside the jar, then slowed down gradually and finally died. That, in essence, is what happened to democracy in Czechoslovakia.

7

MY WIFE AND PARTNER

IN MARCH 1946 I flew from London to Zurich for a series of meetings with Dr. Charles Jucker, a senior partner in Dr. Wettstein's law firm. With me were Glen McPherson, formerly Canada's custodian of enemy property, and Colonel Ernest Magnus, a Canadian army intelligence officer whom I later persuaded to join our organization. As usual we were guests at the Wettstein home, and toward the end of the week Mrs. Wettstein suggested that we take advantage of the glorious spring weather and fly to St. Moritz for a couple of days of skiing.

It didn't take much to persuade me or my two companions that this was an excellent idea. On the way to the Wettsteins' beautiful ski chalet our hostess remarked repeatedly what a pity it was that her daughter Sonja was away and hadn't been able to join us. We were busy going through the multitude of skis and boots stashed away in a cupboard and looking for the right size to fit each of us when the door opened and there stood Sonja. I guess lightning struck the moment I set eyes on her — which may seem strange considering that we had known each other, off and on, for sixteen years.

I had first met her early in 1930 when I was holidaying with my parents in Switzerland. Father and I shared a love for fast outdoor sports, so we decided to sample an icy luge run down a St. Moritz street. We were negotiating a sharp turn, when something went wrong and we landed in a snowbank, at which point a Swiss couple emerged from their house and asked if we were hurt. We weren't, so they helped us brush off the snow, and we returned, a bit chastened, to our hotel.

In the afternoon I was told to make myself respectable because a man whom Father considered engaging as his corporate lawyer was coming with his wife to have tea with us. When the Wettsteins arrived, they turned out to be the people who had come to our rescue earlier in the day, so a friendly rapport had already been established. The meeting went well, and when we were invited to pay the family a return visit, we met the two Wettstein children, a boy of about six and his three-year-old sister Sonja. At age fifteen I can't claim that I was particularly impressed with either of them.

By this time the Depression had set in and the National Bank of Czechoslovakia, like its counterparts in most other countries, tried to conserve foreign exchange by refusing to authorize investments abroad. That was when Father decided to set up a holding company in Switzerland, and Dr. Wettstein came to Zlin to discuss the particulars. Since the new company was to guide the organization's future development, it was to be called Compass. But when a telephone call to Zurich revealed that the name had been preempted by someone else, Dr. Wettstein and Father decided to call the holding company Leader, which conveyed the same meaning.

During the 1930s, I was a frequent visitor in the Wettstein home, and while I didn't devote much attention to the two children, I did develop a close relationship with their father, particularly following my own father's death. One of Europe's top experts on international law, Dr. Wettstein instilled in his children and, I hope, in me a lifelong sense of responsibility and an abhorrence of mediocrity. While his somewhat autocratic and patrician manner might be considered old-fashioned by today's standards, he was also a visionary who dreamed of a united Europe long before the concept became either fashionable or realistic.

The last time I saw him was in March 1939, following my precipitous departure from Zlin a couple of days ahead of the Nazi occupation of Czechoslovakia. For six years I looked forward to our reunion. But early in 1945, when I was about to leave Paris for Zurich on the last leg of my wartime journey, I was saddened to hear that he had lost his long battle with cancer. Not only did I owe him a lasting debt for his invaluable services to the Bata organization, but I had always looked up to him as a role model, almost a surrogate father. When I arrived in Zurich a few days after Dr. Wettstein's death, his widow and children were in deep mourning, and though I shared their grief, I did my best not to intrude on their privacy. But a year later, when I saw Sonja standing in the doorway of the ski chalet in St. Moritz, she was no longer the little girl for whom Mother had occasionally bought toys, or the grieving daughter shrouded in black. She had grown into a beautiful young woman of nineteen, and frankly, I was swept off my feet.

It was a wonderful weekend. We spent the days skiing, the evenings talking and dancing, and by the time we returned to Zurich I knew I had found the girl I wanted to marry. Fortunately she, too, seemed interested in me, and so I embarked on an intensive if somewhat disjointed courtship. Being based in London at the time and trying to rebuild the European organization, I had no trouble justifying frequent visits to Switzerland, all the more so since I needed to discuss with my Swiss lawyers the problems I was having both with the Czechoslovakian government and with Uncle Jan. So throughout that spring, I managed to be in Zurich almost every other week.

Late in May I was once more on my way to Zurich, piloting a plane I had borrowed from a friend. Its maximum speed was 100 miles an hour. With the chief accountant of the Indian company as a passenger, we crossed the English Channel, touched down in Paris for refueling and headed for Switzerland. The weather deteriorated rapidly, I had to fly around a number of thunderstorms and I had a hard time keeping on course. In those days there were no navigation aids for small aircraft, no radio communications, just charts and, failing all else, railroad lines that one could follow. To make sure I didn't get lost, I flew along the Rhine, sometimes at an altitude of no more than 400 feet. But the weather kept getting worse, and finally I realized we would have to turn back. Making a U-turn in the narrow river valley scared the daylights out of my passenger, but we returned safely to Basle, where we hired a car and drove the rest of the way to Zurich.

When I woke up the following morning, the skies had cleared, the weather was beautiful and, to my surprise, I found it was a holiday. Just why Ascension Day, which is a Catholic holiday, should be observed in Protestant Zurich is one of those mysteries I have learned not to inquire into. But since the city was at a standstill and there could be no question of transacting any business, I asked Sonja's brother George if he would drive me back to Basle so that I could pick up my aircraft. He, in turn, invited a friend to join us, so I suggested that Sonja might like to come, too, and fly back with me. She agreed and off we went.

The plane was waiting for us in Basle, freshly serviced by the airport mechanics. I remember Sonja wore a light beige coat, and she gave me a pensive look as she climbed into the two-seater; perhaps she knew better than I what to expect. Normally the flight to Zurich would have taken no more than forty-five minutes, but since it was such a lovely day, we decided to make a bit of a detour and take a look at the mountains. That was when I made up my mind to pop the question, and to my everlasting joy, she said yes. Given what people do under such circumstances, up in the air or anywhere else, it was fortunate that there was no other aircraft anywhere in sight. Right then and there we began planning our future, the number of children we were going to have, the art objects we would buy to furnish our home. The one thing we didn't plan, and something neither of us suspected, was the part Sonja would play in the Bata Shoe Organization.

Later that afternoon I realized that proposing to a girl was easy; the scary part was breaking the news to her mother. Sitting on a garden swing with Mrs. Wettstein, I had a hard time persuading her that at age nineteen, Sonja wasn't too young for matrimony, that it didn't matter if she didn't finish her studies in architecture, that her being a Protestant and my being a Central European Catholic didn't make us incompatible. Mrs. Wettstein claimed that her late husband would have wanted Sonja to graduate from university. Besides, her daughter knew absolutely nothing about cooking or keeping house! While she didn't object to me as a prospective son-in-law, she insisted we should wait at least a year before being married. I argued that this would be a mistake because, unless Sonja became my wife before January 1, 1947, when the Canadian Citizenship Act was due to be proclaimed law, she might find herself stateless at some future date when, by marrying me, she would lose her Swiss citizenship.

Eventually Mrs. Wettstein relented, though there was one point on which she remained adamant: Sonja couldn't be married without knowing how to keep house. So the wedding date was set for October 26, late enough in the year to let Sonja attend a special school where she learned how to make soufflés, choose the right kind of polish for parquet floors and stretch freshly laundered lace curtains back into shape. The Swiss take such accomplishments very seriously.

I was in Canada when the time came to read the banns. There was no way I could get hold of my baptismal certificate, which was the only official document to list my place and date of birth; it hadn't occurred to me, on that stormy night in March 1939 when I left Czechoslovakia, to take it along. However, given the influence of the Wettstein family, the powers that be agreed to settle for my passport, which identified me as Thomas J. Bata. That middle initial was extremely important to me. Throughout the two years I had spent at prep school in England, I had felt disadvantaged because, unlike all the other boys who had two, three or even four initials, I only had one. Years later, at the time of my confirmation, I followed the European custom of adopting my godfather's Christian name, which happened to be Jan.

Then, about a week before the wedding, some kind soul who presumably wanted to be helpful smuggled my baptismal certificate out of Czechoslovakia and sent it to Sonja. That was when she learned that she was engaged to be married not to Thomas J., but to Thomas Alexander Vladimir Ferdinand Bata. I would have loved to know that I had four initials when I was at school but, a few days before our wedding, the news was decidedly inconvenient. Being a well brought up young lady with generations of Swiss probity in her veins, Sonja never thought of destroying or hiding the certificate. Instead she took it to city hall, where the authorities concluded that I wasn't the man she was planning to marry. It took considerable persuasion and a bit of string-pulling by the Wettstein law firm to get them to relent.

We had hoped to be married in a small church near St. Moritz, but, considering the prominence of the Wettstein family and the number of friends we both had, that turned out to be impossible. I was particularly happy that my mother had escaped from Czechoslovakia in time to attend the wedding. In addition to our relatives there were guests from many countries, including Bata executives and my Canadian army friends. From London came the British women who had driven the cars in our convoy to Czechoslovakia. The wedding itself was a lengthy affair, with a civil ceremony one day and a church wedding the day after, followed by a sit-down dinner for more than 100 guests and dancing until late into the night. Though I wasn't exactly an impartial observer, I believe a good time was had by all.

One of the wedding guests, the British consul, presented Sonja with her new British passport complete with a French visa so that we wouldn't have to delay our honeymoon while waiting for the required documents to be issued. Our Swiss friends provided us with generous food parcels to supplement what they assumed would be meager fare in postwar France, but after one meal at La Réserve in Beaulieu, we knew the parcels would go to waste. Never before had I eaten such marvelous food. After a very pleasant week, I developed such a terrible headache that I wondered if I might have picked up some tropical disease during my travels in the Orient. But that wasn't the local doctor's diagnosis. *"Congestion de foie"* he announced gravely after a thorough examination. Congestion of the liver, apparently the result of overeating! For the rest of our honeymoon I was on a liquid diet of vegetable bouillon and Vichy water. When at the end of our two-week stay we were getting into the car that was to drive us to Paris, the hotel manager presented Sonja with a beautiful basket of delicacies and a small bottle of champagne. For me there were dry biscuits and melba toast, along with a large bottle of Vichy water.

From Paris we flew in our airplane to Croydon, which was then London's only civilian airport. I was flying in and out of London so often in those days that I knew most of the immigration and customs people. As we landed one of the immigration officers came up to us, so we both produced our passports for his inspection. But he waved them aside and said, "I know both of you, so let's not bother with documents." Sonja gave me a mighty strange look; obviously she thought I was flying girls to London every week or two. She was wrong, but I had quite a bit of explaining to do.

After a few weeks in London we left for New York and Canada, where we settled into the caretaker's cottage in Frankford — at that time our only permanent home. So Sonja became a landed immigrant in December 1946, and because she was a British subject, she was exempt from the normal residency requirement when the Canadian Citizenship Act became law the first of the new year. About two months later we were in Quebec City, attending a meeting of the Canadian Institute of International Affairs. At dinner Sonja, who had just turned twenty, was seated beside Louis St. Laurent, the secretary of state for external affairs who was soon to become prime minister. She had never heard of him, and though I whispered to her that this was the man whose facsimile signature appeared on her passport, this fact failed to impress her. Apparently in Switzerland passports were signed by an otherwise anonymous civil servant. Sonja at that time spoke little English, but her French was, of course, fluent, so she and Mr. St. Laurent had a pleasant conversation. Having established that she was a relative newcomer to the country, her distinguished neighbor inquired what her citizenship was. Surprised by her answer, he asked how long she had been a Canadian citizen. "As long as you have" came the reply. He was momentarily taken aback, but once he realized that she was right, he roared with laughter, and from that day on we remained good friends. Shortly before he died, we received his last handwritten Christmas card.

But in other ways Sonja was finding life in Frankford confining, to say the least. The caretaker's cottage was a far cry from the elegant house in Zurich and the sophisticated environment in which she had grown up. She used her newly acquired culinary skills to roast a Christmas turkey, but it was clear to both of us that she wasn't cut out to be a housewife in a small Ontario village. In years gone by her ambition had been to become the world's greatest architect. Now that our marriage had put an end to that plan, she decided she was going to help me rebuild and modernize the Bata organization.

I couldn't have been more pleased. Having grown accustomed to wartime and postwar austerity, most Batamen tended to take shabbiness and lack of innovation for granted. Not so Sonja. Because she had spent the war years and studied architecture in Switzerland, where artistic and cultural activity continued to flourish, she aspired to much higher standards of quality and design. Shortly after our marriage, she immersed herself in the development of shoe lines and, with a team assembled from various parts of the organization, she began touring Bata factories with huge sample cases full of new styles. The result? As Sonja says, "Management would roll out the red carpet for me, present me with a big bouquet of roses, nod approval when I made suggestions, and then do absolutely nothing." When she told John Tusa, the head of our British company, how frustrated she felt, he suggested she try to learn more about the business by managing one of our London stores.

Sonja jumped at the idea, and the time she spent running a store in a working-class district of London turned out to be an invaluable learning experience. For a few weeks she did everything from fitting and selling shoes to stocktaking, accounting, ordering and hiring. It didn't take her long to discover that imaginative products aren't necessarily bestsellers, that it doesn't pay to stock avocado green or shocking pink in an environment where women insist on black in the winter and white in the summer. In addition to managing the store, Sonja took courses in shoe design, pattern cutting, grading, even orthopedics. With that background, the impact of her taste and decorative skills soon became increasingly apparent. I remember old Mr. Bally, the head of the venerable Swiss shoe company by the same name, remarking on the improved appearance of our display windows and advertisements and wondering if it was the result of a Swiss presence within the organization.

One of Sonja's more dramatic contributions to product development occurred some years after the war when she detected, long before our competitors, the advance signals of a major upheaval in the world of fashion. At a time when pointed toes were no more than a glimmer on the footwear horizon, she sensed a revolution in the making and worked hard to convert the rest of us to her point of view. It wasn't easy, given all the equipment we had to make stub-nosed shoes and the resistance to change that permeates most large organizations. But she succeeded, and as a result, we were among the few footwear manufacturers who didn't have to clear at nominal prices vast quantities of round-toed shoes.

During the first ten years of our marriage, I traveled almost incessantly, and with few exceptions Sonja always came with me. While I dealt with strategy, operations, government relations and personnel, Sonja would discuss product development and marketing. In those days we were expanding rapidly, so she would become involved in finding architects for new factory buildings and keep in touch with them during the construction period. On the retail side she designed and developed a standard Bata store that included everything from partitions to carpeting, furniture, even shelf brackets. The design, which we adopted worldwide, was based on modules that could be taken off a truck and assembled in little more than an hour.

In the developing countries we visited, Sonja studied the market to see what kind of footwear people might find both attractive and affordable. In Senegal, for instance, the primitive, uncomfortable sandals worn by native women were obviously out of keeping with their multilayered dresses and elaborate headgear. So she designed more suitable sandals and tested their appeal by hiring a few women to parade them up and down the local marketplace. In countries that didn't have enough foreign exchange to import hides or textiles, Sonja searched for indigenous substitutes. Then, in the evening or over breakfast, we would compare notes.

To me, her enthusiasm, her innate good taste, her talents as a hostess and her willingness to share my problems were and remain tremendously helpful. I won't pretend that everybody within the organization was thrilled to see the importance I attached to her views. For one thing, she was still very young, and I daresay some of the old-timers may have resented having the boss's wife tell them what they ought to be doing. Not that she ever held or wanted a management position within the company. Beyond taking on specific projects, her role was strictly that of a consultant. Her advice could be pretty persuasive, but, in the final analysis, local management was free to accept or reject it.

Thanks largely to the competence and devotion of a wonderful Scottish nanny, we were able to continue hopscotching between countries and continents even after we became parents. Thomas George, named after his two grandfathers, was born in Zurich on February 13, 1948, a few days before the Communists seized power in Czechoslovakia. In due course we had three more children, all daughters. Christine was born in 1953, Monica in 1955 and Rosemarie in 1960. While we saw less of our children than many other parents, I believe we did succeed in guiding them in directions that both Sonja and I considered important. One of our objectives was to bring them up to be self-reliant and willing to assume responsibilities at an early age. Young Tom was barely eleven when, during his school holidays, he began accompanying us as a "task man" on some of our travels. On one occasion he was assigned the job of producing a moving picture record of the ceremonial opening of our new plant in Chile. To this day he recalls with horror how, overcome with excitement and faced with the fairly complex equipment of that era, he somehow pressed the wrong button and ended up with blank film. A few years later, when Sonja was unable to accompany me on a trip to India, I invited our daughter Christine, aged thirteen, to come along and act as my hostess. In spite of being scared stiff, she acquitted herself with true Bata aplomb.

Self-discipline was another quality that Sonja instilled in the children. Once when the girls were quite young she took them to the ancient Peruvian town of Cusco, where we were hoping to build a store on property that belonged to a local religious order. With Sonja's help the negotiations were successfully concluded and the abbot insisted that she and the children come to breakfast the following morning. The meal consisted of hot milk with thick skin on top and goat cheese covered with hair. It wasn't easy for the girls to eat this unusual fare, let alone pretend they enjoyed it. But once again, I gather they came through with flying colors.

I daresay there must have been times when the children wished they could go to summer camp and have the same kind of normal holidays as their friends; but in retrospect they look on these trips as invaluable experiences. As a by-product of all this travel, we hoped they would acquire not only self-confidence, but also the ability to feel at home among different people and cultures. It isn't something we preached or even discussed with them; but by taking them along on our trips, by welcoming to our home people of different races and nationalities, by making sure they spoke a number of languages, I believe we did teach them, as our company song says, that "it's a small, small world."

Young Tom went to an English boarding school at the age of

six, which may seem young by North American standards. But I had enjoyed my prep school years thoroughly and I believe our son did, too. Besides, it meant that all the disciplining, all the nagging about untidy drawers and dirty fingernails was done by the wicked matron, while parents were free to indulge their children during the generous British school holidays. I am convinced that my own close relationship with my mother was due, at least in part, to this convenient division of responsibilities.

Inevitably as Sonja and I traveled around the world we wondered what would become of our young children if anything were to happen to us. "We have a rule that members of our family must not fly together," a German shoe manufacturer once said to me. "In that case," I replied, "you shouldn't drive together, either." "As a matter of fact," he said, "we don't." That seemed to us to be carrying precautions a bit far. After thinking it over, we concluded that, if we were to make sure we wouldn't die in the same accident, we would have to live separate lives. So we decided to take our chances.

Both Sonja and I had been brought up to account for the way we spent our pocket money, and we agreed that the same rule should apply to our children — not because we wanted to control their expenditures, but because we believed that they should learn to keep track of their cash flow. I am not sure how successful we were: much later they admitted that the books they submitted to us for inspection weren't always a completely accurate reflection of their financial transactions.

When they were old enough to go to college, we followed my father's system of working out a budget, including tuition, books, living expenses and extras, and giving them enough money to see them through a year. If they were frugal enough to save any part of it, the surplus was theirs to keep; if they overspent, that was their problem. During his first year at university, Tom was a bit extravagant and, as a result, ended up working in a funeral parlor to make up for his budgetary deficit. Christine, on the other hand, managed to save $300, with which she bought a secondhand car. I was furious; it seemed to me the car would cost her a fortune in repairs, besides which I was afraid it wasn't safe. However, when she drove the jalopy without mishap for two years and then sold it for $180, I had to admit she was a chip off the old block.

In addition to her qualities as a wife, mother and business partner, Sonja introduced me to the world of fine arts that, I must admit, had previously been foreign territory to me. A few days before our daughter Christine was born we were walking along Bloor Street in Toronto and there, in the window of a little art gallery, we saw a beautiful painting. I suspect Sonja mentioned the name of the artist, but it went in one ear and out the other. After the baby was born I wanted to give Sonja a present, and it occurred to me she might like to have that painting. So I went back to the art gallery and, to my horror, found the painting was no longer on display. However, I went in and explained to the owner what I was looking for. "Oh," he said, "you mean the Utrillo," and he produced the picture from the back of the store. The name of the famous French painter meant absolutely nothing to me, but I asked what the price was and he said $2,700. "I'll take it," I said. "Please wrap it for me." He had never set eyes on me before and he obviously wondered if my check was any good; there were no bank credit cards in those days. However, I must have looked trustworthy, because he relented and I was able to present the painting to Sonja in the hospital.

The painting now hangs in our living room, where we enjoy its beauty as well as the knowledge that it was one of the best investments I ever made. By the way, I would no longer have a problem identifying a Utrillo, or the works of quite a number of other artists; and after joining the board of the National Ballet of

Canada, I soon learned to look down my nose at those business-men who protested they didn't want to watch men jumping around in long underwear. Music is the one art form I have enjoyed all my life, though not necessarily in a conventional way. Rather than sending me into some sort of trance, a symphonic concert stimulates my thought processes and, occasionally, in-spires me to come up with solutions to intractable problems. No doubt purists would frown on this kind of music appreciation, but it works fine for me.

Meanwhile Sonja was becoming increasingly active in a variety of cultural and educational organizations whose objectives she considered important, and where she thought she could play a constructive role. Because she believed, for instance, that it was ridiculous to teach French to middle-aged civil servants rather than small children, she agreed to help the Toronto French School get off the ground. Similarly, it was her faith in democracy and in the need for an informed electorate that made her take on a succession of responsible positions in youth and educational organizations. She served as a director of the Art Gallery of Ontario, and as her talents became more widely known, she was elected to the boards of such large and influential public companies as Alcan and Canada Trustco. Whenever she agreed to join an organization or to pro-mote a worthy cause, she discharged her responsibilities with a dedication and disregard for personal comfort that I sometimes found astonishing. I have known her to fly halfway around the globe, from New Zealand to Mexico, to attend a Girl Guide council meeting and fulfill what she considered to be her duty.

But the job that gave her the greatest satisfaction was her chairmanship, in the 1970s, of the National Design Council, an organization concerned not only with the esthetic value of design, but also with its impact on people and on the environment they live in. A country such as Canada, she points out, can only compete with low-wage countries by creating quality products that are more attractive, more functional and less likely to pollute the environment. The Design Council's mission, as she saw it, was to steer the government as well as the private sector toward that kind of production.

Given the environmental implications of design, it was only logical for Sonja to become involved in another of her favorite causes: the conservation of nature and of wildlife as advocated by the World Wildlife Fund. Most of the issues — the establishment of parks, the preservation of forests, the protection of endangered animal species — require legislation on the part of governments of Third World countries, so Sonja's activities in this area tied in perfectly with our business travel. Moreover, her work on behalf of the World Wildlife Fund turned out to be, on more than one occasion, an unexpected door opener to the corridors of power. In both Africa and Southeast Asia, heads of state seem occasionally more interested in the fate of the rhinoceros or the tiger than of the Bata Shoe Company.

People occasionally ask me, "What is the secret of a harmonious husband-and-wife business relationship?" While there is obviously no universal formula, I do believe that, in our case, it has been our ability to prevent disagreements in business from spilling over into our personal lives. Over the years Sonja and I have occasionally gone at each other hammer and tongs over such issues as shoe styles, factory design or personnel policy. When two somewhat opinionated people are working together, such arguments are inevitable and, to some extent, even desirable. But at no time have they affected our personal relationship. It's as though we had built a partition between these two facets of our marriage. Not that we planned it that way. It is something that just happened, and I consider myself very fortunate that it did.

C H A P T E R

8

B A T A   V S   B A T A

AMONG THE PAPERS FOUND in my father's safe after his death was an envelope addressed to his half brother Jan. In it was a memorandum, handwritten on draft paper and signed Thomas Bata, according to which Father was selling all his business assets to Jan. The price, to be paid within a year, was fifty million Czech crowns (roughly $1.67 million Canadian). I was still on my way back from Switzerland when the safe was opened, but according to all the eyewitnesses, the alleged sale came as a complete surprise to Jan. "Is this valid?" he asked. No, said the notary, not unless it was signed by the buyer as well as the vendor. Upon which Jan produced a pen, wrote, "I agree to purchase," and signed the document. Later, realizing that he couldn't enter into a contract with a person who was no longer alive, he amended "I agree" to read "That is to say, I agreed, as per oral agreement."

What did my father have in mind when he drafted this strange document? To anyone who knew him it was inconceivable that he would ever sell the enterprise, let alone that he would virtually give it away for a fraction of its true worth. The value of his Czechoslovak holdings alone was estimated at several times the purported sale price. Whatever the explanation may have been, none of us thought of questioning my father's motives or the wisdom of his actions, least of all at a time when we were in a state of shock over his sudden death. Besides, we had no doubt that his overriding wishes were expressed in his "moral testament," the document in which he insisted that the enterprise be managed as a public trust rather than a source of private wealth. In that context the technicalities of ownership seemed almost irrelevant. What mattered was the continued health of the enterprise and its employees, a continuity that Jan's appointment as chief executive seemed designed to ensure, at least in the short term.

At age thirty-eight Jan was one of the most senior managers within the organization; he was efficient, he was mature and he was a Bata — a name that inspired confidence in employees as well as the public. I was yet to turn eighteen and totally inexperienced, so I was clearly out of the running. The only alternative candidate for the top job was Dominik Cipera, my father's brilliant deputy and trusted confidant. But while Cipera was the better adminis-trator and intellectually far superior to Jan, he didn't have the personality or the charisma of a leader. At a time when the Depression was tightening its grip over the industrialized world, that above all was what the organization needed.

Under Jan's leadership the organization continued to prosper. During the balance of the 1930s, he implemented and extended Father's plans for international expansion and invested generously in research and development. In his relationship with me he endorsed Cipera's efforts to provide me with increasingly chal-lenging jobs and opportunities for personal growth. Looking back on those formative years, I am convinced that I couldn't have wished for better mentors.

Even so it wasn't long before Jan began displaying worrisome personality quirks. Foibles such as his insistence on being called "Doctor" on the basis of an honorary degree bestowed on him by the university in Brno were harmless enough. More serious was his penchant for ostentatious behavior, which at times bordered on megalomania. During a visit to the United States, he arranged for police motorcycles to meet him in New York harbor and escort him to his hotel.

Unlike my father, who had maintained a simple lifestyle, Jan loved pomp and circumstance. Having bought a château to serve as a guest house for visiting cabinet ministers, major customers and other dignitaries, he proceeded to use it as the setting for a formal white tie reception on New Year's Eve 1938. That reception caused many raised eyebrows and murmurs of disapproval among the invited Bata executives. Not only was it a radical departure from the Bata family tradition of celebrating New Year's Eve with employees at informal staff parties, worse than that, the elaborate affair seemed a totally inappropriate way to mark the advent of a year that might well prove fatal to our recently betrayed and defenseless country.

At the same time, Jan was becoming an increasingly outspoken critic of Czechoslovakia's government and was doing nothing to discourage those of his friends who began touting him as a potential successor to President Benes. Indeed, my mother, who had always been on the friendliest possible terms with the authorities in Prague, encountered a noticeable chill on the part of officialdom in the wake of Jan's blunt antigovernment pronouncements.

By then I had assumed the duties of deputy general manager of the British enterprise, and in that capacity, I visited Zlin at least once a month to participate in strategic planning sessions. Once during such a visit Jan asked me to come to his office. "Why do you think I wanted to see you?" he asked. I said I had no idea, but, when he insisted, I wondered aloud if there was any truth to the rumors that he intended to go into politics. He said, "I don't suppose you could run the show if I did decide to throw my hat into the ring?" I told him that at age twenty-three, I felt totally unqualified to manage what had become a huge international organization, upon which he changed the subject. But the conversation confirmed my assumption that a change of command was in the cards at some later stage of my development.

During and after the Munich crisis in the fall of 1938, most of us were much too busy worrying about the likelihood of war, the safety of our employees and the survival of the organization to concern ourselves with personal idiosyncrasies or questions of control. Even so, that was the time Jan chose to travel to Germany for a private audience with Hermann Göring, an intimate friend of Hitler's and one of his most notorious henchmen. Personally I am convinced that the trip was motivated more by curiosity and self-importance than by sympathy for the Nazi regime. But given his outspoken dislike of President Benes and, later, his refusal to identify himself with Czechoslovakia's government-in-exile, his pilgrimage to Germany was used after the war by the Communists as proof of his alleged Nazi sympathies.

Following the German occupation of Zlin in March 1939 and my departure from Europe, I became completely preoccupied with the buildup of the Canadian enterprise. Jan, however, was in a quandary. Having fled Zlin in anticipation of the Nazi occupation, he had to decide whether he, too, was going to stay abroad, in which case the Germans would presumably interpret our absence as a hostile act and expropriate the company. If, on the other hand, he were to go back, there was a danger that he might become a virtual hostage in his hometown. After several days of indecision and assurances of safety from the German authorities, he and his family did return to Zlin on the understanding that they would be free to travel to America in the summer for a visit to the World's Fair.

Jan was no stranger to the United States. He had lived there in the early 1920s, after my father had bought a small shoe factory in Lynn, Massachusetts, and appointed Jan as its manager. The venture wasn't a success, which in retrospect is hardly surprising, given the post-World War I recession and the stiff competition from much larger American manufacturers. But in Zlin the general perception was that Jan had mismanaged the enterprise and its failure so infuriated Father that he banished Jan temporarily from the Bata organization.

Following this setback, plans to establish a production facility in the United States were shelved in favor of a strictly centralist corporate philosophy. Specifically, Father reached the conclusion that the company should operate a single superb manufacturing facility in Czechoslovakia and use it to export footwear to the rest of the world. Bata shoes were to be sold abroad partly by the company's own retail outlets, partly by independent agents with access to wholesalers and department stores.

The man Father chose to represent us in the United States was the owner of a Berlin shoe agency, a man by the name of Walter Löwenthal. Mr. Löwenthal argued that in order to impress the top ranks of America's commercial establishment, he would need an impressive title such as Czechoslovakian commercial consul. Having a German Jew appointed Czechoslovakian consul was somewhat unusual to say the least but, as a special favor to Father, the government agreed to overlook the technical difficulties. Armed with his exalted title, Mr. Löwenthal proceeded to establish in the United States an excellent customer network.

Early in the 1930s, in an effort to penetrate the American market further, my father decided to open Bata shoe stores in the United States. The main focus of this retailing activity was Chicago, which, with over half a million inhabitants of Czechoslovakian origin, was home to more of our compatriots than any city in the world other than Prague. It was assumed, erroneously as it turned out, that Americans with Czechoslovakian blood in their veins would buy Bata shoes out of loyalty to their former homeland. Instead we learned then a lesson that Marks & Spencer learned in Canada several decades later, namely that immigrants leave consumer preferences behind in their homelands and quickly adopt the buying habits of their new fellow citizens. The Czechs who had settled in Chicago wanted to become Americans, and if they bought Bata shoes, it was because they were good value, not because they were made in Czechoslovakia.

At the height of that period we had some seventy stores in the United States, and our exports grew to about five million pairs of shoes a year, or between two and three percent of America's total sales. That's peanuts compared to today's shoe imports from the Far East, which add up to some 700 million pairs, or seventy-five percent of total sales in the U.S. But in those days of massive unemployment and business bankruptcies, it was more than enough to turn Bata into a whipping boy of the shoe industry, the trade union movement and protectionist politicians on Capitol Hill.

Another member of this motley anti-Bata alliance was the United Shoe Machinery Corporation, an industrial giant with, at that time, a virtual monopoly in its field. USMC, as it was generally called, insisted on leasing rather than selling its products, so customers were spared the initial outlay for the machinery. But in return they had to buy from USMC all supplies such as nails, wood pegs and sewing yarns, all spare parts (which tended to be extremely expensive) and all maintenance services. In addition, they had to agree that they wouldn't buy machinery from anyone else, and that they would employ USMC mechanics exclusively. These mechanics knew, of course, every trade secret throughout the industry and thought nothing of transplanting from one customer to another good ideas they had picked up along the way.

After years of dealing with USMC, my father decided sometime in the 1920s that he wasn't going to put up with such monopolistic conditions any longer. By then our own engineering division was going strong and machinery manufacturers in Germany and England were emerging as potential suppliers. So Father advised USMC that, as the leases expired, their machines would be shipped back to them. By 1931 not a single USMC machine was left in Zlin. As a result, the company viewed Bata as an archenemy and did its best to arouse American opinion against us.

The combined efforts of so many adversaries made an importer's life in the United States precarious, to say the least. Even while the wildly protectionist Hawley-Smoot Tariff Act was plunging America's foreign trade into a steep decline, the footwear manufacturing industry and its political representatives in Washington were pressuring the government to subject shoe imports to more prohibitive tariffs. And while this danger was averted, we were compelled to negotiate what was probably America's first "voluntary" import quota.

Given the importance of the American market and the restrictions faced by our imports, plans to establish a manufacturing base in the United States were dusted off and reexamined every few months. In 1933, when I accompanied Jan, my mother and about twenty Bata executives on a visit to our American customers, we decided to fan out and survey various cities where a major shoe factory might be located. As a result, Bata bought 2,000 acres of land in Maryland at a place called Belcamp some forty kilometers from Baltimore. There Jan intended to build an American shoe town, a mirror-image of Zlin on the shores of Chesapeake Bay. But we all knew that it was no use tackling the American market unless we were willing to commit large financial and human resources to it, and so the decision to take the plunge kept being postponed. It wasn't until Christmas 1938, with war looming on the European horizon, that the American project finally got the go-ahead.

When Jan and his family arrived in New York in July 1939, construction was already under way, and it was obvious to the American authorities that the flock of Bata employees who accompanied him hadn't come primarily to visit the World's Fair. Though they received temporary work permits to act as instructors in the Belcamp plant, those permits soon ran out and the "instructors" had to leave for other parts of the world.

Meanwhile, Jan's behavior was becoming increasingly erratic. As the chief executive of one of the largest companies in Czechoslovakia and a potential candidate for the presidency of his country, he had developed an ego that didn't take kindly to the diminished status of a small fish in a huge pond.

One day while visiting the Hershey chocolate company in Pennsylvania, he was miffed to find that the owner and chief executive hadn't seen fit to schedule a personal meeting. To remedy the situation he ordered urgent calls to be placed from the Hershey Hotel to India, the Belgian Congo and Chile, even though he couldn't think of anything to say when the calls came through. The only purpose of the expensive exercise was to impress the hotel management and, by extension, Mr. Hershey with his importance and international contacts. The following day the Hershey company newspaper dutifully reported that a guest by the name of Jan Bata had placed all these overseas calls, but the anticipated invitation from Mr. Hershey failed to materialize.

Later that summer Jan moved from Long Island to Washington, where he established a temporary command post on Connecticut Avenue. When I went down to visit him, I was surprised to find him preoccupied with fantastic plans for the postwar expansion of his would-be empire. By then the war was on, the Germans and the Russians had divided Poland between them and everybody was wondering where Hitler would strike next. And here was Jan, sticking pins into various locations on the map where he intended to build factories. Apart from being a waste of time his game seemed harmless enough, though it did make me wonder about his mental equilibrium.

Then one day in November 1939 Jan said to me, "I need Staroba." Staroba was the name of the head of a professional team that I had transplanted from Zlin to launch our Canadian engineering division. Though the division was still operating out of a corrugated iron shack, it was already working on our first war contract so that, as far as I was concerned, Staroba was absolutely indispensable. "For heaven's sake," I said, "what do you want Staroba for?" "Well," he said, pointing at the pins on his map, "he's got to plan the machinery supply for all these factories." I pointed out that those factories weren't going to be built for an awfully long time, that Staroba was a hands-on guy rather than a planner and that he was badly needed for the war effort in Canada. But Jan insisted, tempers flared and there was a good deal of shouting. At one point Jan said something to the effect that I might have to be replaced in Canada by someone more willing to toe the line, and I made it clear that I had no intention of letting myself be replaced. True, the Canadian operation had been grafted on top of the trading company that had existed years before my arrival, and that listed Jan as its president. But I owned all the shares, I had provided the financing and as far as I was concerned it was mine. Finally I said, "Staroba is *not* coming, and that's that!" And I walked out, slamming the door behind me.

When I returned to Washington a week or so later, hoping to make my peace with Jan, I found two letters waiting for me at my hotel. One was a reprimand from my uncle for the way I had behaved the last time we met. Having had time to simmer down, I had to admit he had a point: I had been rude to a much older relative and I deserved to have my knuckles rapped. The other letter was a friendly invitation to lunch at the elegant house Jan was renting in Chevy Chase. After a thoroughly enjoyable family meal Jan and I drove to his office, where he readily agreed to sign a letter addressed to the board of directors of the Canadian company, asking them to accept his resignation from the presidency and suggesting that I be appointed in his place. His willingness to relinquish the title made me feel that whatever his peculiarities, he did have my best interests at heart.

But in the American press Jan was being accused of every conceivable sin, from using child labor to being a Nazi sympathizer. The latter charge struck me as particularly strange given the isolationist rhetoric that was being spouted at the time in the United States. Nevertheless, I urged Jan to make a public statement to the effect that he backed the Allied cause and the Czechoslovakian government-in-exile. But he refused, claiming that such a statement would endanger Bata employees in Zlin. That may have been true as far as it went, and had he simply chosen to shut up, I for one would have sympathized with his predicament. But it wasn't in Jan's nature to keep quiet. Instead he continued to sound off about all kinds of issues, including American politics. Though he was in the United States on a visitor's visa, he went out of his way during the 1940 election campaign to make speeches on behalf of Senator Tydings of Maryland, a bitter opponent of President Roosevelt and his policies. Presumably this didn't endear him to an administration that was already suspicious of his loyalties and his labor practices.

Meanwhile Jan's plans for the creation of a shoe town in Belcamp were going full speed ahead. In addition to the standard

Bata factory, he was building a corporate headquarters, a five-story hotel and a big mansion for himself and his family. The trouble was that he didn't have the money to pay for all these grandiose projects, and when he tried to have a million dollars in Bata gold transferred from Canada to New York, he ran up against the custodian of enemy property, who refused point-blank to release it. In the words of the custodian's counsel, Glen McPherson, "We were determined to prevent Jan Bata from getting any financial assistance from any Allied country unless he agreed to cooperate with us in the war against Germany."

In addition to scrutinizing Jan's political tendencies, McPherson was also trying to unravel the tangled web of interrelationships within the Bata organization. Who exactly owned what? McPherson decided that the way to find out was to speak to Jan. He asked me to come along, and so four of us — McPherson, two partners of the accounting firm P. S. Ross who were on loan to the custodian of enemy property and I — journeyed to Belcamp for a meeting with Jan. Glen's recollections of that meeting are somewhat different from mine, and since Jan didn't allow any of us to take notes, it is hard to tell whose version is correct. I remember Jan being uncooperative and downright evasive, as though he were trying to conceal the true state of affairs. At the time I didn't know much about the ownership structure, but I knew enough to realize that Jan was spinning yarns. I don't, however, remember him saying, as McPherson later reported, "That we [i.e., the British and their Allies] couldn't win the war, and if he didn't cooperate with us, he would regain control of the Zlin company and the world organization." Perhaps I wasn't present when that particular conversation took place.

In any case, McPherson came away from the meeting convinced that Jan was "an arrogant SOB" and, quite possibly, a Nazi sympathizer. He also warned me that in his opinion, Jan was trying to conceal the truth not only from the authorities, but more particularly from me. For the first time it dawned on me that the time might come when I would have to fight for my rights.

By then the Allies had put Jan and all Bata companies in neutral countries on their black list, which meant that no individual or organization in an Allied country was allowed to trade with them. About the same time Jan conceived a truly bizarre scheme, presumably to be implemented after the Germans had won the war. According to this plan, the population of Czechoslovakia was to be evacuated from its homeland and resettled in Patagonia. He reasoned, with considerable logic, that the Germans would be pleased to endorse a scheme that would rid them of their ancient enemies and, at the same time, provide the master race with such desirable *Lebensraum.* Less logical was Jan's assumption that the British would embrace his plan as a "foundation for permanent peace" and a way of expanding their sphere of influence, or that the Americans would be thrilled to have part of the western hemisphere colonized by "a hardworking and cultured nation." And while the Czechoslovaks would presumably raise some objections, Jan was confident that they, too, could be persuaded to see reason.

When I first heard about the Patagonia plan, I couldn't believe that my uncle could have hatched anything so absurd. Surely this had to be malicious gossip spread by his enemies. Unfortunately I was wrong. Nevertheless, I continued to urge Jan to make some sort of declaration in favor of the Czechoslovakian government-in-exile; but none of the vague statements he drafted were explicit enough to satisfy President Benes.

To make matters worse, Jan became the beneficiary of a curious transaction negotiated between a German trading company by the name of Sloman Brothers and the Bata operation in Zlin. Sloman Brothers owned vast tracts of Brazilian land, which they were anxious to sell, presumably because they were afraid the land might be expropriated in case Brazil entered the war on the side of the Allies. In any case, the Czech company bought the land, paid for it in German currency and put it under Jan's control. I imagine the Bata executives who negotiated the deal figured that by acquiring valuable German assets in return for worthless reichsmarks, they were doing the Allies a favor. But to McPherson and his superiors in Ottawa and London, the transaction looked like a thinly disguised Nazi kickback to Jan.

Early in 1941, having been informed by the American authorities that his visitor's visa wasn't being extended, Jan set sail for Brazil, where he planned to manufacture shoes and found yet another Bata headquarters. He left the Belcamp operation to be administered by John Hoza, a veteran Bata manager who, unlike the "instructors" imported from Czechoslovakia, was a U.S. citizen and therefore couldn't be denied permission to stay. With the help of Canada's custodian of enemy property, who finally did authorize a transfer of funds to Belcamp, the American operation emerged from its financial difficulties and eventually became an important part of the Bata organization. But it never did live up to Jan's grand design: the building that was to become a head office now serves as a warehouse, and a monument to thwarted ambitions.

With Jan's departure the organization's center of gravity began to shift. It wasn't that I conspired to usurp his position or to undermine his authority. Rather it was a combination of circumstances, many of his own making, that isolated him from the mainstream of the organization at a time when I was becoming increasingly involved. My management of the Canadian company, my contacts with Jan Masaryk and the Czechoslovakian government-in-exile, the backing I enjoyed from the Canadian government and my army commission all helped to inspire confidence in those Bata executives who were operating in Allied or neutral countries. They compared my activities with those of Jan, who was blacklisted, whose Brazilian enterprise never really got off the ground and who kept ordering Bata enterprises around the world to transfer to him part of their mostly nonexistent profits, and they drew their own conclusions.

The shift became more pronounced when the Chilean company, which had been founded early in 1939, just before the outbreak of war, ran into financial difficulties. Like all our embryonic operations, it had been equipped from Zlin with raw materials, machinery and building supplies, down to the last brick and nail. The team of carefully trained young men, average age about twenty-five, who were sent from Czechoslovakia to operate this budding enterprise were supplied with every conceivable necessity, including crates of toilet paper. In no time at all they had assembled a plant where they were manufacturing shoes and selling them at a respectable profit. Two years later, when Jan stopped off in Chile on his way to Brazil and saw how well the enterprise in Peñaflor, some forty kilometers southeast of Santiago, was doing, he decided to capitalize on what was obviously a good thing. So he bought 1,000 acres of land in a beautiful but somewhat isolated valley and ordered a new industrial city to be built. Unfortunately he forgot one minor detail: there was no money for capital expenditures. Before long the Chilean enterprise was on the verge of bankruptcy.

I appealed to Glen McPherson to release some of the Bata gold for a rescue operation in Chile, and he agreed on condition that we send a capable executive to investigate the situation and an accountant to straighten out the financial mess. Accordingly Ota Mencik, my mother's elder brother who was living in Toronto and who had been associated with the company for a number of years, went to Chile and worked out a plan for the rehabilitation of the enterprise. Since the plan called for the infusion of capital from Canada, McPherson agreed to release some of the Bata gold on condition that the new Chilean shares issued as part of the rescue plan be held by the Canadian company. For the first time Canada became the focus of Bata operations beyond its own borders. As for the Chilean company, it recovered rapidly from its slump and grew into one of the most successful members of the postwar Bata organization.

Though in 1943 peace was still no more than a mirage on the horizon, it seemed to me the time had come to figure out how the various components of the Bata organization were going to re-cover from the rigors of war and what part they might play in the reconstruction process. I therefore proceeded to assemble in Canada some of our most senior executives from around the world. From India came general manager John Bartos; from Britain general manager John Tusa; from Peru a chap named Kacal, who was in charge of our bits and pieces in South America; and from Belcamp John Hoza, who was running the U.S. company.

Getting travel permits and intercontinental transportation fa-cilities for all these civilians was a major achievement and a tribute not so much to my own standing with Allied military authorities as to the reputation these individuals enjoyed in their respective countries. Though I had no legal status other than president of the Canadian company, there was a tacit consensus that someone had to take the initiative. It couldn't be Jan, if for no other reason than that most of us were forbidden by our governments to communicate with anyone who had been blacklisted. Besides, all but a few of the Bata veterans had always assumed that Jan was merely acting as a trustee until such time as I was ready to take over.

At that meeting and, more particularly, at meetings I had with

Bata executives a year later in Europe, the Middle East and India, I could see that all of us were becoming increasingly worried about the likely effect of Jan's blacklisting on the fate of the Bata organization. With the liberation of Czechoslovakia finally in sight, and with the Benes government acquiring a decidedly reddish tinge, it was painfully obvious that Jan's refusal to speak up against the Germans or to support the Czechoslovakian government-in-exile was going to be used to tar him as a Nazi collaborator. No matter how unfair such a charge might be, there wasn't the slightest doubt that a Moscow-oriented regime would find him guilty and that the verdict would serve as an excuse for expropriation. To save the enterprise it seemed essential that I distance myself from Jan and that he acknowledge my right of beneficial ownership.

I therefore asked our lawyer, Wilf Parry, and Antonin Cekota, one of my two Batawa deputies, to go to Brazil and speak to Jan. But Jan refused point-blank to discuss a transfer of control or even a compromise. The way he saw it, he was going to return to Zlin as the owner and chief executive of the organization, and that was that. So divorced was he from any sense of reality that he asked the famous French architect Le Corbusier to propose him for the Nobel Peace Prize. "Of course," says Le Corbusier in his memoirs, "I refused."

In 1946 Charles Jucker, who had succeeded Dr. Wettstein as senior partner of the Swiss law firm, complied with Jan's request to meet him in Brazil. But when he was confronted with a demand to acknowledge in writing Jan's exclusive ownership of the enterprise, Jucker refused, upon which Jan threatened him with all kinds of dire consequences. In the same vein, when he heard about my engagement to Sonja, Jan wrote to Mrs. Wettstein and warned her against letting her daughter marry a criminal who was going to spend years languishing in jail. Eventually the inevitable happened: Jan was tried in absentia by a Czechoslovakian court and sentenced to fifteen years of hard labor as well as confiscation of all his property. It is this sentence that the Communist government of Czechoslovakia used for over forty years to deny my claims for compensation.

Though I made several more attempts to negotiate a compromise with Jan and avoid a family rift, I was rapidly coming to the conclusion that we were too incompatible for any kind of shared responsibility. As much as I disliked the idea of a legal free-for-all, the issue would have to be settled in court one way or the other. The question was where to begin. At the time my father created Leader A.G. as a holding company for Bata enterprises outside Czechoslovakia, he appointed Dr. Wettstein's law firm as trustee of a majority of Leader shares. This meant that for all practical purposes, the Swiss lawyers acted as shareholders of all Bata companies outside Czechoslovakia. Leader became an independent financial institution to which the Bata companies had to apply for additional operating capital or funds to finance their expansion plans.

The minority Leader shares were part of the assets allegedly sold by my father to Jan, though there is no evidence that Jan ever laid hands on them. Instead, they were carried around for years in the briefcase of Frank Muska, Father's financial adviser and one of his most trusted lieutenants. After Father was killed, Muska worked closely with Dr. Wettstein, and his financial expertise contributed immeasurably to the health of the organization. But Muska was a secretive man. Sometime in 1940, without saying a word to anybody except his wife, he removed 826 Leader shares (out of 2,000 shares outstanding) from his briefcase and put them in a safety deposit box in an upper Broadway branch of what was then the Chase Bank. Two years later he died.

When I decided that a court challenge was inevitable, I got in touch with a lawyer whom Sonja and I had met socially and who had impressed us with his knowledge of international affairs. His name was Allen Dulles, and he was a partner in the prominent law firm Sullivan and Cromwell, headed by his brother and future secretary of state, John Foster Dulles. During the war, Allen had been head of the Office of Strategic Services in Zurich and had negotiated the final surrender of the German forces in Italy on behalf of the Allies. Unlike his more famous but dour brother, Allen was a delightful companion, a great raconteur and, in later years, a good friend. Eventually he was appointed director of the CIA, but he never tried to involve me in covert activities, though I suspect it wasn't for lack of trying on the part of his subordinates. The only time I ever set foot in the CIA headquarters was when he invited me for a sandwich lunch in order to tell me, as a matter of courtesy, that he had been approached by a former director of our French company with an offer to mediate a settlement with Jan. I was amused to find that the man who conducted me to Allen's office was my old friend Charles Katek, who had always claimed to be on the staff of the State Department.

At the time of our meeting in 1946, Allen suggested that since his specialty was corporate law rather than litigation, I should engage one of his partners, Inzer Wyatt, as my counsel. That was some of the best advice I ever got. Though the lawsuit was obviously going to be complex and international in scope, Wyatt decided that the test case should focus on the ownership of the Leader shares found in Muska's safety deposit box. Under Czechoslovakian law that prevailed at the time of my father's death, the estate of a person who died intestate was to be split in a proportion of three to one between his offspring and his spouse. Accordingly, in May 1947, I launched a suit on behalf of my mother and myself against the Chase Safe Deposit Company, holders of the shares found in Muska's safe. The essence of the case, in this as in subsequent suits, was simple: had my father really sold the business to Jan? How did the words "rather I agreed to purchase as per oral agreement" come to be added to the alleged contract? During his cross-examination, Jan came up with a story that he kept embellishing, about a walk in the garden during which my father supposedly offered to sell and Jan agreed to buy the enterprise. But he clearly failed to convince Mr. Justice Schreiber of the New York Supreme Court.

When pronouncing judgment in our favor, Judge Schreiber concluded that there never had been an oral agreement, that Jan was a witness "wholly unworthy of belief" and that his testimony was "improbable and unbelievable." Says Robert McCrate, who worked with Inzer Wyatt on the case and subsequently rose to become president of the American Bar Association: "In forty years of practicing law, I have never seen stronger language written about a witness's testimony." Two higher courts dismissed Jan's appeals and reaffirmed Justice Schreiber's decision so that, by October 1953, the case of the 826 minority Leader shares was settled.

But all we had won was an initial battle in a long war. Round two would have to tackle the more complex issue of ownership of the majority Leader shares. In the 1930s Dr. Wettstein had decided, as a precaution against possible German claims, to transfer the shares to a foundation called BSF Stiftung in St. Moritz. Then, during the war, when even Switzerland didn't seem immune to Nazi aggression, a further decision was made to create in the state of Delaware two corporations by the name of Westhold and Red River, and to transfer to them most of the Leader shares as well as shares of all Bata companies not controlled by Germany.

To make sure that Jan couldn't order the Swiss lawyers to hand the shares over to him, our lawyers had already asked the District

Court in Zurich for an injunction forbidding the partnership from disposing of my father's property. In its decision the Swiss court declared my mother and me to be my father's legitimate heirs and ordered the lawyers to act in accordance with our wishes.

The next step was to go to court in Wilmington, Delaware, "to secure recognition of their (the plaintiffs') complete and undivided ownership of Leader in succession of Thomas Bata." Again the court ruled that the alleged sale of the enterprise was "a fiction," and that the Leader shares must therefore be turned over to me and to my mother. Jan tried but failed to persuade the Delaware Supreme Court to reopen the case on the basis of supposedly new evidence. "The Bata litigation has gone on for thirteen years," the judgment said. "The suit in Delaware has lasted seven years. Now, at the last moment, Jan asks us to open the door to a retrial of the case on a theory known to him for at least nine years and expressly abandoned in the Delaware litigation." The United States Supreme Court refused to hear another appeal.

Even so the last word hadn't been spoken. In addition to the Leader shares there were shares of the individual operating companies whose ownership was contested in court actions in Argentina, India, Denmark, England, Holland and Switzerland. The only jurisdiction where we lost was Holland, whose courts concluded that Jan was the owner of the Dutch enterprise. While that was a blow, it was a minor setback in the context of the important victories we had won in the United States and Switzerland. But every battle was hard fought, and Jan pulled out all the stops in his determination to win. At one point he actually tried, unsuccessfully, to persuade the pope to intervene on his behalf.

Finally, in 1962, during yet another court case in New York, Mr. Justice Greenberg threw up his hands and said in effect, "This has been going on long enough. You, Jan Bata, haven't got a leg to stand on, so why don't you try to work out a settlement with Tom?" It seemed like good advice, and with the judge's encouragement, it took only two months to reach a "comprehensive settlement" whereby Jan renounced his claim to all Bata operations except the ones in Brazil and Haiti. As part of the financial terms of the settlement, I agreed to pay $700,000 into an escrow fund, which the Central Penn National Bank of Philadelphia was to remit to Jan once he had complied with his part of the bargain. We were convinced that we had finally reached the end of this painful and expensive family feud.

As it turned out, we were wrong. Jan, who had switched lawyers several times along the way, had by then engaged as his counsel Harold Stassen, the perennial candidate for the Republican presidential nomination, who had temporarily traded his political ambitions for a law practice in Philadelphia. When Stassen heard that my counsel, Inzer Wyatt, was about to become a judge and would therefore have to leave his law firm, he thought he sensed an opportunity to upset the settlement. In a letter to Robert McCrate, who had taken over from Wyatt as my counsel, he renounced the agreement, which, he claimed, was based on "fraud," "duress" and "lack of consideration." Since Stassen had previously insisted that the settlement be governed by Pennsylvania law, we had to go to Philadelphia to fight this latest challenge.

After another two years of litigation, Judge Alessandroni dismissed as delaying tactics Stassen's repeated attempts to introduce "newly discovered" evidence.

Two more appeals by Jan were also dismissed and at last it really was over. For the first time, on December 6, 1966, I could claim to be the legitimate head of the organization. For almost twenty years I had been, so to speak, a chief executive on approval, backed by my associates as long as I lived up to their expectations. What would have happened had I lost? There never was any doubt in my mind that, back in 1932, Jan was the right man to succeed my father. But by the same token I am convinced that, as head of the postwar organization, he would have been a disaster. He was a man who clung to the past, who refused to acknowledge change or adjust to it. After six years of global war, political upheaval and technological breakthroughs, he thought he could go back to Zlin and pick up where he had left off, presiding over an all-powerful central organization. Failing that, he would have tried to build a new Zlin in Brazil and, in the process, bled the organization to death. I am sorry to say that we never saw each other again — he died in 1965.

And what would my father have said had he known that his fictitious sale would cause a twenty-year-long court battle for control of the organization? My guess is that he would have been delighted. As I look at his portrait in my office, I can almost hear him chuckling and saying, "So the kid had to fight for the business. It didn't just fall into his lap. Isn't that marvelous!"

9

WINDS OF CHANGE

S OMETIMES I FELT I was running a three-ring circus. Even
while I was fighting a legal battle with Jan and a political
battle with the government of Czechoslovakia, my associates and I were embarking on the reconstruction and
expansion of what had become the Western Bata Organization.
Inevitably I was handicapped by the tremendous amount of time
and energy I had to devote to the litigation. Some initiatives had
to be postponed pending settlement of the lawsuits and clarifica-
tion of the situation in Czechoslovakia; others didn't receive the
attention they deserved.

Yet, in a curious way, the need to fight on three fronts spurred
all of us on to greater efforts. Throughout those early years after
World War II, the enterprise grew and prospered, almost in
defiance of external problems. This growth is all the more remarkable considering the potentially crippling impact of the loss of
Zlin. Compared to the highly centralized nature of the prewar
organization, we were like a body without its head, like Ford
without Detroit. The research center, the product development
center, the machine shops, the large colleges were all gone; so
were the financial resources of the parent company. Indeed, some
of our companies were desperately short of money. Once, while

visiting Germany, Sonja and I invited our local bankers to a restaurant for a rather expensive dinner. After the meal we retired to a wine cellar, where the record player was blaring out the current hit song *"Wer kann das bezahlen?"* roughly meaning, "Who's Rich Enough to Pay the Bill?" We were so broke that the question seemed tailor-made for us. Sonja and I looked at each other and spontaneously chimed in with the singer.

What we did have, however, was a cohesive, highly motivated group of managers who were determined to build a bigger and better organization than the one grabbed by the Communists. Every year they set themselves ambitious goals and then went on to exceed them. One year they were going to produce 100 million pairs of shoes, then 200 million, then 300 million. Nothing seemed impossible. Years later at a business seminar a Northern Telecom executive told his audience that the three essential ingredients for success are confidence, competence and common purpose. We were fortunate enough to have large doses of all three, with special emphasis on common purpose.

In addition to the three Cs we were blessed, during that postwar period, with a fair amount of good luck. In England, in the 1930s, we had opened a number of retail outlets for footwear produced by our British company. Partly for reasons of economy, partly to avoid antagonizing British wholesalers who were buying large quantities of Bata shoes imported from Czechoslovakia, our general manager in Britain had located these stores away from the mainstream in decidedly unprepossessing neighborhoods. Even so, the expense seemed considerable at the time. As a young understudy to the general manager, I was horrified in those prewar days when my boss signed leases that committed us to pay, for twenty-one years, rents that ran as high as 200 pounds a year.

After the war these leases, which didn't expire until the mid-1950s, were as good as money in the bank. By then 200 pounds a year was a bargain, and in a market where consumer goods were still scarce, British customers didn't mind shopping around the corner from main street as long as they got value for their money. Our advantage was, of course, purely temporary, and unfortunately it lulled us into a false sense of security. But for a decade or more those low-cost stores, along with a booming export business, turned the British company into a beacon of profitability and a source of funds for foreign expansion.

To a lesser extent the same could be said of France. When I first visited France after the war, the political situation was so precarious that I wondered whether we should commit any of our limited resources to a country where the Communist party seemed poised to seize power. Fortunately Marcel Fribourg, one of our outside directors and a Jewish concentration camp survivor, persuaded me that my fears were groundless, that the country was perfectly capable of withstanding a Communist challenge. So we decided to reinforce our French retail chain, which, unlike its British counterpart, commanded prime locations in major cities such as Strasbourg, Metz, Nancy and Mulhouse. But in order to appease the powerful Pillot retail chain, which carried Bata shoes in its stores, we had agreed before the war to stay out of the center of Paris. This unfortunate decision was to haunt us for years to come.

Eventually two events came to our rescue. One was the liquidation after the war of the Pillot chain, whose owner had been convicted of wartime collaboration with the Germans. The other was the advent of shopping centers. Because of my involvement with the North American business scene, I was familiar with the strip plazas that began springing up in Canada and the United States in the 1950s, and I was aware of their appeal to customers. But I had a heck of a time persuading the managers of the French company that they should adopt this newfangled American notion. But persuade them I did, which is how we established a foothold in suburban Paris. Ours was the first major footwear chain to make an appearance first in strip plazas and later in major shopping centers. It was one of many occasions when the ability to transplant experiences from one part of the world to another proved invaluable to the organization.

Then, one day in 1955, the general manager of the French company, Robert Vogt, said to me, "Mr. Bata, there is in the center of Paris a chain of thirty shoe stores called Phit-Easy, which their owners are willing to sell. We should buy them." My hair stood on end when I heard what the price tag was, but I knew Vogt was right: it was an ideal opportunity to close or at least narrow that Paris gap. So we borrowed the money and bought the stores. As a result of these moves, plus a fast developing export business to francophone Africa and the Caribbean, the French company became another mainstay of the organization.

But while business in Western Europe was booming, international political tensions were assuming increasingly threatening proportions. Almost half a century later even those of us who were around tend to forget the atmosphere of impending doom that hovered over the world in the wake of the Second World War. For almost twenty years we lurched from one crisis to another, from the Berlin blockade and airlift to the Korean War, from the Suez debacle to the suppression of the Hungarian uprising and the Cuban missile crisis. The tense international situation was one reason why, in building a global organization, it seemed desirable to have strong independent companies capable of standing on their own feet rather than hanging on to the apron strings of a dominant parent. Never again would the loss of a head office threaten the existence of our organization.

The threat of war wasn't the only, or even the main, reason we opted against a centralized structure. To begin with, local auton-omy acted as an incentive for managers to hone their entrepre-neurial skills and be rewarded or penalized in accordance with their success or failure. Second, it enabled each company to adjust its operations to specific markets. In this respect we were quite different from multinationals such as Coca-Cola, IBM or Dupont. Unlike soft drinks, computers or chemicals, shoes aren't an item that can be transplanted without change from one part of the globe to another. Their sale depends on climate, time of year, cultural differences and shifts in fashion. Winter boots that are in great demand in Canada would be of no use to the people of Southeast Asia, and what appeals to British customers may be of no interest to their French cousins, or vice versa.

Yet another advantage of decentralization was its appeal to the emerging countries of Africa and Asia. Governments of newly independent nations were obviously going to be more kindly disposed toward enterprises that looked and behaved like their own corporate citizens rather than subservient offspring of for-eign parents. And so, just as Edward Spears had made sure before and during the war that the British company draped itself in the Union Jack, we now set out to create autonomous enterprises with local boards of directors and extensive decision-making powers.

Unlike most companies with worldwide operations, we are multidomestic rather than multinational. The head of IBM Ger-many, for instance, makes decisions with regard to employment practices, government relations and compliance with German legislation; but marketing strategies, technological initiatives and research programs are determined at the corporation's Euro-pean headquarters in Paris. Our local managers are far more independent, much more part of the countries in which they operate. I have always considered it a compliment when, during my travels, I introduced myself to strangers and someone in India or Chile would say to me, "I always thought Bata was an Indian [or a Chilean] company."

Yet no international enterprise is ever completely centralized or decentralized. While some lean more one way or the other, all are hybrids and all are constantly subject to conflicting pressures. Even while we were building multidomestic companies and endowing them with extensive autonomy, I was busy creating a headquarters that would guide, cajole and, failing all else, order individual managers to adopt policies that were considered basic to our philosophy or essential to success. Without such central direction, the organization would degenerate into a group of independent fiefdoms devoid of a common thread or raison d'être. In an article about the Bata organization published in the American magazine *Footwear News*, the author wondered whether we were an octopus or a bunch of squids. The truth of course is that we are neither. But we have to be constantly on guard to make sure we don't become one or the other.

There were times when our head office people were exasperated because they didn't have the authority to impose their will on operating managers. Store design is a case in point. Sonja, who had studied architecture and was anxious to improve the esthetic standards of the organization, was impressed by the work that had been done in 1951 at the Festival of Britain by a young Polish-born architect named Bronek Katz. So Katz was engaged to design the prototype of a modern shoe store, which was so light and airy that it set the style for decades to come. But when Philip Cowell, who was in charge of the commercial section at Bata Development, set out to sell this new, dramatically different look to the heads of individual companies, it seemed he had embarked on mission impossible. The European managers, most of them Zlin veterans of prewar vintage, made it clear that they weren't about to adopt the newfangled ideas of my young bride and her avant-garde architect.

As a last resort, Cowell suggested to the head of our company in Cyprus that he adopt the new design for the store in Nicosia. As far as the other managers were concerned, seeing was believing. When they realized how attractive and successful the Cyprus store was, they promptly fell into line, and before long we had an architectural office in London designing stores for all our companies. Obviously it would have saved a lot of time and bother for me to say, "This is the way it's going to be done." But in this particular instance persuasion seemed like the better part of valor.

On the other hand, we would have courted chaos if we hadn't centralized functions such as the purchase of machinery and, in the mid-1960s, the introduction of computers. More important, the company's dedication to customer service, its color-blind employment policies and its unconditional ban on the giving or receiving of bribes had to be applied across the board.

Creating and maintaining the optimum balance between local autonomy and corporate policies is a never-ending challenge for any large organization. There is no perfect solution that, once achieved, can be maintained. The equilibrium shifts with changes in the political and economic environment, and it is up to the chief executive to keep adjusting the balance. Any permanent formula would inject rigidity into the system and probably destroy it. Perhaps that is the Russians' problem, that having adhered to one formula for so long it has become, so to speak, part of their genetic code, and now that they want to change it they don't know how.

In my own case, the moment of truth came with the creation of the European Economic Community in 1957 and the European Free Trade Association three years later. Though these two organizations were mere stepping stones toward a Common Market, their effect on the business environment was dramatic. Just as the erection of tariff barriers and other import restrictions had led my father in the twenties and thirties to build manufacturing plants outside Czechoslovakia, so the crumbling of these same barriers in the fifties threatened the survival of our European companies. Designed as they were to serve domestic markets first and foremost, our closely integrated manufacturing and retail enterprises were ill equipped to compete with the sudden influx of merchandise from the rest of Europe, let alone with low-cost imports from the Orient.

For instance, in Holland, where the only shoes previously available had been the solid, conservative variety made in Dutch factories, retailers were now able to import and offer for sale highly fashionable Italian shoes along with inexpensive rubber and canvas footwear made in Japan and, later, Korea or Taiwan. In a sense, the Italians and Orientals were doing to us in the 1950s what we had done to Europe twenty-five years before. At that time, it had been our inexpensive quality merchandise that had taken the European market by storm. Now the shoe was, so to speak, on the other foot.

We were not alone, or even the hardest hit. Instead of having a captive market of about fifteen million, Dutch footwear manufacturers found themselves besieged from all sides by competitors whose merchandise was either more attractive or less expensive than their own. Inevitably the domestic industry shrank, from several hundred factories immediately after the war to no more than a handful by the mid-sixties. The same thing was happening in Sweden, Germany, Denmark and France, though the French, in their inimitable way, managed for a number of years to block imports even while proclaiming an open market. A good deal of the labor-intensive leather footwear industry migrated to southern Europe, where wages were substantially lower and manual skills continued to flourish. Meanwhile the manufacture of canvas and rubber footwear, which had been the mainstay of our organization, found a more hospitable habitat in Oriental countries, whose low wages, undervalued currencies and enviable work ethic added up to an insurmountable advantage.

We tried to fight back by way of specialization, in the hope that the Dutch or the Swiss company would become Europe's prime producers of women's walking shoes or men's industrial footwear. This plan might have worked if it hadn't been for the combined effect of inflation and currency fluctuation. In my experience there is no deadlier alliance. Holland, for instance, was transformed from one of the lowest cost countries to one of the most expensive, mainly because of the rise in the value of the Dutch guilder. In France, a business that ordered expensive machinery from the United States might find that by the time the machinery was ready for delivery, a devalued French franc had inflated the price at the very time when the bank was cutting the business's line of credit. It was the type of scenario that drove many an enterprise into bankruptcy.

That was when I took possibly the most momentous decision of my business career. Throughout the history of the Bata organization, our stores had been the main if not the only retail outlets for footwear produced in our factories. While we were willing to sell through other channels, most independent retailers perceived us as competitors and were therefore reluctant to carry our products. Only in countries where our own retailing strength was limited, notably the United States and, to a lesser extent, the United Kingdom, were Bata shoes sold to any appreciable extent in stores other than our own. By the same token our stores didn't, as a rule, carry footwear made by our competitors.

But given the moves toward a common European market, it became clear to me that we had to change, specifically that the retail arm of our organization had to be split off from manufacturing. In order to survive, our stores had to be free to offer their customers the widest possible selection of merchandise, regardless where it was produced or by whom. That meant that, rather than relying on captive markets in the shape of Bata retail chains, our plants would have to compete for business with other suppliers. On the other hand, they would be free to market their products abroad without using the local Bata enterprise as their agent. If, for instance, Bata Holland had a product that might sell in the United Kingdom, it could bypass the British Bata company and strike a deal directly with individual British merchants. Indeed, there would no longer be a single head of the British, or French or any other company; instead, there would be two heads, one in charge of manufacturing and the other of retailing, both reporting to their local board of directors.

There was no doubt in my mind that this was the way to go. But divorce is never pleasant or easy, no matter how logical it may be. When our Dutch stores, for instance, began buying footwear from the Orient because our plant across the street couldn't match the price of imports, we promptly found ourselves with a vastly oversize manufacturing operation. It was a traumatic experience, watching that plant shrink from some 3,000 employees to 1,000 and eventually 600; but we simply couldn't keep on producing merchandise for which there was no market. Fortunately Europe was prosperous at the time, modern industries were being created and most of our employees had no difficulty finding new jobs, often at higher wage levels than we could afford to pay.

A more difficult problem, from the human point of view, was the inability of many of our retail managers to take advantage of their newfound freedom. It wasn't entirely their fault. The best manufacturers, in Italy and in the Orient, had their order books filled by existing customers and weren't exactly panting for new business. But it is equally true that our people, who had been champing at the bit to break loose from the shackles that bound them to our manufacturing plants, didn't know how to locate suppliers outside their captive orbit or select the styles most likely to appeal to their customers. Somewhat naively we had assumed that this type of expertise would descend on them like manna from heaven once they had the opportunity to use it. It didn't, and we paid dearly for our illusions.

Paradoxically enough, our problem was compounded by the strong ties that bound so many of our senior managers to their roots in Czechoslovakia. For years these men had been the backbone of the organization, the glue that held it together throughout the war. But ten or fifteen years later they still viewed "the way it was done in Zlin" as gospel, the golden rule that transcended all other considerations. They simply couldn't adjust to the fact that, in an age of dramatic changes in technology, economic conditions and business practices, the way it was done in Zlin had become largely irrelevant. Sure, lifetime employment had been an important part of our corporate culture, and I would have loved dearly to hang on to it. I, too, hated to see people laid off, and I sympathized with plant managers whose products were being spurned in favor of imports. But when stocks were piling up, when capital was tied up and losses were mounting, drastic surgery became inevitable.

We could have tried to solve our problem by going outside the organization in search of managers with the required expertise. But people with marketing qualifications as well as a background in the shoe business were hard to find, and for most management functions it is essential to have a thorough knowledge of the industry. For all I know it may be possible for a bright young university graduate to join a brokerage firm and become, from one day to the next, a productive member of the team. Similarly we do go outside to hire professionals such as chemists or engineers or financial experts. But to assume responsibility at a senior level for, shall we say, the selection of fashion footwear a person needs a good deal of experience, starting at the retail level and working up to corporate management. Obviously such people do exist outside our organization and, in recent years, we have been lucky enough to find them. But in those postwar days we were more apt to discover, too late, that we had inherited someone else's castoffs.

As I surveyed the situation in the 1950s, I concluded that by and large, our policy of promotion from within had served us well in the past and that, with some modification, it would serve us equally well in the future. The modification that was required was greater emphasis on management development. During the stewardship of my father and, later, Uncle Jan, management development had been mostly a matter of sink or swim. Graduates of the Bata Schools advanced quickly from the assembly line to managerial jobs, initially as understudies to store or department managers who made sure they were equipped to succeed them once they themselves were promoted to higher positions. But that was the end of any kind of apprenticeship. From then on people were expected to acquire as best they could the skills they needed to discharge increasingly difficult responsibilities. In the words of Tony Daicar, a Bata veteran with over fifty years of service, "You learned on the job if you wanted to survive." Daicar should know. Having started out cleaning shoes outside the Zlin factory gates, he quickly climbed the ladder to regional retail manager and, a little later, corporate manager of textile purchasing. This involved going to Egypt to buy cotton — quite a challenge for a young man who had never seen a bale of cotton before.

As a way of awakening the entrepreneurial talents of young people, the system proved highly effective in its time. But it wasn't designed to develop executives with modern management skills or to equip them to compete in the vastly more complicated postwar world. The colleges we had built or expanded in Europe, and the new ones we built in Chile, Kenya and what was then Rhodesia provided an invaluable combination of academic study and practical experience. Yet it was clear to me that the colleges were only the beginning. Given the rapid changes we were experiencing both within and outside the organization, there was a constant need for the young graduates and, more particularly, the older managers to have their knowledge and skills upgraded.

In the forties and fifties, saying that education is a lifelong process wasn't the truism it is today, and there was no way of telling how seasoned executives might react to such a concept. Since, back then, intercontinental transport involved weeks on board ship, European or North American managers who were stationed in tropical countries qualified for several months of overseas leave every three or four years. Many of them spent the time roaming around Bata companies, trying to find out what was going on. So we decided to formalize the learning process and put on courses for their benefit in such subjects as marketing, purchasing, production and store management. Once the courses were set up, we decided to make them available, not only to people on overseas leave, but also to the up-and-coming local managers recruited in Africa, Latin America and Southeast Asia. The next logical step was for similar courses to be made available locally as part of career development rather than something to do while on leave.

Today we have literally dozens of courses that deal with every aspect of the organization and are attended by people in every part of the world, from first-line supervisors to senior executives. We also try to make sure that people are given the time and the opportunity to use what they have learned. It is no use exposing employees to new concepts if they then return to desks piled high with unanswered correspondence and all kinds of urgent matters to be dealt with. Chances are that, by the time they have cleared the decks, both their newfound knowledge and their enthusiasm will have evaporated.

Apart from their educational value, the courses and conferences that were launched as part of our postwar development had two beneficial side effects. One was the opportunity for people from various parts of the world to get to know one another, exchange experiences and keep in touch after they returned home. Suppose, for instance, a chemist in Chile is experiencing a problem because of the discoloration of a rubber compound. He remembers that a chemist from Zimbabwe whom he met on a course seemed particularly knowledgeable in that area, so he picks up the telephone or sends off a fax, and chances are he will have a solution to his problem the same day, possibly within a few minutes.

That is vastly different from what would happen in a hierarchical organization. There the Chilean chemist would take his problem to the local manager, who would try to contact the appropriate person at head office and ask to be referred to an expert. Assuming the head office executive could be reached — he might be traveling in a remote region of India — he won't necessarily know who in all the world might have encountered and solved similar problems. The whole consultative process could take weeks, and the Chilean chemist might never get an answer to his question. We have literally hundreds of long-distance telephone calls and faxes crisscrossing the organization every day, conveying information directly to the people who need it, regardless of rank. The contribution of this informal communications network to the efficiency of the organization is incalculable.

The other side effect of the courses and conferences is the opportunity to identify management talent. At some of the larger gatherings there may be half a dozen executives who spend their time observing the participants, trying to pinpoint the most promising ones, compiling lists of candidates for promotion. In addition to all the usual attributes such as initiative, integrity and good judgment, we look for people with an international outlook. That may seem obvious, since we are a global organization. But an equally important reason is the fact that we are heading into an increasingly interdependent world where there will be no room for people with a narrow nationalistic horizon.

Ideally the international outlook should, of course, go hand in hand with international experience. In recent years that kind of experience has, unfortunately, become more difficult to find, partly because North Americans, and increasingly Europeans, are reluctant to leave their home turf. But an additional and, to my mind, equally regrettable factor is the refusal of many newly independent countries to grant work permits to foreigners. While I appreciate their desire to provide their own nationals with career opportunities, some of these countries have gone overboard to the extent where they are retarding their own economic development. Ironically it is easier, in some African countries, to get a work permit for a European than for a citizen of a neighboring country.

Such barriers were largely absent during the early postwar period. In those days we had few problems in transferring people to almost any country and, in the process, developing a management team with the experience and ability to serve anywhere in the world. Suppose, for instance, a young Chilean with obvious leadership potential served under a manager who was also young and not likely to retire or move for a number of years. If a management position opened up in Colombia, we would give him the opportunity to transfer rather than have him wait in Chile for his own command. Some big companies appoint, as a matter of policy, only citizens of the host countries to head their foreign subsidiaries. But when you look behind the facade, you may discover that the so-called chief executive is a figurehead and that his expatriate deputy or chief operating officer, who is a citizen of the parent company, is the chap who really runs the place. We prefer to tell it as it is.

As far as we are concerned, color and nationality were and remain irrelevant. At the time I started writing these recollections, the American company was run by a Swiss, the Mexican company by a Brazilian, the Caribbean area by a Lebanese, the Colombian company by a Chilean and the Canadian trading company by an East Indian. Nevertheless, we cannot be completely oblivious to national prejudices or sensibilities. It would be extremely difficult and probably counterproductive to have an Indian manager in Pakistan (or vice versa), or to have the citizen of one African country running a company in another African country, or to appoint a Jewish manager in a strictly Muslim country. These are facts of life, and as much as we regret them, we can't pretend they don't exist.

To make sure we promoted the most suitable people, we developed what we called our deputization program shortly after the war. During those long periods that managers spent on overseas leaves, we appointed from a list of potential candidates for promotion someone to run the show on an interim basis. On the face of it, the absent manager's second-in-command might have been the obvious person to take over. But as a rule we chose someone from a different part of the world partly because it was a way of providing promising people with mind-broadening experiences, partly because we hoped the newcomer would inject new ideas into the enterprise. Last but not least, this program gave us an opportunity to observe the deputy in action and see if he did indeed have what it took to manage a company. A problem developed later when, with the advent of air travel, the periods managers spent away on overseas leave became substantially shorter. However, with the help of sabbaticals and temporary assignments, we have managed to keep the deputization program going not only for the top positions, but also for two or three rungs down the ladder.

Thanks largely to the development of a new generation of innovative managers, we ended up with a leaner but healthier organization in Europe. In the meantime our problems in the Old World were more than offset by our explosive growth and successful development in Asia, Africa and Latin America. Even while our manufacturing operations in Holland and Switzerland were shrinking, we were building an overseas organization that, in many ways, exceeded anything my father had dreamed of. Between 1946 and 1960 twenty-five new factories and 1,700 retail stores were added to the organization. During the same period footwear production in Bata plants increased almost fourfold.

For a number of years after the war, Europe and, particularly, Great Britain had underwritten and kept alive many of our embryonic overseas enterprises. Now it was the turn of some of the children to take the lead and point the organization in new directions.

FROM COLONIES TO NATIONS

THOUGH I NEVER SET FOOT in India until my wartime visit in 1944, I had been virtually brought up to think of the subcontinent as a natural extension of the market for Bata shoes. I was an impressionable eleven-year-old when my father returned from his first tour of India, full of stories about the beauty of its architectural treasures and about the poverty of its people. Appalled to find that the servants in his luxurious Bombay hotel were barefoot, he had dipped into the cases of samples that he carried with him and presented each of the servants with a pair of canvas shoes. A few weeks later, after he had toured most of northern India, he returned to the same hotel and found, much to his surprise, the same servants still hurrying barefoot across the marble floors. One of the reasons, he learned, was that the hotel's European clientele liked Indian servants to be barefoot because, that way, the sound of their feet was less likely to intrude on their conversations or after-dinner naps. But an additional reason, Father was intrigued to discover, was that most of the servants had taken their shoes to the local market and sold them at a handsome profit.

As far as my father was concerned, this incident proved what he had suspected all along: there was an enormous demand in India for shoes. True, Japanese imports were already pouring into the country, and thousands of small artisans were producing everything from crude sandals to the beautifully crafted shoes worn by India's elite. But there was no domestic enterprise to provide millions of Indians with quality shoes at reasonable prices, and Father decided it was up to him to fill that void.

He started out by engaging distributors to sell Bata shoes in and around Bombay, Calcutta and Karachi. Then, in 1932, following his flying tour of the Middle East and Southeast Asia, Father decided that rather than continuing to ship shoes halfway around the globe, he was going to build a plant in India and use it as a source of supply for a retail organization of his own. The location he chose for the first overseas Bata factory was in the vicinity of Calcutta, a city that was then, as it is now, beset with appalling poverty, overpopulation and widespread unemployment. As soon as he returned home he selected forty graduates of the Bata School of Young Men, all in their early twenties, to launch this new outpost of the organization. Along with all the machinery and building materials for a new factory, plus enough cases of shoes to stock the first 100 stores, they set sail for India.

The first few years weren't easy. With few exceptions none of the young pioneers spoke English, let alone any Indian languages, so communications were largely confined to sign language. Shortly after his arrival in the Punjab in northwestern India, one of the young men set out to explore possible locations for retail shoe stores. In one town, as he was getting off the train, he was surprised to find a man on the platform shouting something unintelligible and trying to push him back into the carriage. Undeterred he went into town, but when he found all the shops closed and painted with white lime, he returned to the railway station where the same man was still shouting the strange word.

Back at his home base in Lahore he looked up the word in a dictionary and was horrified to find that it meant "plague." Fortunately he was none the worse for the experience.

The Indian company expanded rapidly during the balance of the 1930s. By the time war broke out it was producing rubber and leather as well as canvas shoes, had its own tannery and was operating more than 600 retail stores. One must keep in mind that there were millions of Muslims as well as followers of other religions living in India, so leather shoes were very much in demand, even though, strictly speaking, Hindus weren't allowed to touch them. But in India, as elsewhere, the war sent the production of consumer goods into reverse gear. Rubber and chemicals became all but unavailable for nonmilitary purposes, there was a serious shortage of such basic materials as nails, glues and packing cases, and transportation facilities were allocated on a priority basis. To supplement the sagging production of shoes and provide store managers with sufficient income, the Bata pioneers proceeded to manufacture related merchandise such as suitcases and handbags and organized a cottage industry for the production of socks. Even so, 100 retail stores had to close down for lack of merchandise.

These problems, however, were insignificant compared to the critical military situation that developed in the wake of the outbreak of war in the Pacific. After the fall of both Singapore and Burma, when enemy forces invaded the eastern part of Bengal and began bombing Calcutta, it seemed that India or at least parts of it might become the next victim of the Japanese juggernaut. The authorities urged industries to decentralize, and our people responded by opening up new tanning and manufacturing operations hundreds of kilometers up the Ganges River. Though painful and expensive at the time, this move turned out to be a blessing in disguise. After the war, when we concluded that small units were more efficient and more responsive to change than huge dinosaurs, the Indian company considered itself fortunate to have taken at least some steps toward decentralization.

To compound the wartime hazards, Bengal was hit in 1943 by a famine that threatened the lives of millions of the province's inhabitants. Britain's Field Marshal Wavell, who was then viceroy of India, asked our people to use their business experience to organize the distribution of food to the population. The sales department was mobilized, plans developed and, within weeks, hundreds of distribution centers were opened up in Calcutta and throughout the province. When the viceroy inspected these centers, he was so impressed that he introduced some features of the Bata planning system into government operations. Our people, for their part, decided to emulate the detailed, minute-by-minute schedules that Wavell's staff prepared for their boss's public appearances. Years later, when my wife and I visited Pakistan, the program called for me to deliver a three-minute speech to be followed by "roaring applause." Apparently nothing was to be left to chance.

During the war, it became obvious that even though India was still technically a British colony, its citizens were playing an increasingly important role in the government of their country. One person who was clearly destined to emerge as a leader was Sir Mohammad Zafrullah Khan. I had met him before the war while I was living in England, where he had introduced me to the Indian high commissioner. From the beginning we got along so well that the two of them plotted to have me married to one of their stunningly attractive compatriots. Though I disappointed them by showing no interest in the young lady, my relationship with Mohammad Zafrullah Khan developed into the kind of friendship that ideally exists between a father and his adult son. After the partition of India, he became Pakistan's foreign minister,

At nine months of age, with my father, Thomas Bata, Sr.

Posing in a new suit and hat at the age of six.

In my auto–racing days with my date Bozena Vavreckova. Married years later to Vaclav Havel, she became the mother of the famous defender of human rights and current Czechoslovak president Havel.

Sonja and I cutting our wedding cake after our marriage in October 1946.

Zlin, the city my father transformed from a village into an industrial center, featured everything from factories to modern housing, schools, health-care centers and sports facilities.

Lt.-General Sir Edward Spears (far right), chairman of the British Bata company, and I(left), discussing London antiaircraft defenses during the Second World War.

To find out about new technological and marketing developments, senior Bata executives toured Canada and the United States in 1946. I'm second from the left.

Prime Minister Nehru inspecting Bata-made army boots flown to India from Canada at the time of the Chinese invasion.

Throughout my career as chief executive, I made a point of personally handing out 25-year service awards to Bata employees.

Mother Teresa welcoming Sonja and me to one of her orphanages, a "Partner in Progress" in the Bata organization.

Then U.S. Vice President George Bush greeting Sonja and me at a World Wildlife Fund meeting in Washington.

With customers in Old Delhi, India.

In 1974 Sonja and I met General Yakubu Gowan, Nigerian head of state.

With Sonja in June 1983, after she was invested as an Officer of the Order of Canada. I became a Companion of the Order in December 1971.

The Bata family posing for a Christmas portrait. BACK, LEFT TO RIGHT: my son, Thomas G.; son-in-law Peter Schmidt; daughter Christine Schmidt; son-in-law Sam Blyth; me; Sonja; son-in-law Regis Pignal. FRONT: my daughter-in-law Sarah Bata; daughter Rosemarie Blyth and daughter Monica Pignal.

After turning 70, I handed over the chief executive's responsibilities to my son, Thomas G. In the background hangs a potrait of my father, Thomas Bata, Sr.

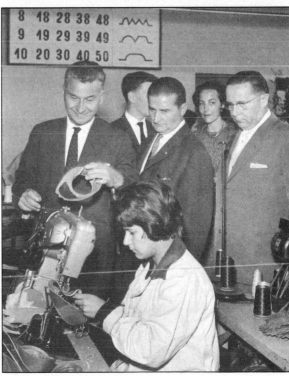

Examining a pair of uppers during a visit to our factory in Peñaflor, Chile.

Sonja and I in Prague during our extraordinary trip to Czechoslovakia in December 1989. Behind us is a Civic Forum poster.

then president of the United Nations General Assembly and finally chief justice of the International Court in The Hague. During my 1944 visit to India and, indeed, on many subsequent occasions, I felt privileged to enjoy the benefit of his vast wisdom and knowledge of world affairs.

Another impressive personality whom I got to know during that wartime visit was Sir Ramashwani Mudaliar, the minister of finance. I raised with him the issue of excess profits taxes, which were being levied in India at a rate of 100 percent on all profits above those realized two or three years before the war. Part of the tax was supposed to be refunded sometime after the war, so it was really a form of enforced saving. But meanwhile we were being hard hit, all the more so since we had grown rapidly in the years immediately preceding the war so that the tax was particularly punitive. I pointed out to him that under these circumstances, it was impossible for the company to accumulate resources for postwar reconstruction. He assured me that many Indian businessmen had raised the same point and that their pleas were more likely to sway the Indian government than those of a foreigner like myself. It was a perfectly friendly and, for me, enlightening conversation. It certainly left me with the impression that the days of the British Empire were numbered, at least where India was concerned, and that a highly capable, brilliant ministerial hierarchy was willing and able to assume the reins of government. What I didn't suspect was that the transition would be so violent and that it would cost the lives of millions of innocent human beings.

One night during my 1944 stay in Delhi I joined a couple of managers for a visit to a Muslim wholesaler. It was pitch-dark because of the blackout, and we had to climb three flights of stairs in what looked to me like a dingy building. But inside the door we were welcomed by a number of delightful people and a table full of refreshments. We had no idea what on earth we were imbibing, in those days there were no bottled soft drinks in India, but refusing that kind of hospitality was out of the question. Fortunately I seem to have an iron constitution; though I have had to consume at times literally gallons of liquids whose origin was, to say the least, uncertain, I have never suffered any ill effects.

At the time of our arrival our host had put garlands of flowers around our necks. I thought mine seemed rather heavy, but it wasn't until I took it off that I realized it was full of gold sovereigns. There must have been forty of them. I said to John Bartos, the general manager of our Indian company, "I can't accept this kind of gift from Rashid." But Bartos assured me that returning the sovereigns would be a mortal insult, so I had no alternative but to keep them. Fortunately I had no idea that possessing gold or transporting it was illegal, or I might have reconsidered. It took three months of negotiations to get the stuff to Canada.

In 1946, when the powers that be decided that the subcontinent should be divided along religious lines into two countries, one Hindu (India) and the other Muslim (Pakistan), they agreed that Pakistan would consist of two wings, separated by more than 1,500 kilometers of Indian territory. (The smaller of the two, East Pakistan, would later become Bangladesh.) The demarcation line between India and West Pakistan was going to be drawn along one of the irrigation canals that ran between Lahore, whose population was predominantly Muslim, and Amritsar, which was essentially Hindu. The question was which one.

During the war we had built, in a place called Batapur just outside Lahore, a factory that was somewhat smaller and more modern but otherwise similar to our original plant in Batanagar. For several weeks, while the border commission was locked in argument, Batapur shifted back and forth between India and Pakistan. Eventually it ended up about four kilometers inside West Pakistan, which was fortunate as far as we were concerned.

It meant that we had a fully integrated industrial enterprise in each of the two countries, each fully equipped to do everything from tanning hides and milling rubber to producing finished shoes. It also meant that either of the enterprises could absorb many of our agents and employees, whether Muslim or Hindu, whom partition had turned into refugees.

The Rashid family were among millions of Muslims who fled to West Pakistan with nothing but the clothes on their backs. A number of years later when I happened to be in Karachi, Rashid's son, who had become our agent following his father's death, invited me to dinner and placed yet another garland around my neck. While this one contained only five gold sovereigns, I was deeply moved because I realized that as a proportion of the man's total wealth, that gold represented an infinitely more generous gift than the forty sovereigns presented to me by his late father.

In addition to the trauma of partition and the human tragedies it created, India, in the late 1940s, faced the awesome challenge of unifying within one country millions of people whose one common denominator was their colonial heritage. Far from being the homogeneous entity the British had hoped to vacate, prewar India was a crazy quilt of languages, cultures and traditions, a mixture of provinces ruled by a British bureaucracy and semi-independent princely states headed by powerful maharajahs. Some of the differences and ancient animosities survive to this day. Yet, considering all the problems, the creation of what is today the world's most populous democracy was a major accomplishment, a lasting tribute to its political leaders as well as to the civil service originally created by Britain.

Perhaps because neither Czechs nor Canadians carried the stigma of colonialism, we enjoyed from the very beginning a cordial relationship with the Indian authorities. I was fortunate in that I had met Jawaharlal Nehru way back in 1937 when he was our houseguest in Zlin. Not that anybody suspected in those days that Nehru might ever become prime minister of an independent India; the very thought would have been preposterous at a time when, in the opinion of most Westerners, the British Empire was destined to last forever. That view wasn't, however, shared by our Indian directors. Even though in the 1930s the articulate young lawyer and associate of Mahatma Gandhi was spending much of his time in British jails, our directors were sufficiently impressed with his leadership qualities to suggest that while touring Europe, he should stop over in Zlin. He was the first leader of world stature I ever met, and his visit made a lasting impression on me.

That first meeting established a link between us, and after Nehru became prime minister I always called on him whenever I was in India. He, in turn, came to see Batanagar, unfortunately at a time when I wasn't there to welcome him. It is symptomatic of the country's diversity that in Batanagar, he had to use English to make himself understood because he didn't speak Bengali, the native tongue of most of our employees.

My most memorable meeting with Nehru occurred in 1948. I knew from our past encounters that he had a way of firing questions like so many bullets at visitors who were expected to come up with equally concise answers. But when he asked me how the Communists had succeeded in hijacking Czechoslovakia's democratic government, he didn't insist that I condense my answer into a few words. I could tell he was concerned not so much about Czechoslovakia as about the Communist challenge his own government was facing in India, and he listened attentively while I outlined in some detail the events and circumstances that had led up to the coup d'état in Prague. Our meeting, scheduled to last for twenty minutes, stretched to well over an hour. Not until I left did I realize that Lady Mountbatten, the wife of the last British viceroy, was waiting for him to join her for lunch. Though

I was totally unaware at the time of any romantic link between them, I felt flattered that he was sufficiently interested in what I had to say to keep such an important personality waiting.

In spite of the painful birth pangs of independence, it wasn't long before India's economy recovered to the extent where our production capacity was barely sufficient to satisfy the domestic market, let alone take full advantage of the export opportunities that were opening up. Expanding our plant in Batanagar was out of the question. Not only was it already too big and unwieldy, it was also weighed down with all kinds of barnacles — restrictive rules and regulations that had accumulated over the years and that made it difficult or impossible to operate efficiently. We weren't allowed, for instance, to move workers from jobs where they were no longer needed to areas where there was a shortage.

Such barnacles, spawned by governments or trade unions, aren't, of course, confined to India or to the developing world. But in Europe or North America they are easier to live with because they apply to everybody, which creates a level playing field. But in a country like India, your competitors aren't other manufacturers; your real competition is the poverty of the people. If the barnacles force you to raise prices, your customers may no longer be able to afford the shoes you produce.

Clearing Batanagar of its barnacles would have been next to impossible, so in 1950 we decided to build a new Indian factory. The location we had in mind was the west coast, preferably in the vicinity of Bombay. That would place it on the opposite side of the country from our Bengali manufacturing complex, near a major harbor through which both imported raw materials and exported finished goods would have to flow. I was visiting the plant we had built during the war in Patna, about 500 kilometers up river from Calcutta, when I got a message that the newly elected president of India, Mr. Rajendra Prasad, was also in the city and wished to see me. Along with our Indian chairman, Motilal Khaitan, and our managing director, John Bartos, we were invited to the governor's palace to have tea with the president, who, it turned out, was accompanied by the minister for refugees and rehabilitation.

Together they described the monumental challenge of resettling millions of Hindus who had fled from the newly established state of Pakistan. The refugees were destitute, subsisting in the type of primitive camps that were to become all too familiar in later years. One such camp with some 50,000 inhabitants was located near a small village called Faridabad, some thirty kilometers outside Delhi, and the government had decided to convert it into a model community. The idea was that the refugees themselves would build the infrastructure, including roads and sewers, as well as kilns, where they would manufacture bricks with which they would build their own homes. The challenge was to provide the community with opportunities for employment in business and industry. Were we, the president asked, willing to change our plans and build our new plant in Faridabad instead of on the west coast?

I asked the president why he was putting this proposal to us rather than to Indian entrepreneurs. He replied that Indian businessmen were being approached to help in other ways, but that he wanted us to spearhead this particular project because he was confident that we would build a modern enterprise complete with recreational facilities and proper housing for our employees. He hoped, he said, that we would establish a standard for other people to follow. For its part, the government would provide the land and would further assist us by releasing immediately the refundable portion of the wartime excess profits tax. It was an irresistible opportunity to help ourselves as well as our host country and thousands of homeless people. Even though the location was a long way from the coast and therefore not ideal from our point of view, our team agreed unanimously that we should rise to the challenge.

So we went ahead and built in Faridabad a supermodern plant that featured the latest technology and work methods. In appearance Faridabad's "industrial park" bore little resemblance to its counterparts in North America. Most of the enterprises that joined us there within the first few years were no more than shacks. But some of their owners made up in ingenuity what they lacked in esthetics or financial resources. One particularly imaginative fellow bicycled every morning to Delhi, where he and his children scoured the streets for waste thermoplastic materials. Back in Faridabad at night they used their bicycles and leg power to run extruders that recycled the scrap material into inexpensive hoses for sale to Delhi's growing population.

Whenever I was in India, which in those days was at least once a year, I made a point of stopping in Faridabad and inviting the members of the industrial association to tea. With the exception of an American-educated young lady who ran her father's small air-conditioning plant, the members neither looked nor acted like entrepreneurs, and Sonja's attempts to communicate with their wives were met by shy giggles behind raised saris. Twenty years later some of these same entrepreneurs were employing scores of people, driving substantial automobiles and sending their children to college. Today Faridabad is a thriving city with a population of several hundred thousand and industries that overshadow, in size if not in quality, our own enterprise. Most of our 1,500 Faridabad employees own agricultural land or shops that employ their wives and children and provide them with independent income.

As for the Indian government, it adhered meticulously to its commitments. The refundable portion of the excess profits tax was repaid promptly, whereas other enterprises, which the government considered less cooperative, had to wait for years, by which time inflation had eroded the value of the money. And though the country suffered at times from a severe shortage of foreign exchange, we were never asked to stop or defer the payment of dividends to foreign shareholders. Even in 1962, when China's invasion of northern India created a grave military crisis, our routine application for the remittance of dividends was approved without delay.

In a number of other ways, however, the Nehru government's attitude toward big business in general and foreign-controlled enterprises in particular was, shall we say, less than enthusiastic. Espousing the socialist dogma that radiated from post-World War II Great Britain, the ruling Congress Party wasted no time in nationalizing public utilities as well as a number of other industries, particularly those controlled by the British. Some of these acquisitions provided the newborn country with valuable technology. But others, having been deliberately neglected by their parent organizations in anticipation of decolonization, ended up being more of a burden than an asset.

Enterprises such as ours, whose ownership wasn't challenged, were subjected to heavy taxes on profits as well as excise taxes on materials. These taxes didn't apply to small businesses with fewer than fifty employees and less than two horsepower energy consumption. Everybody knew that, in many instances, three or four shoemaker brothers divided up the work so that one cut the leather while the second sewed the uppers to the soles and the third did the finishing. Since each enterprise employed no more than forty-nine people none was subject to tax. But since such small entrepreneurs were the backbone of India's economy, it seemed fair enough that they should enjoy a tax advantage.

Nor did I have any quarrel, during the postwar years, with Nehru's insistence that expatriate managers be replaced as quickly as possible by Indians. In the days of the Raj most senior positions, and quite a few intermediate ones, had been held by highly paid and, occasionally, incompetent foreigners whose only claim to fame was their European ancestry. Since this was clearly wrong, we had made a determined effort, years before independence, to develop and employ Indian talent, and by the end of the war, we had a strong Indian management team in place. So the government's policy did not cause us any problems.

More serious and, in my opinion, more ill advised was the legislation that eventually made it impossible for enterprises such as ours to build new factories or expand existing ones. Indeed, even to produce a new type of footwear we would have to apply for a special license, wait for months while the application wended its way through the bureaucratic channels and then find, assuming it was approved, that it was so narrowly defined as to be almost worthless.

To make matters worse, the government announced, just after we had developed a highly automated plastic footwear business, that the production of such footwear would be reserved for small industry. That, frankly, was a cockeyed idea. The production of plastic footwear requires expensive equipment, which small village shoemakers couldn't possibly afford, so most of the beneficiaries were the well-heeled sons of prominent officials. However, rather than sulk, we offered to supply these entrepreneurs with machinery, molds and technical know-how. Within three or four years there were some twenty domestic enterprises making plastic shoes for us. True, we could have produced the same footwear more economically and with better quality control. But under the circumstances it was a mutually beneficial compromise.

Seeing that cooperation with outside suppliers of plastic footwear was so successful, there seemed to be no reason why the same approach wouldn't work equally well in other areas. There were in India's towns and villages literally thousands of tradesmen producing handmade leather shoes. During the war, in the ancient city of Agra, famous as the site of the Taj Mahal, we had begun to sell in our stores merchandise produced by such local cobblers. A technical assistance team and, later, a research center were installed to help the shoemakers upgrade the quality of their products. As communications improved, we began sending out European designers and patterns that enabled the Indian shoemakers to produce up-to-date, fashionable footwear made of local materials and marketed through our retail outlets. It was good for them and good for us.

And so, gradually, our growth in sales became fueled not by our own factories, which weren't allowed to expand, but rather by merchandise produced by these outside associates. This relationship later developed into what we call our "Partners in Progress" program, whereby we buy hundreds of thousands of shoes from independent businesses in India as well as other countries in Southeast Asia, Africa and Latin America. Some of these people are previous employees who decided to become entrepreneurs; others came to us and said, "I would like to start up a shoemaking business." Either way we lend or lease them the required machinery, provide them with technical assistance and indicate what we would like them to produce, and we agree to market the shoes for them.

In India alone we now have between sixty and seventy Partners in Progress, including one of Mother Teresa's orphanages, which produces shoe polishing brushes for sale in our stores. I don't know of any other corporation doing this, certainly not in the shoe business. European or American importers who arrange for footwear to be shipped from the Orient usually deal with investors who can afford to set up large manufacturing operations; we prefer to deal with small entrepreneurs and sell on the domestic market.

In the early 1960s the Indian government began pressuring us to go public. We weren't exactly enthusiastic about departing from our 100 percent ownership policy, but, given the importance of the Indian market and the risk of alienating the government, we agreed to sell sixty percent of the shares to the public. That, however, turned out to be easier said than done. As we soon discovered, floating a public issue in India involved many decisions and the input of countless individuals, none of whom seemed in a hurry to get the job done. After years of bureaucratic foot-dragging and having our licenses held up, I finally asked for an appointment with Mrs. Gandhi, who, in the meantime, had become prime minister. During the twenty minutes that was all the time I was told she could spare, I tried hard to persuade her to help us resolve our problem. But she didn't seem particularly interested and we were about to be dismissed when I mentioned that Sonja would like to say a word or two about "Project Tiger."

It was as though I had found the key to a secret door. Mrs. Gandhi's attitude changed instantly, and for the next half hour she listened while Sonja described the World Wildlife Fund's plans to save India's tiger population. A secretary reminded the prime minister repeatedly that the next visitor was waiting, but Mrs. Gandhi paid no attention to him. Finally, on our way out I asked, "Madam, what about our public issue?" In reply she suggested that I go to the office of Professor Dar, her economic adviser. "Explain to him what you want done," she said, "and I'll see that it's expedited." I did as I was told, the approval was granted and the Indian company's shares, floated on the Calcutta and Bombay stock exchanges, were snapped up by local investors. Incidentally, the visitor we had kept waiting was the Soviet ambassador, which pleased me no end.

While the licensing restrictions have since been relaxed, I am sorry to say that little or nothing has been done to lift the ban on the import of non-Indian managers and professionals. The Indianization policy made eminently good sense in the early days of independence, but attempts to perpetuate it in the 1990s seem to me anachronistic and self-defeating. In an age of growing globalization the government's refusal to permit the employment of foreigners deprives the country of technological and scientific know-how at the very time when many Indians are making major contributions to science and technology in Britain, the United States and Canada.

On balance, however, India achieved nationhood with less turmoil than most other countries in Southeast Asia. For the first quarter century of its existence, the newly independent state of Pakistan was rocked by rapid changes of government, political assassinations and armed clashes with its Indian neighbor. From the point of view of business, the investment climate wasn't exactly hospitable, and the 1971 partition of the country did nothing to improve conditions in either of its components. Pakistan's president, Zulfikar Ali Bhutto (father of Benazir Bhutto, elected prime minister in 1988), was pleasant enough whenever I paid him a courtesy visit, which I tried to do every time I was in the country. But at the same time he nationalized banks and a number of homegrown industries, and though he didn't touch us, his neo-Marxist policies created a difficult environment in which to operate.

Meanwhile, in the newborn state of Bangladesh, a succession of military coups and presidential assassinations, combined with the expropriation of jute mills and other enterprises, tended to dampen one's entrepreneurial spirit. We already had one plant built in what had been, before partition, East Pakistan, and for a while that seemed plenty. When we eventually decided to add a plant in Bangladesh and provide employment for 1,000 people, we ran into licensing roadblocks that seemed designed to outdo their Indian counterparts. Each time we agreed to a set of conditions, a new one was added. After several months of this cat-and-mouse game, we were about to abandon the project, when I happened to be in Dacca to attend a seminar run by an organization called Business International. By then President Ershad had assumed power, so I went to see him, explained the problem and said I hoped he would announce a change of policy in his opening statement to the seminar. He did just that.

Inevitably news of the plant to be built in Bangladesh reached Pakistani president Zia ul-Haq, who in 1977 had overthrown Bhutto. "Why in Bangladesh?" he asked the next time he saw me. "Why not Pakistan?" I replied that the sixty percent duty levied by Pakistan on imported machinery would increase our costs to the extent where a new plant wouldn't be profitable. He turned to his finance minister and asked, "Is the duty really that high?" "Yes, Mr. President," the minister said. "That duty was introduced by the Bhutto regime." I was amused to find that, in Pakistan as in Western democracies, any flaws in the system are attributed to one's predecessors. Apparently nothing is ever the fault of the politician in power.

Zia immediately suggested that we apply for a remission of the duty and assured me that our application would be approved. On the strength of this assurance we decided to build a second plant in Pakistan, far superior to the one in Batapur, which was beginning to show symptoms of old age. We selected a beautiful site in a place called Maraka and commissioned a noted Canadian architect, Raymond Moriyama, to design the building, complete with an interior mosque. True to Zia's promise, the government approved a duty remission on machinery for all new industrial projects, and construction of our new plant proceeded according to plan. But shortly before opening time, a number of serious problems threatened to scuttle its existence. When Zia inquired what the problems were, our people handed him a list of fourteen issues that remained to be resolved. Among the most serious was the electric utility's refusal to guarantee a power supply; the absence of a telephone link between the old and the new factories was another.

When I arrived in Islamabad a few days later, Zia invited me to lunch and informed me that all our problems had been resolved. Obviously he was treating the creation of a new industry in an impoverished part of the country as an event of major importance, and he was using his personal prestige to remove any roadblocks that might jeopardize its completion. When I landed in Karachi on my way to the plant, my aircraft was surrounded by military vehicles and a senior officer welcomed me as a guest of the president. After spending the night at the provincial governor's house, I was flown in the presidential aircraft to the factory, where Zia joined me and made the appropriate speeches to mark the official opening. Nor was this some sort of favoritism. He was genuinely dedicated to economic development and made a point of showing up at any function that served that purpose.

Which is not to say I advocate military dictatorships, in Pakistan or anywhere else. Nor would I describe Zia as a warm human being. He did try to smile and be pleasant, but the military personality always shone through and projected a sense of distance that seemed impossible to bridge. However, he did impress me as a man who not only refused to be corrupted by power, but did his utmost to keep corruption under control among his associates. Throughout his eleven years in office he continued to live in the relatively modest house he had occupied as army chief of staff and never moved into the palace that had been started in Islamabad by his predecessor. But he did have his office there the last time I saw him, two years before his 1988 death in a mysterious aircraft crash. That was the occasion when he presented me with a beautifully illustrated copy of the Koran, with the English translation beside the Arabic.

A couple of years before that last meeting, Zia loaned Sonja and me his helicopter so that we could visit some of the remote areas in the Hindu Kush Mountains bordering on Afghanistan. It was an area ruled by tribal rather than Pakistani law, utterly primitive but tremendously beautiful and exciting. Quite apart from its scenic rewards, the trip enabled us to visit customers whom we might otherwise have found inaccessible. I was happy to see that all of them wore shoes.

The only "hotel" accommodation in the area cost the equivalent of fifty cents a night, which was, if anything, more than it was worth. Fortunately we were invited to spend the night in the officers' quarters of a military post that turned out to be a strange relic of the colonial era. More than thirty years after the creation of independent Pakistan, the army personnel behaved as though the British had never left. The flag-raising ceremony in the morning, the sounding of taps at night, the bagpipes, the spit and polish — nothing seemed to have changed. In the shelter of a pavilion built by the British, we sipped tea while we watched a polo game staged for our entertainment. The rules of the game were, however, intriguingly different from any that I had ever known. While both teams started with the same number of horses, individual players from the team that was gaining the upper hand would switch sides to make the game less lopsided and more interesting.

People sometimes ask me whether political stability is one of the prerequisites for doing business in a given country. My reply is that in most parts of the world, stability is as unpredictable as the weather. For several years after World War II Southeast Asia was a caldron of religious, political and racial strife. In Malaysia the government was fighting an insurrection inspired by Communist Chinese, and while Singapore was spared the horrors of guerrilla warfare, it, too, was a hotbed of Communist intrigue. The first time Sonja and I visited that part of the world we had an armed escort with machine guns pointing out of the windows as we drove at high speed from Singapore to our Malay rubber plantation. The plantation manager, who lived in a comfortably furnished bungalow on a hilltop, slept in a cast-iron bathtub, which he hoped would stop any stray bullet that might penetrate the walls. He was a truly heroic chap, working under tremendous pressure, and I hope our visit provided him with a little moral support.

For a while after the war, conditions were as bad or worse in what had been the Dutch East Indies. In 1945, when our management team emerged from Japanese prison camps, the Dutch were fighting stubbornly to regain control of their colonial empire, armed bands of self-styled freedom fighters were roaming the country, looting was commonplace. One of our managers, a man by the name of Karel Vytopil, was ambushed on his way to work by a group of guerrillas and dragged to what was presumably to be his place of execution. Fortunately a Chinese storekeeper who had witnessed the incident yelled at Vytopil's captors: "He is not a white man. He is from Bata." It was as though he had uttered a secret password. "Not only did the guerrillas let me go," Vytopil recalled later, "they actually apologized to me."

But these warm feelings toward Bata were not shared by Sukarno, first president of independent Indonesia. A Communist sympathizer whose messianic faith in central planning was matched by a total lack of administrative skills or experience, Sukarno wasted no time in propelling his once affluent country to the edge of bankruptcy. Under his system of "guided democracy" inflation soared out of control, raw materials became all but unobtainable and people were literally starving.

At that time, the only oasis of peace in the area was Sri Lanka, or Ceylon as it was called before decolonization. When I first went there in the late 1940s, it was a Shangri-la full of smiling people, ambling elephants and king coconuts with delicious milk to quench one's thirst. Almost in defiance of the horrors that were raging all around it, Ceylon was an island of tranquility and racial tolerance. Forty years later the Indian subcontinent, along with Singapore, Malaysia, Thailand and Indonesia all enjoy peace and varying degrees of prosperity, and our enterprises in these countries are among the strongest pillars of the Bata organization.

But in poor Sri Lanka, racial hatred has destroyed a model community and put an end, in most instances, to goodwill among people. I say in most instances because some of our employees have been nothing short of heroic in risking their lives to shelter their Tamil or Sinhalese co-workers. Unfortunately they couldn't save them all.

None of us has a crystal ball to tell us what the future may bring, and entrepreneurs who aren't willing to ride out occasional storms had better not venture beyond their home turf. But let us remember that, regardless of political upheaval and even bloodshed, people still have to earn a living. Even while Western news media were inundating us with pictures of massacres and civil war, ordinary citizens in Bangladesh, Malaysia and more recently Sri Lanka continued to go to work and collect their wages.

That is why most of our managers are willing, even eager, to stay at their posts, even in the midst of wars and revolutions. One day in 1949, while I was in New York, I got a cable from John Bartos, our regional coordinator for Southeast Asia, informing me that he proposed to build a sizable expansion to our plant in Saigon. If I had any strong objections, I was to let him know within twenty-four hours. The idea seemed questionable to say the least. In what was then Indochina, fighting against the French colonial troops had all the earmarks of a long and bitter struggle. Even in the context of the violence that was raging throughout that part of the world, Saigon didn't sound like a healthy place to be. But I was on my way into court for an important hearing concerning the litigation with my uncle Jan, so I stuffed the cable into my pocket and promptly forgot about it.

In the absence of instructions to the contrary, Bartos went ahead with the expansion and the plant proceeded to operate successfully throughout the war against France and, later, during the Vietnam War. Its Dutch manager stayed on the job and refused point-blank to obey Bartos's order to leave, even after the Americans had pulled out of Vietnam and the fall of Saigon was imminent. Fortunately I was in Singapore at the time, so I insisted that he and his wife join me there "for a discussion of future developments." They arrived only just in time.

CHAPTER

11

THE MANY FACES OF AFRICA

ACCORDING TO AN ANECDOTE that has become part of Bata folklore, two salesmen were sent overseas to explore the possibility of selling shoes in Africa. One of them cabled home: "Nobody wearing shoes. No market possibilities. Returning home soonest possible." The other one, a true Bata disciple, had a completely different reaction. "Everybody barefoot," he informed head office. "Tremendous sales opportunities."

While details of the story may well be apocryphal, the message was as valid in the 1940s as in the organization's early days in Zlin. Though missionaries had in the meantime persuaded many of their converts to cover their bodies with clothes, they apparently didn't consider bare feet to be either immodest or unhygienic. Countless Africans continued to walk around barefoot, and their ranks were being swelled every year by millions of new babies. For a business with an avowed objective to put shoes on every pair of human feet, Africa was the place to be.

Though I paid brief visits to Kenya and the Sudan during the war, my real acquaintance with Africa and its people dates back to 1947 when I embarked on a reconnaissance tour that took six of us — two pilots and four passengers — to more than a dozen African countries. In our little unpressurized De Havilland Dove we hopscotched from Morocco down the west coast all the way to South Africa, then back along the opposite side of the continent to Abyssinia, the Sudan and Egypt.

The trip was a crash course in geography, political science and some of the characteristics that distinguish the peoples who coexist in that part of the world. What it wasn't was a luxury trip. We slept wherever we could find accommodation, including hammocks with nothing but mosquito netting for shelter and hotels where we could count the previous occupants by the number of rings of dirt inside the bathtub. I learned that Douala in Cameroon is probably the soggiest city in the world, and that landing there during one of its daily thunderstorms, with the mighty Mount Cameroon hidden in the clouds and no radar to guide you, can be an unnerving experience. And I was intrigued to find that hotels in French colonies, whose standards of cleanliness left a good deal to be desired, produced delicious meals whereas immaculate British hostelries served food that tasted like cotton wool.

Wherever we went we visited Bata enterprises, ranging from tiny operations to fairly substantial ones. Though they had all been cut off during the war from their traditional sources of raw materials, equipment and expert advice, they had survived or even expanded, thanks largely to the dedication and inventiveness of our people. From next to nothing before the war, major enterprises had materialized in Morocco, Senegal, the Belgian Congo, Rhodesia and Kenya, marketing embryos had sprung up in a number of other countries and there was a modest shoe manufacturing factory in Johannesburg. But it was also clear that a great deal of work would be needed to convert these technologically primitive operations into modern enterprises.

Inevitably I came across instances where managers were either inefficient or out of touch with modern concepts. In Nigeria, I was horrified when I was shown the design for the prototype of new stores. When I asked the managers why they proposed to put up such primitive, unattractive buildings, they explained that that was what most stores in Nigeria looked like. I, in turn, informed them that we had our own standards to live up to, besides which we had no business being in a developing country unless we could improve on the status quo. We had quite an argument. But though Sonja and I had only been married for a year, she had already imbued me with her ideas about the importance of good design, and so I stood my ground. Even though she wasn't with me, the modern Bata stores that were built in Nigeria owe a great deal to her innovative spirit.

A different kind of confrontation occurred toward the end of our trip when we stopped for refueling in a place called Wadi Halfa, a dusty little town on the border between the Sudan and Egypt. Rather than wait around, I decided on the spur of the moment to go into town and take a look at the local Bata store. After admiring, a day or so earlier, the immaculate appearance of our stores in Khartoum, I was in for a shock. Attired in his pajamas, the store manager was sitting on a bench smoking his water narghile; the shelves were covered with a mixture of dust and dead flies; cats and chickens were roaming around the aisles. It was a horrible mess. Back at the airport I had a few pungent words to say to the retail manager who had boarded our plane in Khartoum. To this day throughout the Bata organization, Wadi Halfa is shorthand for an unmitigated disaster.

On balance, the two-month trip reinforced my conviction that Africa was a continent with tremendous potential for an organization such as ours, and that we had a good base to build on. As far as I was concerned, this view was perfectly consistent with the desire for independence that was obviously stirring in many of the countries we had visited. After talking to African customers, to business people and to government officials, I knew that these freedom movements were real and that they were gathering strength. But contrary to conventional wisdom within the business community, I found the prospect of decolonization more exhilarating than threatening. Sure, there were going to be problems. While a number of African countries could boast of ancient cultures, few had a history of nationhood to use as a basis for self-government. Worse still, borders had been drawn arbitrarily by the colonial powers without regard to tribal loyalties or economic realities. Under such circumstances, decolonization was bound to be painful and, in some instances, bloody.

On the other hand, many of our people had been in Africa long enough to become almost part of the local fabric. Those who came from Czechoslovakia, a country free of the stigma of colonialism, were perceived as allies rather than oppressors. Indeed, on some occasions they were at the receiving end of the same discrimination that afflicted the native population. They were not eligible, for instance, for membership in exclusive British clubs. Instead they joined clubs patronized by local people and became their friends. At the same time, a postwar generation of our European employees were largely immune to their parents' colonial notions of superiority. In those days, in places like the Belgian Congo, ours were the only commercial enterprises where an African was welcome to enter through the front door and be waited on like anyone else by a salesclerk who might be black, white or some color in between. This policy, which was nothing short of revolutionary at the time, paid rich dividends in years to come. Unlike many of their fellow Europeans, our people didn't panic at the prospect of decolonization.

But in 1947 independence in most parts of Africa was no more than a mirage on the horizon. Yet their colonial status notwithstanding, places such as Kenya were basking in newfound prosperity. Having been paid generously for housing and feeding British troops, and with the added benefit of high commodity prices, Kenya had emerged from the war in a state of affluence that its debt-ridden mother country could only envy. This prosperity was reflected in the demand for merchandise on the part of consumers starved by six years of wartime austerity. With the added advantages of being part of the vast sterling area, the prospects for organizations such as ours could hardly have been better.

At that time Kenya, Tanganyika and Uganda were all part of an East African federation that operated like a common market. By selling made-in-Kenya footwear throughout this area we were able to provide people with shoes at incredibly low prices and still make a healthy profit. In fact, we were doing so well that we thought of building a second plant, also in Kenya. But with the approach of independence and the emergence of nationalist pressures, it was suggested to me that, in order to spread the wealth, we might locate the new plant in Tanganyika. I discussed this proposal with Julius Nyerere, Tanganyika's chief minister under British rule and obviously the country's future head of state. At the time he impressed me as a young, dynamic leader, and when he described to me and Philip Cowell, one of our most senior executives, the marvelous welcome that awaited foreign investors in independent Tanganyika, we decided to change our plans and build the new plant there.

During a private conversation following the plant's official opening, Nyerere shared with me some of his concerns about the future of East Africa. By becoming independent a year or two apart, he explained, Tanganyika, Kenya and Uganda would have time to develop the trappings of sovereign countries complete with national flags, anthems and, inevitably, all the jealousies and rivalries that abound between neighbors. In the process the East African economic community, whose benefits all of them had enjoyed in the past, would be destroyed. "What the British should do," he said, "is make all of us independent at the same time. That way we could become some sort of federal state and all of us would be better off."

His ideas sounded eminently sensible to me, and I discussed them with a number of influential people in Britain. To paraphrase Henry Higgins's song in *My Fair Lady*, they listened very nicely, then went on to do precisely what they had intended to do all along. In due course Nyerere's predictions all came true. Tanganyika, or Tanzania as it is now called, became independent in 1961, Uganda in 1962 and Kenya in 1963. With independence came a breakup of the three countries' joint monetary, transportation and postal systems and, for a quarter century, an almost complete severance of trade links. Only recently have steps finally been taken toward some sort of regional economic cooperation.

What Nyerere hadn't predicted was his own change of personality and political orientation. When neighboring Zanzibar, where an Albanian-style Communist regime had perpetrated terrible massacres, became part of Tanzania, Nyerere presumably thought that the Zanzibarians would mellow under his benign influence. Instead, it was a case of the tail wagging the dog. Before long Nyerere began dressing like Mao and behaving more like a Zanzibari than the man we had known. But the straw that broke the camel's back was Egyptian President Nasser's state visit to Tanzania.

Ever since its beginnings in the 1930s, our Egyptian enterprise had enjoyed the support of the various regimes that ruled the country. Even after Nasser came to power and began expounding his socialist dogma, our relationship with the government remained good enough for the minister of industry to come to Alexandria to be on hand when the hundred millionth pair of Bata shoes rolled off the assembly line. To commemorate the occasion the street where our large new factory was located was renamed the Thomas Bata Street. Then came the 1956 Suez War and Nasser's decision to place all Western companies, including ours, under government control.

After the armistice I wangled an entry visa to Egypt, and with the help of the Canadian embassy, we persuaded the authorities to withdraw the government commissioner. But our Egyptian board chairman, a retired general who, incidentally, had been appointed on Nasser's recommendation, warned me that our reprieve might prove to be temporary. Nasser, he told me over dinner at Cairo's newly rebuilt Sheppard Hotel, was determined to create a system whereby every kind of business and every source of income would be either owned or totally controlled by the government. So I was not altogether surprised when, a couple of years later, the ax fell. To make it all seem legal, the government allocated to us nontransferable bonds with a face value of approximately ten percent of the real worth of our enterprise. It was a ridiculous subterfuge, and we never accepted it as compensation.

A few years later, after Tanzania's 1965 plebiscite had confirmed Nyerere as the country's president, Nasser arrived in Dar-es-Salaam for a state visit. According to a witness who was in the car that carried the Egyptian president and his host from the airport into town, Nasser expressed surprise at the number of foreign-owned enterprises that lined the road. "Why do you put up with all these exploiting imperialists?" he asked. Nyerere protested that they were doing a pretty good job. Besides, he had neither the money to buy out the owners nor the management talent to replace them. "No problem," Nasser said. "Just take over the enterprises and promise to compensate the owners out of profits.

That's what I've done, so I know it works." As for management, the incumbents were sure to sit tight in their cushy jobs until such time as Nyerere was ready to replace them with his own people.

Shortly after Nasser's departure, Nyerere announced that sixty percent of the shares of all foreign enterprises were henceforth the property of the state. The former owners, he said, would be compensated out of future profits, and in the meantime, they were welcome to stay on as managers of their enterprises. A week or two later in Montreal I was attending the world congress of the International Chamber of Commerce, when I caught sight of the chief executives of the half dozen or so companies affected by the decree. We promptly huddled together, and within a few minutes, we reached a unanimous decision. "We're going to resist Nyerere's arbitrary action," each one of us vowed. "We're not going to sign up on his terms." Sixty days later Bata was the only holdout — all the others had buckled under and accepted the sixty percent solution. Personally I had no intention of condoning the breach of Nyerere's solemn promises, nor of attempting to operate in an increasingly antibusiness, chaotic environment. So we withdrew our foreign personnel and left the government-appointed board to manage as best it could.

About a month later in Nairobi local representatives of the same multinational companies were summoned to a meeting by a group of Kenyan government ministers. It seemed as though Kenya was about to follow Tanzania's example. Instead the managers were given a tongue-lashing for their weak-kneed response to Nyerere. Kenya, they were told, had no intention of nationalizing their enterprises. "But think of the political problems with which you have saddled us by crying to high heaven that you would resist the takeover, and then giving in without a whimper."

But our troubles in East Africa were far from over. In 1969, on the eve of the anniversary of independence, Uganda's President

Obote invited several businessmen to dinner so that they could discuss the economic content of his anniversary speech. It was, by all accounts, a pleasant evening and Obote seemed interested in his guests' suggestions. They were all the more surprised the following day when, in the middle of the obligatory patriotic platitudes, he paused for a momentous announcement. "As of this moment," he told a wildly cheering audience, "sixty percent of the shares of all industrial enterprises belong to you, the people of Uganda." The formula was distressingly familiar, and so were the names of the victims. They were the same enterprises that had been taken over by Nyerere in Tanzania.

I was in London at the time and, within minutes of Obote's announcement, my telephone began ringing. "We must stick together," every one of the chief executives who were calling said. "We mustn't let them get away with it." But I had learned my lesson. "After all the promises you've made and broken," I told them, "here's what we're going to do. We'll sign up with Obote as quickly as we can on the most favorable terms we can get without discussions with anyone else." Which is exactly what we proceeded to do. In due course an agreement with the Ugandan government was ready for signature. Our representative, Philip Cowell, flew to Singapore to join Obote, who had been attending a conference of Commonwealth prime ministers, and together they left for the signing ceremony in Kampala. They got as far as Kenya when news reached them that Obote had been overthrown and that Idi Amin was the new president.

Incredible though it may seem, most freedom-loving people welcomed Amin as a liberator. It was, after all, Obote who had created Uganda's notorious secret police and initiated the persecution and torture of political prisoners, and it took both the Ugandans and outside observers some time to realize that his successor was every bit as bad or worse. One of the first things

Amin did was to rescind Obote's nationalization decree, so the agreement we had negotiated was torn up. Even when Amin began expelling Ugandan Asians and confiscating their business assets, he showed no antagonism toward foreign-owned enterprises. Yet a few months later, without any warning, the police turned up at our factory, occupied our offices and installed a government commissar. Once again we were out in the cold.

The official explanation, that we had been smuggling machinery out of Uganda, was patently false; in fact, we were expanding at the time and had actually been shipping machines into the country. So the Canadian high commissioner and I flew to Kampala and, with the help of willing informants, we soon found out what had happened. In order to make better use of our resources, we had been shipping the expensive molds needed to make plastic shoes back and forth between our factories in Uganda and Kenya. The customs people of both countries had approved the arrangement, so there was nothing secret or underhanded about it. But some well-connected person had seen those molds being loaded onto a truck and, convinced he had witnessed a dastardly deed, considered his discovery important enough to phone Amin during a cabinet meeting. Apparently Amin answered the call, listened for a moment, then turned to the minister of the interior and said, "Take over Bata."

Hoping that a face-to-face meeting might clear up the misunderstanding, I made an appointment to see Amin. It was the first time I had met him, and though he wore civilian clothes, I thought he looked like an overfed sergeant major with a strange predilection for fondling two of his little sons. At the time he refused to commit himself one way or the other, but, in due course, I was informed that we were to be denationalized once again. So the government commissar was withdrawn and we picked up where we had left off. We have continued making and selling shoes in

Uganda ever since, while dictators came and went and civil wars were ravaging the country. Now that some measure of political stability seems at last to have returned to Uganda, perhaps its delightful people will be able to enjoy the peace and prosperity they have been so sadly lacking for so many years.

In Egypt, as well as Tanzania, suggestions have been made on several occasions that we might consider coming back. During President Sadat's regime in Egypt, negotiations to privatize our company or to establish some sort of joint venture were well under way. But as Anwar Sadat discovered then and Gorbachev has found out more recently, it is much easier to grab property than to give it back. By the time a new hierarchy becomes entrenched in managerial positions, it is often impossible or politically too damaging to dislodge it and turn back the clock.

As for Tanzania, we have refused to contemplate any kind of deal simply because we believe it is impossible to operate in a country whose economy has been so abominably mismanaged. A quarter century of Julius Nyerere's concept of "independence" has turned what was the most affluent part of East Africa into a country of beggars; and though Nyerere himself has retired, his legacy lingers on. All the companies that originally agreed to operate as minority owners have long since departed, and the compensation they had been promised never materialized.

Tanzania has, however, become the darling of the foreign aid fraternity, to the extent where the World Bank announced a few years ago that it intended to finance the construction of a Tanzanian shoe manufacturing complex. I warned the Canadian director of the bank that this wasn't likely to be a good investment, that the plan to export from Tanzania fine footwear to Europe was nonsensical, if for no other reason than the nonavailability of high-quality hides. But the would-be benefactors had clearly made up their minds, and I realized I was wasting my breath. The shoe manufacturing complex was built and promptly became a white elephant, a monument to good intentions gone awry.

Meanwhile we were busily expanding into francophone Africa, an area where we had maintained little more than a token presence before the war. With the help of the French government, which was paying higher than world prices for the agricultural products of its former colonies, the economy was booming in countries such as the Ivory Coast, Cameroon, Senegal, even Upper Volta. New buildings were going up, tourists were flocking to modern hotels and sunny beaches, and foreign investment was eager to locate in a newly affluent and surprisingly sophisticated market. With the welcome mat rolled out for private enterprise, there was no country in that part of the world where we didn't establish ourselves as the number one supplier of footwear. Indeed, in some tribal languages the word for *shoe* is *bata* because, for a long time, that was the only kind of footwear local people had ever known.

To the extent some of these countries later indulged in xenophobia, it was directed against their neighbors or tribal minorities rather than outsiders like ourselves. The lone exception, and one that left a particularly bitter taste in my mouth, was Algeria. Having spent some time there with my mother when, at age sixteen, I was convalescing from a bout of undulant fever, I had a soft spot for the country, and after the Second World War, when we decided to build an Algerian factory, I made sure that it was particularly modern and attractive.

In spite of the bitter war of independence that broke out in 1954 and engulfed the country for eight years, business was excellent and so, initially, was our relationship with the newly established Algerian government. Even when state enterprises were built to compete with our own, I agreed to participate in government-sponsored seminars that told potential investors about the wonderful welcome that awaited them in Algeria.

But it wasn't long before we were "asked" — "ordered" might be a more accurate word — to sell thirty percent of our shares to the government. We would be paid, we were told, in three installments spaced three months apart. Unfortunately the Algerian government was split down the middle between a faction headed by the minister of commerce, who wanted to nationalize everything in sight, and a less radical faction headed by the minister of finance, who favored a limited role for private enterprise. While they were feuding among themselves, we waited in vain for our money.

Finally I went to Algiers, where the minister of finance promised to see me but kept me waiting for an appointment during the first two days of my stay. On the third day I sent word to him that I had to catch a flight that afternoon to Ibiza, and the minister replied that he would see me at five o'clock. As for my flight, I wasn't to worry: he would arrange for a government aircraft to fly me to Ibiza.

The meeting was attended, in addition to the minister of finance, by representatives of two other ministries, and the three of them kept squabbling about whose responsibility it was to pay. Finally the minister of finance said to me, "Mr. Bata, I am terribly embarrassed that a year has gone by without a single installment being paid. Let me assure you that by the time you get home . . . " He paused and I was convinced he was about to say "the money will be in your bank account." Instead he came up with a promise that he would launch an inquiry to find out what was holding up payments, and make sure that the department concerned paid immediate attention to the matter. I was furious, all the more so since I knew that Canada was pouring foreign aid money into Algeria. But there was nothing further I could do.

The little twin-engine Piper Apache that was waiting at the airport didn't strike me as an ideal conveyance for a nighttime flight across the Mediterranean Sea. But the weather was good, so I headed for the aircraft, when a woman came running up to us shouting, "Monsieur Bata, the check, please!" Apparently the minister had kept his promise to provide me with a plane, but he expected me to pay the bill. In this instance, however, I had the last laugh. Since it was the chief financial officer of our Algerian company who signed the check, the money came out of the government's pockets when they took us over completely.

As time went on, Algeria's minister of industry became increasingly irritated with our ability to run a successful business while all his state enterprises were losing huge amounts of money, so he decided to "buy" from us the remaining seventy percent of our shares. Once again we were told we would be paid, this time by way of a rebate on our purchases of Algerian exports. But pretty soon the country was running out of everything that was exportable, even sheep and goatskins, which had been plentiful before. All we ended up getting was a display of sleazy behavior.

On balance, however, our problems with the governments of decolonized African countries have been far outweighed by success stories and friendly relationships. As for the few instances where we suffered expropriation, it is well to remember that Africans didn't invent this particular game. Our biggest losses occurred not in the Third World but in Central and Eastern Europe. The enterprises we lost through nationalization, confiscation or whatever Communist governments cared to call it in Czechoslovakia, Poland, East Germany, Yugoslavia, Romania, Hungary and Bulgaria accounted for close to three-quarters of our total assets. Nor were we the only victims. While proportionately not as traumatic as ours, the losses suffered in Eastern and Central Europe by Unilever, Michelin and a number of oil companies were also enormous. So the Third World had plenty of examples to follow, and plenty of inspiration to derive from the socialist rhetoric that was being spouted in pre-Thatcherite Britain, in Scandinavia and, during the first Mitterand regime, in France.

When visiting a country, in Africa as in other parts of the world, I always made a point of calling on the head of state and on cabinet ministers in charge of industrial development. Since we were invariably one of the largest employers in the land, most of these leaders seemed more than willing to meet me and discuss with me economic issues of interest to their countries. One of the advantages of such high-level contacts is the deterrent effect they have on corrupt underlings. Once these people know that we have an entrée to the corridors of power, they are less likely to hold us up for ransom before expediting a routine application.

It is not that Africa has a monopoly on corruption. Convincing suppliers and government officials, even in some so-called developed countries, that Bata people neither accept nor dispense bribes can be a difficult and, occasionally, a painful process. There have been instances where our more accommodating competitors have paid only a fraction of the duties and sales taxes to which we were subjected by government bureaucrats. But once these rascals realize that we are on friendly terms with the boss and that he might find out what they are up to, they tend to discontinue such practices.

My conviction that it is always best to deal with the top decision maker was confirmed by an incident that occurred in Nigeria in 1965. Shortly after Prime Minister Balewa had cut the ribbon and made a speech at the ceremonial opening of a new factory of ours, I was approached by the British head of an international food processing company. Apparently his company was about to complete a large new sugar mill in Nigeria, and he had been told that having the prime minister officiate at the opening would cost a huge amount of money. He wondered how much we had paid.

The conversation took place during a flight from Lagos to London, and since the head of our Nigerian company was on the same plane, I asked him to answer the question. "We didn't pay anything," he replied indignantly. How about a gift? "Yes," he said, "we presented the prime minister with a token present, a volume of the works of Shakespeare bound in leather from our tannery." The reason for the discrepancy, it turned out, was quite simple. The British company's executives had approached a friend of Balewa's and asked him to intercede on their behalf; the substantial fee they had been quoted would, no doubt, have disappeared into the friend's pockets. Our man, on the other hand, went straight to the prime minister's office and, as a result, didn't pay a cent. I suspect that at least some of the African leaders owe their bad reputation to this kind of corruption at intermediate levels.

Over the years I have gotten to know most African presidents and prime ministers, and with few exceptions, I have found them courteous and helpful. I haven't had the dubious pleasure of meeting Colonel Gadaffi of Libya, nor did I meet King Farouk of Egypt, though a member of the latter's entourage once had the gall to approach Sonja with an invitation to spend a weekend with the notoriously lecherous monarch. On the other hand, many of the leaders of the emerging francophone countries were highly intelligent, well-educated individuals steeped in French culture.

Leopold Senghor, for example, who was to become Senegal's first president, was known in his younger days not only as an up-and-coming official in the colonial government, but also as the author of creditable French poetry. I first met him at a dinner party shortly before Senegal achieved independence. That evening our host, the French governor, was holding forth on the subject of education. Africans, he said, should concentrate on technical schools rather than trying to copy European concepts of higher learning. Mr. Senghor turned to me and said, "What our French friends don't understand is that, in order to build a new nation, we need people with a general education, with a knowledge of philosophy and law and political science. If we need technicians, we can hire Frenchmen or Belgians or Germans. We might even hire Russians." His logic seemed impeccable to me.

In the formerly British part of Africa I have enjoyed my acquaintance with Jomo Kenyatta, the legendary freedom fighter whose forces terrorized the white population before he became the first president of independent Kenya. The first time we met was when I called on him at Government House, formerly the British governor's residence. A smallish, hefty fellow with a beard and humorous eyes, he didn't look at all ferocious as he came down the stairs dressed in a baggy suit with a flyswatter in his hand. He spoke excellent English, and though he was reputed to be a radical Marxist, our conversation left me with the impression that his ideology was, to say the least, flexible. At one point he asked me if I had chased him in the woods in the 1950s during the Mau Mau uprising. I said that I might have done just that had I lived in Kenya at the time. "But there were no Mau Mau in Canada." He was clearly amused at the thought of me chasing around the Canadian woods in search of African rebels.

Under Kenyatta's pragmatic leadership Kenya developed into a prosperous country with an essentially capitalist economy. That doesn't mean we didn't have disagreements. The main one occurred when the government decided to Africanize the retail trade. Handing over our stores to Kenyans was no problem as far as we were concerned. We continued to own the buildings or leases, we were paid for the merchandise and since we had made a point of training African managers and sales staff, there was a pool of competent Kenyans ready to assume full responsibility for the stores. Unfortunately that wasn't what the government had in mind. "You may not hand the stores over to your managers," we were told by the authorities. "We will designate the people who will own those stores." Most of the government appointees were prominent citizens or their wives who proceeded to fire the trained staff and replace them with the cheapest help they could find, or with the most useless members of their families. Either way it was a serious problem.

But now, twenty-five years later, the problem has largely resolved itself. Some of the original owners have learned the ropes and have become successful retailers, while others have sold out to more competent individuals. These days many of them call on us for help with personnel selection and training, window displays and management know-how. For us, working with such associates is a real pleasure.

Equally enjoyable is our relationship with a number of our Partners in Progress. In Africa, as in Southeast Asia and Latin America, we have helped small enterprises improve their production, install up-to-date machinery, train their work force and market their products. In Nairobi, for instance, Printpak Company was a small print shop until Bata Kenya helped it acquire machinery and the technical skills to manufacture boxes. At last word Printpak was employing 375 people and exporting its products to other East African countries.

In neighboring Zambia a similar success story concerns the industrial footwear that is worn by thousands of workers employed by the country's mining industry. In colonial days what was then Northern Rhodesia imported such footwear at considerable cost from Europe and the United States. Following independence, our managers in Zambia decided to manufacture it locally and taught a modest manufacturer of pots and pans near Lusaka how to make the steel toe caps that are the boots' most essential safety feature. The world standards for that particular product are extremely stringent, and the temptation to cut corners at the expense of quality is almost irresistible. But the Bata people insisted and, in the process, helped management become more quality conscious with regard to the company's other products.

The unfortunate part of the story is that we also manufacture industrial safety footwear in Kenya and in Zimbabwe, which means that the market is fragmented and the product that much more expensive. The Zambian pots and pans outfit could, without further investment, triple its output of toe caps and supply the entire region, probably at a twenty-five percent cost saving. Meanwhile, someone in Zimbabwe could manufacture zippers or some other metal product for sale in the other two countries. But the neighbors aren't on good enough terms to permit that kind of rationalization — at least not yet. Negotiations to join a number of eastern and southern African countries in new structures have so far proved slow and laborious.

Zimbabwe had, of course, traveled a particularly tortuous road from colonial status to nationhood. During the immediate post-war period, our factory in what was then Southern Rhodesia grew rapidly from a tiny nucleus to a highly successful operation with close to 3,000 employees. At that time Bata shoes made in Rhodesia were being sold by the hundreds of thousands, not only in our expanding Rhodesian retail chain but also in Europe and South Africa.

But the growing polarization between the black and white communities led to repressive measures and, in 1965, to the white government's Unilateral Declaration of Independence. I personally refused to go to Rhodesia during the UDI period because I didn't want anyone to think I was endorsing that type of racist regime. But none of our products was subject to the sanctions imposed against Rhodesia by the international community, so the company wasn't violating any rules or, as far as I was concerned, any moral standards.

The UDI interlude happened to coincide with the period of student radicalism in Canada, so when I was invited to address a student meeting at the University of Toronto, I had a pretty good idea what to expect. During the question-and-answer period, one of the students asked how I could reconcile my opposition to the Nazis' racial policies with our continuing presence in Rhodesia. I replied that, if we were to walk out of our Rhodesian factory, the plant would be taken over and operated by the government. Therefore nothing would be gained. What would be lost, however, would be our efforts to groom Africans for managerial positions.

I went on to tell them about our training scheme for black Rhodesians, a number of whom were working at that very moment in different parts of our organization in Britain, Australia and New Zealand in anticipation of their own country's independence. Others were pinch-hitting for white managers who were subject to military service and who therefore spent months on end in the army. This gave the understudies a chance to demonstrate their competence and, in case they experienced any difficulties, to receive guidance before their next stint at the helm. Finally I told them that, even if we could close down our operations, it would be wrong to throw thousands of people out of work, many of whom were the only breadwinners for large families.

The students said they would like to withdraw and discuss their response to my remarks among themselves. When they came back, their spokesman said, "If you're really treating your black employees well and giving them opportunities for promotion, then we believe that you should stay."

When independence came and a number of our white employees joined the exodus from Rhodesia, we were able to replace them with fully trained and experienced black managers. One person who didn't leave, significantly enough, was our managing director, a Rhodesian of Scottish descent by the name of "Duffy" Fraser. He had been a colonel in the Rhodesian reserve army, and I couldn't help wondering how an officer of his rank, who had spent part of his life fighting the recently appointed cabinet ministers, would be able to function in the new environment. The first time I visited independent Zimbabwe I was amazed to find him introducing me to the prime minister, Robert Mugabe, and to several of his cabinet colleagues. Some years later Fraser was transferred to Canada, but eventually, when he retired, he went back to live in Zimbabwe.

From a political, as well as an economic point of view, Zimbabwe has surprised many prophets of doom by becoming a successful, tolerant, multiracial society. In spite of the country's chronic shortage of foreign exchange and the resulting restrictions on the remittance abroad of dividends, our business in Zimbabwe has continued to grow and prosper.

I wish I could say the same about South Africa. After the war, the first plant we built in South Africa was located on the outskirts of Durban in an area with a predominantly Asian population. The economy was booming and business was so good that we built or acquired over the next twenty years four more factories, two of them in Kwazulu, the home of the most populous black group. All told we ended up employing some 3,500 people, most of whom had never had a job before. We provided them with transportation, canteen meals, maternity leave, day-care centers and medical services. By almost any standard it was a good place to work.

While we couldn't openly defy the apartheid rules, we found that by and large, foreign-owned businesses could get away with a good deal more than domestic ones. Then came the agitation, mainly in North America, that organizations such as ours should get out of South Africa. Personally I was convinced that we should stay, partly because by training Africans for leadership roles, international businesses were doing their best to put an end to apartheid, partly because I don't believe in putting people out of work simply because I disapprove of a political regime. To me that is an immoral act.

We spent uncounted hours preparing reports to an office set up by the Canadian government to monitor the policies and practices of Canadian-owned firms in South Africa. The administrator of that office, a retired ambassador named Albert Hart, gave us a clean bill of health and, in return, was lambasted mercilessly by the press. It seemed strange to me that our news media and, for that matter, academe, both of whom claim to be champions of freedom of speech, should refuse to listen to any views incompatible with their own. It seemed equally strange that an organization that had pioneered, in many parts of the world, the development of people of different races should be singled out for attack by a predominantly white community. But strange or otherwise, we had to face facts. The pressures were becoming intolerable.

In the end it came down to a choice between keeping our headquarters in Canada or staying in South Africa. So we decided to sell, and the Canadian government heaved an almost audible sigh of relief. But for us it meant abandoning people, many of whom had worked for us for twenty-five years or more. Fortunately we fended off the vultures that hovered around in the hope of picking up a bargain and stripping it of its assets. Instead we found a Swiss buyer who promised to continue our employment practices. Even so, I was then and remain convinced that pulling out of a country because you object to its government is the wrong thing to do. Bata operates in many countries whose regimes aren't necessarily to our liking. Governments come and go. What doesn't change is the people's need to earn a living.

There have been other setbacks. In francophone Africa, where, a quarter of a century ago, we were welcomed with open arms, punitive taxes are making it increasingly difficult for local plants such as ours to compete with Korean and Taiwanese footwear that is being smuggled by the shipload into Africa and sold at bargain-basement prices. In the Sudan, the superbly equipped factory we had built after the war was nationalized in 1970 and later returned to us in such a deplorable condition that we were glad to sell it back to the Sudanese government.

Yet to me, Africa always was and remains a tremendously exciting and important part of the world. Recent developments such as the independence of Namibia and the gradual dismantling of apartheid in South Africa suggest that some of the continent's most intractable problems are being overcome. Improvements in the educational system and in people's standard of living are producing a new generation of Africans willing and able to work toward the economic and political betterment of their countries. I believe our organization has made substantial contributions to that development: I am proud of the many outstanding African managers who have come up through our ranks, and of the independent entrepeneurs whom we have helped develop and prosper. Far be it for me to pretend that we were motivated by some sort of missionary spirit. We expanded into Africa in order to sell shoes, not to spread sweetness and light. Yet I can honestly say that for both Sonja and me, seeing our enterprises contribute to the improvement in our employees' living standards was one of the most satisfying experiences in our lives. It was a real thrill to watch people acquire their first bicycles, eventually buy their own homes and then one day come and say, "My son is going to university. He is going to be an engineer, or a doctor, or a businessman."

When my father wrote in his moral testament, some sixty years ago, that the business was to be managed as a public trust, I'd like to think that this is the sort of thing he had in mind.

PAS UN PAS SANS BATA: THE JOYS OF MARKETING SHOES

I N A GLOBAL ORGANIZATION such as ours, genius often flares in the unlikeliest places. During a business trip in the early 1950s, the aircraft in which Sonja and I were traveling touched down for a refueling stop in Tunis. In those pre-hijacking days airports were popular gathering places, and though it was almost midnight, a delegation of our local Bata personnel came to meet us and to show us their products, including a poster they had designed. It featured a family with three or four children, each carrying a shoe box, and a caption that read *Pas un pas sans Bata*, Not a step without Bata. No advertising agency could have come up with a better marketing tool. It was an instant success and soon became a kind of Bata trademark throughout the French-speaking world. To this day a flight attendant who has noticed my name on the passenger list will occasionally come up to me smiling and say, *"Ah, Monsieur Bata, pas un pas sans Bata."*

The message was all the more relevant since the well-shod family depicted on the poster was far from typical. "Half of mankind is still barefoot," my father told his employees in 1932, shortly before he died. "That goes to show how little we have achieved so far and how much remains to be done." I could have said the same thing in the forties and fifties, when we began expanding in a big way into Africa, Southeast Asia and Latin America. The world was still full of people who had no shoes, and in the widely dispersed settlements where they lived, shoes were either unavailable or priced way beyond their means. Some tried to protect their feet by cutting soles out of old tires and using straps to hold them in place. Our challenge was to develop an attractive and comfortable, yet affordable substitute for these crude contraptions.

Once again the winning idea came from far afield. It was our manager in Senegal who suggested that good-looking and durable shoes could be made of polyvinyl chloride, the inexpensive plastic substance that was becoming widely available in the 1950s. He came to Bata Development in London to plead his cause, and being a persuasive man, he sold us on the idea. For some long-forgotten reason we christened the shoes Sandaks, and in Senegal, where the manager promoted his brainchild with all the devotion of a proud parent, they sold like hotcakes. But when it came to marketing Sandaks in other countries, we ran into a wall of passive resistance. Our idea was that for testing purposes, individual companies should buy a small number of pairs and try to sell them as though they had been manufactured locally, that is to say, deduct from the price the duty and transportation costs that wouldn't apply to domestically produced merchandise. If the customer reaction proved favorable, local production facilities could be set up. But partly because of the "not invented here" syndrome, partly because some managers rebelled instinctively against the idea of selling anything at a loss, Sandaks were mighty slow to catch on outside their country of origin.

In Madagascar, for instance, the French manager of our modest operation did put a limited number of Sandaks on the market, but at a price that included the exorbitant duty applicable to imported merchandise. When predictably they didn't sell, he advised us that "after extensive study," he had concluded that there was no demand for this type of footwear. A short time later he was succeeded by a younger and more aggressive Frenchman who had spent some time at our head office in London and who shared our faith in the new product. Undeterred by his predecessor's verdict, he introduced Sandaks to Madagascar and scored a huge success.

On the opposite side of the globe Mexico, an attractive country with a rapidly growing population, looked like another promising market for Sandaks. But on two separate occasions emissaries sent to reconnoiter the market reported back that the only kinds of footwear Mexicans would buy were traditional lace-up leather shoes for men and elegant high-heeled pumps for women. How about Sandaks? I asked. "No way," our informants replied. At best, they said, we might be able to sell a few thousand as beachwear in such tourist resorts as Acapulco.

That didn't make any sense to me. Obviously if we were to expand successfully into Mexico, we would have to appeal not to the affluent middle class in the cities or to sunbathing visitors on the ocean front, but to the millions of poor people all over the country who needed good-looking, inexpensive, durable shoes. Since no such footwear was available, it seemed ridiculous to claim that there was no demand for it. So we began manufacturing Sandaks in a garage in Mexico City, equipped with a single automatic injection molding machine. Three years later Mexicans were buying five million pairs a year, and we had a dozen machines trying to keep up with the demand.

Nor was the appeal of Sandaks confined to the poor and disadvantaged. As our managers and their staffs became converted to the concept, shoes originally designed for barefoot Africans proved popular with more sophisticated customers in other parts of the world. Even the fashion-conscious French, who, our local executives had insisted, would never consider wearing anything so primitive, decided it was just what they wanted. In due course wordwide sales soared to seventy million pairs a year and accounted for approximately thirty percent of our profits.

Thongs were another Bata product that went through difficult and protracted birth pangs. Around 1954 when a detailed proposal to manufacture this Japanese-style footwear was sent out to all our managers, only two of them were sufficiently impressed to agree to produce a prototype. I was considered a naive optimist for suggesting that 100,000 pairs worldwide might be a realistic target. In due course our sales of thongs on the Indian subcontinent alone exceeded fourteen million pairs a year.

Such success stories weren't, of course, due to the merits of the products alone. As many would-be entrepreneurs have learned to their grief, it isn't good enough to invent a better mousetrap and expect customers to beat a path to your door. An important part of the job was to disseminate information about the product, make sure our own personnel were familiar with it and provide potential customers with an opportunity to see it. Unfortunately many well-intentioned international organizations fail to realize that the key to industrial development isn't manufacturing as such, but bringing the right merchandise to the consuming public.

In those postwar years Sonja and I spent more than half our time traveling around the world like a flying circus, with dozens of suitcases full of shoe samples. Along with a team of executives who specialized in marketing, product development and administration, we displayed our samples, made speeches, staged presentations, suggested to our local managers new types of footwear they might introduce and told them about improvements that had proved successful in other parts of the organization. Equally important, we listened to their suggestions and needs.

In the Third World a major challenge was informing people about the advantages of wearing shoes and about the affordable footwear that was available to them. In countries whose population was widely dispersed, too poor to own radios and, more often than not, illiterate, posters and billboards were only part of the solution. In addition we produced cartoons and films, which we screened in remote villages. We equipped buses as wholesale shoe stores to supply Oriental bazaars, local markets and backwoods shops. We told people about the deadly worm that can enter the body through cracks in bare feet and causes a debilitating parasitic disease called bilharzia. Sonja organized fashion shows, choosing the most attractive girls in town to display our products. Once in Saigon, when she scheduled such an event to begin early in the afternoon, she found most of the models were still in bed, presumably recovering from a strenuous night. She had quite a time getting them dressed in time for the show.

From my point of view, the most important part of these tours was the opportunity to visit local marketplaces and stores, go to the villages and the small towns where merchants were selling our shoes and talk to customers and suppliers. When it comes to finding out what people really want, how well or badly we meet their needs and what opportunities there may be for providing further services, there is simply no substitute for this kind of personal contact. To me, getting close to the grass roots, meeting people of different nationalities and in different walks of life has always been the most enjoyable part of my job. No doubt that is one reason why I have devoted a great deal of time — too much time according to some of my critics — to this type of activity. Yet in recent years business gurus have begun talking about the Japanese practice of "management by walking around," as though it were some dramatic new invention. To me it has always seemed obvious that, as the saying goes, "there is no better fertilizer than the farmer's footsteps." There may be some businesses that can be managed effectively from the confines of an executive suite, but ours isn't one of them. No doubt managers should delegate all those functions that can be handled as well or better by capable subordinates. But as far as I am concerned, delegating one's interaction with the marketplace amounts to abdication of responsibility.

All too often executives who complain about inadequate internal communications, about knowing only what their subordinates want them to know, are guilty of barricading themselves behind a hierarchy of informants. In our organization it has always been understood that senior managers must spend a great deal of time traveling, that they must visit stores and markets and factories, that they must talk to customers and suppliers, to government people and trade union leaders. As long as they do all that, any attempt to mislead them or to withhold information is apt to be counterproductive.

One of many lessons we learned during our travels concerned the differences between the buying habits to be found in African countries, depending on whether they had been part of the French or British colonial empires. It isn't just a matter of tastier food in French-speaking parts of the world, or their relatively casual approach to hygiene. In Africa, as in the West Indies, the inhabitants of the former French colonies are much more fashion conscious than their formerly British neighbors. While we are perfectly safe in shipping footwear to Jamaica and Antigua by sea, stores in Guadeloupe and Martinique have to be supplied by air in order to keep up with the latest fashion trends. I was intrigued to find that green beans, one of Africa's major exports, are sorted and cut differently depending on whether they are to be flown to London or Paris. Apparently the French like them long and thin, the British short and chunky.

Another lesson concerned the danger of offending, no matter how unwittingly, a religious group or a social custom. In the Sudan, for instance, our people were upset when the display boards they put up beside the roads kept being torn down. The culprit, it turned out, was the picture of a shoe on the billboards. Apparently in the Sudan shoes were considered an intimate piece of apparel not to be displayed in public. The problem was resolved when the offending picture was replaced with one of a family whose members, parents and several children, all carried the familiar Bata shoe boxes.

Linguistic nuances are a minefield of potential misunderstandings. While visiting the Middle East one of our managers, a man with the perfectly good Czech name of Victor Kos, was busily handing out his business cards until he discovered that, in the local Arabic, *kos* was a vulgar word with sexual connotations. In response to a flood of indignant phone calls, our local office quickly produced new business cards that identified the visitor as K. Victor.

Sometimes we were lucky. In a number of African and Middle Eastern countries, laws passed in the postcolonial era ordered all posters and billboards to have the Arabic text ahead of the French or English. We were concerned about the cost of having to replace all our publicity material until it was pointed out to us that, since Arabs read from right to left, no changes would be required. In Kenya we discovered belatedly that Jumbo, the name we had given to the elephant whose picture adorned our popular canvas sneakers, is the Swahili word for *good morning*.

While that suited us just fine, we have tried to avoid surprises, pleasant or otherwise. A recent incident in Bangladesh, where part of a picture of Chinese wind chimes on the insoles of our shoes was mistaken for a rendition of the word Allah, has served as a reminder that, when it comes to national or religious sensibilities, a global organization can't be too careful.

Like cultural and linguistic differences, regional consumer preferences have proved largely impervious to the globalization of business. True, high fashion tends to be increasingly international: like the latest creations of French couturiers, famous Italian shoe designers rule the high-priced market all over the world. The members of the upper crust who buy Dior ball gowns and drive Rolls-Royces wear Faragamo or Gucci or Roger Vivier shoes whether they happen to live in Paris, New York, Rio de Janeiro or Tokyo. Interestingly enough, the high-priced shoe designers have all remained small, apparently determined to cater exclusively to a clientele whose primary concern is high fashion rather than comfort or durability, let alone price.

Some of these designers have made a tremendous contribution to the industry in terms of creativity and their willingness to test or even initiate new trends. But the small, affluent elite that buys their shoes isn't the focus of the Bata organization. While we do have customers among members of so-called high society, the bulk of our clientele consists of fashion-conscious, middle-class consumers, people who are more likely to buy a Ford or a Volkswagen than a Mercedes or a Maserati. And among this clientele regional preferences continue to play an important part. Within Germany, for instance, the merchandise sold north of the line running from Frankfurt am Main to Wiesbaden is quite different from that sold in the south just as, in North America, we don't sell the same shoes in New York as in California or Quebec. People in Hamburg buy fewer sandals and more rain-resistant footwear than their Bavarian cousins, and the double-soled, sturdy shoes worn by children in the north are quite different from the light, flexible variety that is popular in the south.

Many of the regional preferences are too deeply rooted in custom, climate or the national psyche to be affected by the removal of international trade barriers. Though the Benelux countries have functioned as a common market for over twenty years, we can't have the same people selecting shoe styles in Belgium and in Holland. There are exceptions, of course. Just like Levi's jeans, brand-name athletic footwear has succeeded in becoming a universal status symbol with a whole generation of consumers. But, by and large, lower- and middle-income shoppers are apt to be influenced by local traditions and climatic conditions rather than global fashion trends.

Furthermore, differences in taste apply not only to the product itself, but also to marketing methods. In North America, for instance, shoppers love bargain hunting. Rather than haggle with shopkeepers as they might in India or the Middle East, they lie in wait for the opportunity to buy merchandise whose price tags have been reduced by ten, twenty-five or even fifty percent. At the time when our North Star athletic shoes were at their peak, a prominent Canadian businessman told me proudly that his wife had taken advantage of a half-price sale at the neighborhood department store to equip their three children with North Stars for years to come. In Canada and the United States retailers as well as manufacturers have learned to cater to this consumer sport with a year-round parade of sales. But the same strategy doesn't work in Switzerland. The Swiss look for quality rather than slashed prices, and they are willing to pay for what they get.

Given this kind of variety in consumer preferences and regional idiosyncrasies, any attempt to impose uniform marketing tactics would be doomed to failure. While we have standardized the design of our stores and developed a corporate identity program, we rely on local buyers, merchandisers and retailers to decide how best to serve their customers.

Yet for all the diversity in consumer tastes, worldwide changes in technology and economic climate have had a dramatic effect on ways of catering to those tastes. Given the speed of modern communications, it wouldn't make much sense nowadays for me to travel around with suitcases full of shoes. Instead our local or regional managers get on a plane and fly to a conference where new shoe styles are on display and where experts are on hand to discuss production and marketing methods. Alternatively we fax our latest designs from Italy to Southeast Asia or Latin America, where, depending on the time of year, they may be reproduced and offered for sale long before their counterparts reach the stores in Milan. And, looking into the future, it won't be long before we have a worldwide network of computer-assisted design departments, all transmitting their creations to one another in vivid Technicolor. Television has, of course, added a new dimension to marketing strategy. In 1986, for instance, some of our most effective billboards were located in Mexico City at either end of the field where the world soccer championship was being played. Since we sell hardly any shoes under the Bata name in Mexico, those posters probably meant nothing to the local soccer fans. But they were not the audience we were targeting. Our objective was to have the Bata name projected onto millions of screens in Western Europe and any other part of the world where people were watching the championship matches on television.

In the wake of the divorce of retailing from our manufacturing organization, some of our plants moved almost entirely out of the retail arena and elected to concentrate instead on the production of industrial safety footwear. The Dutch factory, for instance, sells mainly to large companies through industrial distributors. In other countries our plants have, from time to time, filled large orders from the armed forces. But from our point of view, doing business with the military is a decidedly mixed blessing. On the plus side it has enabled us to keep a lot of people employed at times when the economy was on a downward slide and the shoe business was slow. Another advantage was the efficiency achieved by producing large volumes of identical shoe styles. Yet contrary to a widespread misconception, defense production in my experience has never been highly profitable. For one thing, contracts are almost invariably put out to tender and the lowest bidder gets the order. Even in those few instances where the price is negotiated, it is subject to renegotiation so as to make sure the manufacturer's profit doesn't exceed governmental guidelines.

Moreover, specifications for military footwear are, on average, twenty-five years behind their civilian counterparts. The Vietnam War is a case in point. During the early stages of the war, our regional coordinator in Southeast Asia suggested to the local American ordnance people that our Saigon plant could supply them with the kind of boots that Malaysia's military had found highly satisfactory in difficult jungle terrain; having them manufactured locally seemed to us particularly desirable. When the Americans protested that specifications for military footwear would have to come from the United States, our man took his case back to Belcamp, Maryland, where an appointment was arranged with the appropriate authorities in Washington. After further, lengthy negotiations the Saigon plant finally got a small order just as the war was approaching its sad end.

For a while it seemed that we might fare no better with our American-made DPV boots. Though the ordnance people expressed an interest in this type of footwear in the early sixties, negotiations dragged on for a number of years. But eventually we did receive a small order, followed by much larger ones when the Vietnam War began heating up. We designed boots for American troops that didn't rot, that had no stitching to be attacked by fungi or bacteria and that didn't stick in the mud. An additional feature was a steel inlay that stopped spikes from penetrating the sole.

Contrary to a popular saying, armies don't march into battle on their stomachs. Most of them march in boots, and when those boots are inadequate or unsuitable for the terrain, the country may be at risk. At the time of the Chinese invasion of India in 1962, Indian troops sent to stop them were wearing boots designed for jungle terrain rather than high altitude mountain warfare. One of the reasons they were losing ground was that many of them were suffering from frostbite. We made solid footwear for the Canadian forces, so we sent enough winter boots to India to equip a whole batallion. But by the time our boots reached the troops in the Himalayas, the Chinese had withdrawn from India, so we can't claim to have made a difference in that particular confrontation.

On the retail side of the organization, the use of the Bata brand name became an increasingly important issue. Fortunately the Communist government of Czechoslovakia, in its rush to dissociate itself from anything that smacked of capitalism, had done us an inestimable favor by dropping the use of the Bata name. But once our stores began selling footwear made by a variety of manufacturers and Bata-made shoes began being sold by retail outlets other than our own, we had to decide when and under what circumstances we should use our brand names or allow them to be used by others. The answer varied from one country to another. In Pakistan, for instance, most shoes made in our factories carry the Bata name, no matter where they are sold or by whom; but in India, where our retail chain is much larger, our name is not available to merchants outside the Bata organization.

In some countries we chose not to use the Bata name at all, because in the initial stages, we weren't sure the local product would project the right kind of image. In at least one instance that concern proved unjustified and unfortunate. In the 1960s, when we began negotiating for a joint venture with the Japanese, we thought their quality standards and styling might not be good enough to be called Bata. It wasn't long before the quality and styling of the Japanese merchandise was so superb that we would have been proud to have our brand name associated with it. But by then that joint venture's own brand names were well established, and much to our regret our partners had no wish to switch. The Japanese, incidentally, manufacture under license almost every brand of high-priced European shoes, and in most instances, their products are superior to the originals.

In recent years this type of licensing or franchising arrangement has become commonplace, to the extent where the notion that a brand name identifies the manufacturer or the country of origin is rapidly becoming obsolete. For instance, Bata shoes are being manufactured and marketed in Argentina by an enterprise that pays us royalties and a service fee, while Adidas sports footwear is manufactured and distributed by Bata in Kenya, India and Zimbabwe. As for most American brands, the bulk of their manufacturing is now done for them in Korea, Taiwan or Indonesia.

The net result is that for anyone outside the industry, it is virtually impossible to tell where a shoe was made or by whom. Recently a young hostess on Singapore Airlines repeated to me what unfortunately is a familiar refrain: "I wore Bata shoes all the time when I was a little girl, but I don't anymore." I happened to know that the stylish pumps she was wearing as part of her uniform had been made for the airline by our Singapore factory. But since they carried a neutral brand name, there was nothing to identify them as a Bata product.

But, then, there is mighty little brand loyalty among young, fashion-conscious shoe buyers. Most of them shop around until they find what they like in a store that suits their taste and pocketbook. Those who want to save money at the cost of service and convenience patronize discount stores, while others are willing to pay the price for the more hospitable environment of shopping centers or elegant boutiques. In a sense this distinction is reminiscent of our experiences in postwar Africa, where the cost of rent and electricity and wages boosted the price of shoes sold in our stores by thirty percent or more. The chap in the market stall across the street, who also sold Bata shoes but who had no overhead, presumably said to himself, "To feed my family takes ten shillings a day. Therefore I need to sell ten pairs of shoes, and charge a shilling more than I paid for each." So he charged eleven shillings for shoes that we sold for fifteen, but we provided a service and an environment for which some customers were willing to pay the extra four shillings.

While the current range of outlets is clearly good for the consumer, the proliferation of shoe stores in shopping centers should be a matter of concern to the industry. Assuming that the total sales volume in any one center is more or less constant, it stands to reason that the slice of the footwear pie available to any one store shrinks as the number of stores increases. Faced with this turnover squeeze, plus the high cost of air-conditioning, parking facilities and communal housekeeping and other amenities, some stores could be forced to price themselves out of the market. The survivors will be those whose superior merchandise and service attract more customers, and whose higher sales will, in turn, translate into lower costs and reduced prices. Our experience indicates that staff training and additional sales staff during peak periods results in substantially improved business. Alternatively retailers will succeed by carving out for themselves a distinct niche in the market. Athletic footwear is a case in point. Our Athlete's World stores, which sell our own as well as our competitors' brands, are perceived by their customers as offering a specialized service and selection that aren't available in larger shoe stores, let alone in department stores.

Identifying the future needs of consumers in this varied marketplace is an art rather than a science. People seem to assume that fashion trends are dreamed up and flogged by the advertising industry. That isn't true. Advertising can take a trend and run with it, but the initial impetus originates invariably with consumers. It was the desire for change after World War II that paved the way for pointed toes just as, some thirty years later, North Americans' newfound health consciousness led to a phenomenal demand for athletic footwear. What's more, consumers' shopping habits have become almost as unpredictable as their taste in fashion. Up until a relatively short time ago, members of the upper class would have been mortified to be seen in a discount store. Not anymore. Today it is considered positively chic for members of London's or New York's high society to shop for bargain-priced basics in discount stores while relying on luxury boutiques for caviar and designer clothes. Similarly, an Indian woman who wears Western dresses to the office is apt to change into her sari and matching slippers when she gets home. When Sonja and I were in Teheran in January 1979, a few days before the departure of the Shah, we saw two attractive Iranian women arrive at a pro-Khomeini demonstration. They parked their Volkswagen, kicked off their high-heeled shoes and, having draped themselves in the traditional veils, became indistinguishable from the fundamentalist throng.

What it all adds up to is a somewhat confusing, highly competitive but tremendously exciting marketplace. Sure I wish that *Pas un pas sans Bata* were as true today as it was forty years ago, when we were virtually unchallenged in large parts of the world. On the other hand, I have had it drummed into me since early childhood that the customer is king, that the purpose of our organization is to satisfy the needs of consumers. And by providing the public with a better selection, better quality and lower prices, that is exactly what we are doing.

C H A P T E R

1 3

RIDING THE LATIN AMERICAN ROLLER COASTER

D
OING BUSINESS IN Latin America means learning to live with political upheaval. Throughout most of the Latin American countries' century and a half of independence, presidents have often succeeded each other at a breathtaking pace. In that part of the world political parties have sprung up not so much for ideological reasons as to follow a charismatic individual who promises heaven on earth to the desperately poor populace. Military dictators, neo-Marxists, Peron-style populists and genuine democrats have fought and, all too frequently, died in the pursuit of power.

Yet for all the volatility of the political climate, the health and development of the embryonic enterprises that our people had established in Latin America during World War II depended less on whatever regime happened to be in power than on the peaks and valleys in worldwide economic cycles. In countries where mining was the main source of income, good years were invariably followed by lean ones. When commodity prices were high, the balance of payments was healthy and foreign exchange was plentiful. At such times we would rush to order enough new machines, spare parts and raw materials to tide us over the inevitable ban on imports that would accompany a plunge in metal prices — or governmental splurges on palaces and armaments.

This strategy enabled our Chilean operation to grow within fifteen years from a sickly wartime infant into a successful enterprise with 2,000 employees. When we decided that the time had come to expand even further, we set out to look for a suitable site where we might build a second plant. An important criterion, in Chile as anywhere else, was that it should be a green-fields location. We had no wish to acquire someone else's plant, or to locate in a manufacturing center where our approaches to management, human relations, technology and marketing might run up against ingrained, archaic practices. The site should be near a small- to medium-sized town and no more than a couple of hours' drive from a major city. It would have a good highway, access to a reliable supply of water and electricity and, ideally, enough available land for us to build houses and social service facilities for our employees.

After scouring the country by land, air and even on horseback, our people found exactly what they were looking for about seventy-five kilometers southeast of Santiago, in a little town called Melipilla. Not only did it meet all our criteria; as an additional bonus it was situated in a beautiful valley with rolling hills on either side and a river in the center for swimming and boating. So we took options to buy the land and announced our decision to build a first-class shoe manufacturing and tanning complex in Melipilla. With our son Tom, who had accompanied Sonja and me to Chile, we decided to take a look at the site. As we approached Melipilla, we were met by a welcoming committee of town fathers who informed us that they had declared a holiday for the afternoon. After sampling their homemade wine, we were escorted by a cavalcade of some 200 cars and motorcycles to the top of a bandstand in the middle of the Plaza de las Armas, Latin America's traditional town center. Bands played, speakers extolled our virtues and the crowd cheered. No conquering hero could have wished for a better reception.

While having one's ego massaged is admittedly an enjoyable experience, I was concerned about the impact of all this adulation on my seventeen-year-old son. "Remember, Tom," I said to him in the midst of the festivities, "people's attitudes toward their employer can change mighty fast, particularly in politically volatile countries. I wouldn't be at all surprised if, two or three years from now, we were to have a hell of a strike." The important thing, I told him, was to see both peaks and valleys in their proper perspective. "In other words, don't let yourself be overly impressed by the hymns of praise you hear today, or by the attacks to which we may be subjected in the future. Neither extreme is an accurate reflection of the way people feel about us or about our organization."

We proceeded to build a state-of-the-art plant in Melipilla, complete with the most modern machinery and antipollution devices. We built houses for our employees and provided them with every conceivable service, including a day-care center. Twenty-five years later Melipilla is still one of the most modern footwear centers in the world. And sure enough, we did have a strike two or three years after its opening. It was a difference of opinion rather than a bitter confrontation and it left no aftermath of ill will. Nevertheless, it served as a reminder that, in business as in politics, popularity is a fragile commodity.

Similar swings of the pendulum characterized our employee relations in other Latin American countries. In Bolivia, as in Chile, the small band of pioneers who had founded the company during the war had chosen a beautiful site, a village in a spectacular Andean valley near the city of Cochabamba, some 200 kilometers southeast of La Paz. By the time of my first visit around 1950, the enterprise, while relatively small, was firmly established and profitable. But of all Latin American countries, Bolivia in those days had the most volatile political climate; and while successive governments did little or nothing to raise the standard of living, they were good at employing agitators and whipping up latent passions. At any given moment relations with our 200 to 300 employees depended on the political situation and on the local consumption of a potent brew made of fermented maize batter. Chicha, as this drink is called, was supposedly made by having the batter chewed by old women whose rotten teeth produced the bacteria required for fermentation. About once a year, when the political tensions exacerbated by extra doses of chicha reached some sort of peak, the workers would march our executives at gunpoint out of the factory and install them in the local hotel. No one ever came to any harm; the workers were basically wonderful people. The following day, when tempers had cooled, they invariably invited the executives to come back.

Whenever I visited a plant, in Bolivia or anywhere else, I made a point of meeting with the union leaders and discussing their concerns with them. While I had no intention of interfering with local management, I wanted them to know that I was interested in their point of view. Usually these talks were very pleasant, but at times of political turbulence within the country, the atmosphere could turn nasty. On more than one occasion confrontations were timed to coincide with my visits, when the union leaders figured they could put management under a certain amount of pressure. Once, when six of us had barely missed being on a scheduled flight that crashed in the Andes, we arrived in Cochabamba in an ancient DC-3 that had been loaned to us by a mining company. There was a telecommunications strike, so I couldn't even inform Sonja, who hadn't accompanied me because she was pregnant, that I was safe. On this particular occasion I found the atmosphere in the factory explosive and the union leaders' demands unreasonable, to put it mildly. They didn't call a strike, but it was a decidedly unpleasant encounter.

A couple of years later the pendulum had swung all the way in the opposite direction. On our way to Cochabamba Sonja and I were surprised to be met at the airport by hundreds of our employees and their families. Now in Bolivia you don't just greet people by shaking hands; you are expected to embrace every one of them. I consider myself to be physically fit, but embracing some 300 women, all decked out in their local costumes with numerous petticoats, some of which had never encountered a washing machine, was quite an endurance test.

Another memorable experience awaited us the following morning. Over the years I had entered factories on a bicycle, in a truck and, on one occasion, on the back of an elephant. But never before had I been carried into one of our factories on the shoulders of union leaders. The local bishop said mass at a mobile altar that had been erected in the middle of the garden, after which we were treated to a performance by the Diabladas, a dancing group with fantastic costumes and masks whose name literally translated means "devilry." Finally everybody adjourned to an enormous lunch washed down with large quantities of chicha. It was a truly memorable day.

Nothing quite as spectacular ever happened in Peru, at least not with regard to employee relations. On the other hand, Peru is probably the only country in the world where a Bata enterprise began operating in defiance of the law. During and after World War II, the largest shoe manufacturer in the country was Manuel Prado, who also happened to be the president of Peru. To ensure his hegemony Prado had issued a presidential edict specifically forbidding the establishment of a Bata factory. But when a group of Bata pioneers began producing footwear near Lima, the constables sent to close them down quit the police force and signed up as employees instead. A quarter century later, when the decree was finally rescinded, we were employing 4,000 Peruvians.

Lima in those postwar years was a beautiful, modern city and our relationship with the community and our employees was excellent. But once successive governments tried their hand at expropriation and Communist-dominated trade unions became increasingly powerful, investment dried up and the economy began deteriorating. In the late 1970s one of the successive military dictatorships decided to bypass the unions and establish the so-called "Communidad Industriale." Under this system every enterprise had to pay a percentage of profits into an employee-owned fund that converted the money into equity shares so that, ultimately, the employees would own fifty percent of the organization. Part of the deal was that trade union officers could not sit on the board of a Communidad Industriale. But faced with the prospect of losing power, the Communist union leaders found ways of infiltrating the system and, eventually, destroying it.

From then on conditions went from bad to disastrous. Twenty years ago the Peruvian company was still one of the top five within the Bata organization, and Lima was one of the ten most beautiful cities in the world. Since then the city has spawned slums, the economy is in a shambles, inflation is out of control and insurgents are terrorizing the population. The bombing of stores, office buildings and banks has become commonplace, and along with many others we have had our factory in Lima blown up. Fortunately no one was working at the time and there was no loss of life.

All things considered, we decided not to rebuild on the same site and to decentralize our production among smaller units. Interestingly enough, trade union organizations in various parts of Latin America keep bombarding me with protests against the closure of the Lima factory, even though we haven't laid off any of our employees.

One unfortunate by-product of situations such as the one in Peru is the increasing difficulty of persuading capable people to serve in that part of the world. True, we now have a large pool of Latin American managers to draw on. But given the decline in purchasing power and the threat to personal security, they, too, look for transfers or for alternative employment in more stable parts of the world. And it isn't only managers who are leaving. In Nicaragua our biggest problem is hanging on to skilled workers who know they can make their way to Guatemala, then to Mexico and eventually to the United States. When that happens it isn't just our organization that suffers a loss; the national economy as a whole is deprived of valuable human resources.

Chile is another country that has lost some of its most productive people, both under the Allende and Pinochet regimes. North Americans tend to think of Allende as a martyr crucified on the altar of democracy. My associates and thousands of Chilean refugees remember him as a bumbling president surrounded by ruthless Marxists, the type of leader one might find in Cuba. Though ours was one of the sixty odd enterprises that the government had earmarked for a "negotiated settlement," we managed to hang on longer than most thanks to our trade unions, which were emphatically opposed to nationalization. Finally, under intense government pressure, our regional coordinator, a man named Batek, began negotiating with the minister of finance. But each time they reached an agreement as to the price of the shares, and Batek secured the approval of the shareholders, the minister claimed that the situation had changed and the shares weren't worth as much as before. On one hand, this tactic enabled us to delay the "settlement" in the hope of political change; on the other hand, price controls were draining us of resources to the extent where we didn't know how long we could hold out.

People desperately wanted change. Spiraling inflation and economic mismanagement had produced severe shortages of such basic necessities as soap, sugar and bread. Money was worthless, and the only way to obtain food was by bartering something tangible in return. To help our workers, we negotiated a deal with the union whereby all our employees and each member of their families would receive free of charge three pairs of shoes per year so that they could trade the shoes for food on the underground market. But we had desperately little time left. If political change came before we ran out of money, we would win; otherwise we would lose.

At that point the government committed a fatal blunder. Just before our newly appointed regional coordinator, my cousin Fred Mencik, arrived on the scene, Allende decreed the nationalization of road transport. Chile had only one north-south railroad; all other transport depended on small trucking companies. In response to the nationalization decree the owners drove their trucks off the roads, took the keys out of the ignition and overnight paralyzed the country's transportation system. As a result, shortages that had already been severe became intolerable. From his hotel window Fred watched huge antigovernment demonstrations, with women dancing around fires in Santiago's main square and shouting, "*Que se vaya*," or "He must go." It was as though the witches in *Macbeth* had been joined by dozens of look-alikes.

As a last resort, Fred asked for an appointment with Allende and, to his surprise, was told that the president would see him. At the appointed time a man in civilian clothes called for him and escorted him into the palace through a side door, out of sight of the demonstrations at the main entrance. The conversation was a three-cornered affair with Fred speaking English, Allende Spanish and an "assessor" or economic adviser acting as interpreter. "You're stalling. You're not negotiating in good faith," Allende fired as an opening salvo. Fortunately Fred had brought along all the documentation he needed to prove that it was Flores, the minister of finance, who had repeatedly stalled the negotiations by coming up with new demands. At that point Allende, who didn't realize Fred spoke fluent Spanish, turned to the interpreter and said, "That so-and-so Flores never tells me anything."

Clearly Flores, whose Extreme Left party was much more radical than Allende's Communists, was determined to engage in outright expropriation, with or without the president's approval. The following day, when Fred informed the minister of finance that the shareholders had approved the sale of eighty percent of Bata stores to the Chilean government, Flores laughed in his face. "We don't want eighty percent of your stores," he said. "We want them all."

That same evening, as Fred prepared to leave Chile, he assumed he wouldn't be back. "We only have enough money to last for two weeks," the chief financial officer told him. "After that we'll have to turn everything over to the government and forget about compensation." Three days later the government was overthrown, Allende was dead and Pinochet's military junta had assumed power.

Just why the armed forces, who were believed to be Allende's staunchest supporters, decided to rebel against him remains a matter of conjecture. According to Admiral Merino, the senior naval officer, it all started when the naval officers' suspicions were aroused by a sudden increase in the number of "sailors" on board their ships. Rather than launch an investigation within the government's earshot, they sailed out to sea, identified all bona fide sailors and threw the political informers who had infiltrated the crews overboard. They then contacted the commanders of the army and the air force, explained what had happened and persuaded them to join in overthrowing the government.

Be that as it may, Pinochet was hailed as a liberator by most Chileans. As in so many cases of revolution and counterrevolution, the liberator turned out to be far from benign. Also, as in many other parts of the world, we have been subjected to severe criticism for continuing to operate under a regime notorious for violating human rights. It is a criticism that I reject, whether in Chile, South Africa, Uganda or Nicaragua. I don't believe it is morally justifiable to fire 3,000 people, regardless if the man in power happens to be Pinochet or Allende. Besides, what do the critics mean when they urge us to pull out of Chile? Do they want us to turn our operations over to a regime they profess to hate? Or do they want us to close down our factories and stores and let our employees starve for the sake of our moral principles?

Fortunately a return to democracy may soon render these questions irrelevant in Chile as it has in other Latin American countries. Bolivia, for instance, was at one time an almost impossible country in which to operate. A string of bloody revolutions, skyrocketing inflation, the nationalization and mismanagement of the tin mines and kidnappings of businessmen, including our general manager (the same man who had hung on so bravely in Saigon), all threatened to plunge the country into anarchy. When such conditions arise, as they do from time to time in different parts of the world, we don't run away. Instead we find ways to overcome the raw material shortages, we try to produce the spare parts we can't import, we barter shoes for other necessities and we wait for conditions to improve. In recent years Bolivia has beaten inflation, balanced its budget and held two democratic elections.

On the other hand, we never did get started in Argentina, partly because we could see what was happening to the country under the Peron regime and subsequently during the "dirty war," partly because we didn't want to compete with a company called Alpargatas, which was buying our machinery. We were all the more surprised when the owner, the scion of a Scottish family named Robert Fraser, informed us that he was planning to build a rubber footwear plant in Brazil and suggested that we do the same. "Why do you want us to compete with you?" I asked. Fraser explained that the Brazilian market was so enormous that his company wouldn't be able to satisfy it in the foreseeable future. He was concerned about fly-by-night, inadequately financed entrepreneurs who might rush into the vacuum, try to undersell one another and end up flooding the market with fire sale merchandise. "No doubt you'll be tough competitors," he said. "But at least you know how to cost your products and you'll pay your bills."

The Brazilian economy was booming, so we decided to manufacture molded plastic footwear in Brazil. In a country where newcomers weren't exactly welcome and where we had no previous experience, the choice of a dynamic chief executive was particularly important. I remembered a young French manager I had met a year or so earlier in a tiny African country called Dahomey. His name was Joe Mauss, and I had been so impressed with the efficiency and appearance of the Bata stores in that obscure part of the world that I made a mental note to find out more about him. It turned out that he had been a retail manager in Senegal when he heard about the Dahomey stores being badly run-down, and that he had asked for the opportunity to go and rehabilitate them. For six months he and his wife had worked tirelessly to make the stores attractive and profitable, and they had done a superb job.

Mauss was our unanimous choice to head up the new Brazilian operation. Never mind that he spoke no Portuguese and that, as a marketing man, he knew next to nothing about production. A couple of crash courses would overcome those hurdles. But he wouldn't need any coaching in resourcefulness or determination to succeed. From his base in a nondescript hotel room in Rio, Mauss saw to it that the company was incorporated, a factory building rented, machines installed and workers engaged and trained. But when the first molded shoes emerged on April Fools' Day 1961, not a single merchant was willing to buy something so new and different. Mauss finally persuaded two shopkeepers to display the shoes without paying for them. They were promptly snapped up. Within the following eight years, the Brazilian company grew to employ over 600 people and to sell six million pairs of shoes annually.

Today we operate three Brazilian plants, including one in the poverty-stricken Pernambuco area where we went essentially at the suggestion of the Brazilian government. Even so, our growth in Brazil has been modest, partly because we were a bit late off the mark; by the time we got going, some of our competitors had stolen the march on us. Fortunately that didn't happen in Mexico. In that country we were the pioneers, the first major organization to provide quality footwear for the mass market.

The reason why in the postwar years most of our competitors steered clear of Mexico was the country's legislation that required businesses to have at least a fifty-one percent Mexican shareholding. At that time we had a 100 percent ownership policy, and while some sort of interlocking shareholding might have produced the appearance of Mexican ownership, we weren't interested in that kind of masquerade. The situation seemed hopeless until our lawyer discovered a clause in the legislation that entitled the president to waive the ownership requirement as long as the business didn't engage in activities specifically reserved for Mexicans. The lawyer, therefore, suggested that we get three people, whose names didn't suggest any connection with Bata, to petition the president for permission to establish in Mexico a shoe manufacturing company with a capital of $5,000. The application went forward under the name Calzado Rex, and much to our surprise, it was approved within four weeks.

Calzado Sandak, so named when Calzado Rex turned out to be registered by someone else, began its existence in a garage with a set of molds and a single machine. Today Calzado Sandak employs around 2,000 people and operates three factories as well as a chain of retail stores. These stores sell substantial quantities of shoes made by other Mexican manufacturers with whom we have an excellent relationship. So, instead of coming in like a bulldozer, we grew quietly by plowing back our profits, and we never had any trouble.

There was another wave of nationalism and efforts to Mexicanize industry during the Echeverria presidency in the 1970s and, in response to protests from the international business community, the president invited a number of us to a weekend conference at his summer villa. Our managers in Mexico tried hard to dissuade me from going; they argued that the ownership of our company was bound to come up for discussion and that there was nothing to be gained by risking a confrontation on the subject. But I don't believe in ducking sensitive issues, so I decided to go.

The guest list of about thirty included the heads of such corporate giants as Coca-Cola, IBM and Bechtel; none of the Europeans were able to come, so I ended up being the only non-American. As it turned out, Echeverria was less interested in foreign investment than in his concept of a new economic order, a subject on which he held forth most of the morning. Finally it was time for lunch, which was served at tables for ten. When my neighbor introduced himself as the director of Mexicanization in the Department of Economic Affairs, I decided to take the bull by the horns. "Did you know that we have an enterprise in

Mexico?" I asked. "Yes," he replied. "Calzado Sandak, isn't it?" I asked him how he knew, seeing we had kept such a low profile. He explained that, while holidaying in the mountains, he had gone to buy a pair of shoes for his six-year-old son. The merchant produced a pair of Sandak sandals, which he said would be just right for the terrain. "But are they good quality?" the father asked. "Yes, indeed," came the reply. "They're manufactured by the world's number one shoemakers — the Bata organization."

Since he seemed so friendly, I asked him what he thought we should do about the ownership issue. He replied that, as long as we were employing Mexicans and providing customers with good value for their money, his advice was to carry on as before. That is exactly what we have done ever since. We are happy in Mexico and, to the best of my knowledge, Mexico is happy with us.

One of these days I hope we will be able to say the same about all Latin American countries.

C H A P T E R

1 4

THE NORTH
AMERICAN CITADEL

THE UNITED STATES OF AMERICA emerged from World War II as the technological and commercial center of the footwear industry. Most of the European factories were in ruins and Japan was temporarily out of the picture. It was in the United States where the most modern machinery was being produced, where the best equipped design and research facilities existed, where the top scientific and marketing talent was concentrated. With remarkable generosity, the Americans chose, in the aftermath of the war, to share their expertise with other, less fortunate nations.

My first encounter with that generosity occurred shortly before the outbreak of war when I went to Nashville to meet Maxie Jarman, chairman of the Jarman Shoe Company and, at that time, president of the Shoe Manufacturers' Association. I had arrived in Canada earlier in the year and had met with a solid front of hostility from both the American and Canadian footwear industries. Conscious of our market penetration in other parts of the world, manufacturers on both sides of the border lobbied for all they were worth to keep us from establishing a foothold in either country. Not so Maxie Jarman. "If they're better, we'll learn from them," he told his colleagues. "If they're worse, they'll go down the drain." His was the only voice in the wilderness.

In May 1939 I accepted an invitation from Jarman's president, a man by the name of Henry Boyd whom I had met at a Rotary meeting on my way across the Atlantic, to visit the company's head office. Nashville at the time was a hard-drinking city in a dry state, and most of the passengers on my flight from New York were representatives of liquor companies. They told me Tennessee was about to hold a referendum on whether to go wet or stay dry, and they were all hoping it would stay dry so that liquor could be brought in tax free from neighboring states.

Maxie Jarman, on the other hand, was a Baptist and a strict teetotaler. The day I was invited to his house for dinner, the Boyds suggested that I'd better not have a drink at lunchtime because Maxie would be upset if he detected liquor on my breath. I was careful to follow their advice.

In spite of this somewhat daunting preamble, Maxie and I liked each other from the word go. I was pleasantly surprised when he offered to show me around the plant and explain some of the ins and outs of the shoe business in America. Unlike most European shoe manufacturers who wouldn't dream of allowing competitors inside their gates, we had always welcomed visitors both in Zlin and East Tilbury; but this was the first though by no means the last time I encountered the same open-door policy on the other side of the Atlantic.

During the following five years, our plant in Maryland struggled to keep on manufacturing shoes in the face of financial problems and, after Pearl Harbor, shortages of materials for the production of consumer merchandise. But once the war was over that same plant became a successful participant in America's industrial boom. Before long it had grown to the point where we decided to build a second U.S. plant in Indiana and, eventually, a third one in West Virginia. Along with a chain of three plants we had purchased in northern Wisconsin, our American manufacturing operations became an important component of the global organization.

To a large extent this growth was fueled by the development and application of new technologies. Take polyurethane, a substance that plays an important role in the manufacture of athletic footwear. When it was first developed, polyurethane was suitable as a filler for cushions but lacked the resilience required for footwear. Then one day, while a group of our European managers were visiting American suppliers, someone at Dupont said to them, "By the way, we now have a type of polyurethane with good abrasive qualities. Would that be of any interest to you?" Before long our Belcamp plant was turning out tennis shoes with polyurethane soles. They were a great success and, for a number of years, we had that technology all to ourselves. That kind of head start, by the way, is a thing of the past. Nowadays we consider ourselves lucky if it takes competitors six or nine months to catch up to one of our new developments.

Another innovation pioneered in the United States by our American company was the direct vulcanizing process, whereby rubber soles are fused rather than stitched to canvas or leather uppers. We had developed the DVP technology before the war in Czechoslovakia, but it was virtually unknown in the U.S. or Canada. Strangely enough, Americans, who are so enterprising in many ways, tend to be ultraconservative when it comes to buying shoes, particularly shoes of a utilitarian character. While the high-fashion clientele accepts and indeed demands constant change, people are suspicious of even minor variations in work boots, nurses' oxfords or casual loafers. Though the DVP process is particularly suitable for work boots and industrial safety footwear, we had a hard time persuading department-store buyers that our vulcanized boots were lighter, more durable and more water-proof than their stitched counterparts.

The equipment for this type of footwear was imported from Canada, where our engineering division was at last pursuing its original purpose, namely designing and producing machinery for the global organization. Unlike its American counterpart, our Canadian company had, during World War II, maintained no more than a token presence on the shoe market. Having put most of its resources and facilities at the disposal of the armed forces, it had to start almost from scratch manufacturing shoes, building up a retail organization and converting our engineering division from defense to shoe machinery production. It was a tall order, and for a while we were badly strapped for cash, to the extent where I learned how to assure suppliers that "the check was in the mail." But we never failed to meet the payroll, thanks partly to our bankers, who proved far less evil-minded than I had been taught to believe by my father. Even so, I was taken aback when at age twenty-six I was told that as a condition for obtaining my first, rather modest bank loan, I would have to take out a $100,000 life insurance policy. In 1940 that was an awful lot of money.

Strangely enough, the editors of Canada's widely read *Maclean's* magazine chose this period of postwar austerity to publish a three-part article about me entitled "The Fabulous Shoemaker." According to the author, I was living in the lap of luxury, flitting all over the world, hunting big game in Africa, playing polo in India and socializing with the rich and famous, including Anthony Eden with whom I had supposedly shared a seaside holiday in Hawaii. At that time I had never been to Hawaii, I didn't know Anthony Eden and I have never hunted big game or played polo. Most of it was pure fiction, and I dismissed it as a prime example of creative journalism.

But shortly after the articles were published, a Department of

National Revenue official called from Ottawa and said he would like to see me. He turned out to be a dignified, pleasant chap who explained that there appeared to be a discrepancy between the lifestyle described in the magazine articles and my tax returns. There was a possibility that the minister might be asked questions about me in the House of Commons, so they had decided they'd better do an audit.

They spent a year and a half delving into financial statements all over the world, sorting out expense accounts and deciding whether to use the official or the real rate of exchange in such countries as Chile. It took an awful lot of my time, but while I can't claim I enjoyed it, I must say there was never any discourtesy or unpleasantness. In the end, the auditors discovered, somewhat to their embarrassment, that I had actually overpaid taxes for income from the Chilean company, so they owed me quite a bit of money. Luckily for them, they then found that the Chilean company had claimed as a business expense contributions to a reserve fund that had been set up to pay for travel expenses incurred by expatriate managers who qualified for home leave. Apparently we weren't supposed to claim our contributions to that fund until the expenses were actually incurred, so the two findings more or less canceled each other out.

As part of our postwar strategy, we were determined to expand the modest chain of stores we already owned so that we would have a secure outlet for at least part of our footwear production. The problem was that our customers, particularly small retailers, resented having our stores compete with theirs, while Canada's two dominant department stores, Eaton's and Simpsons, insisted on buying only from manufacturers who had no dealings with the other group. Trying to be fair, and be perceived to be fair by the three types of customers — our own stores, large-volume merchants and independent retailers — was a constant battle. Developing new brands to be sold outside our own stores was only a partial solution. Fortunately I discovered that this type of conflict exists in most multichannel organizations, and none of them has yet figured out a way to please everybody. One American marketing manager told me that if, by ten o'clock in the morning, he hasn't had at least three complaints from customers who believe they are being treated unfairly, he feels something is wrong.

For all these reasons our progress in Canada during the immediate postwar period was slow, and while we had some reasonably good years, there were also times when we experienced serious losses. The turnaround came in the early 1950s when an inventor came to see us and suggested that a process used to make squeaky plastic toys might be adapted to manufacturing shoes. It sounded like an excellent idea, so we engaged that individual and, in cooperation with our production people and chemists, developed a system for converting liquid polyvinyl chloride into durable, waterproof footwear. Developing the proper molds and the semi-automatic machinery for this process was the kind of technological challenge I have always enjoyed and I was happy to participate in tackling the inherent problems. The resulting technology put us way ahead of our competitors in that type of footwear. Besides being the mainstay of our Canadian operation, slush-molded boots are also produced in our factories in Europe, in Chile and in our joint venture in Japan. Furthermore, we have sold the technology to the Russians and Chinese.

Around 1960 we began to wonder whether we should move the organization's headquarters back to Canada. Back in 1945, when Western Europe was struggling to recover from the damage inflicted by six years of war and when Eastern Europe was disappearing behind the Iron Curtain, it had seemed essential, from a practical as well as a psychological point of view, to be near our factories and stores in the areas of reconstruction. Fifteen years later Europe was back on its feet, and given the advances in telecommunications as well as passenger travel, the need for a European headquarters no longer existed. Besides, North America was, at the time, the epicenter of shoe manufacturing and the biggest, most dynamic footwear market in the world. Indeed, by pioneering the export of our European-made shoes to this flourishing market, we had the satisfaction of having made a modest contribution to Europe's recovery.

From a personal point of view, Sonja and I both felt that Canada was a more congenial place than Europe for bringing up our young family. We were Canadian citizens, two of our children had been born in Canada and I had a sentimental attachment to the country that had welcomed me in 1939 as a refugee from my native country. The question was, would it be wise to uproot an operation that was working efficiently in London and start all over again in Canada? After careful consideration, we decided the answer was yes.

At first sight it seemed that the logical place to establish a Canadian headquarters was Batawa, where our plant was located and where we had recently built ourselves our first family home. But having lived for a while in East Tilbury in England, I was aware of the problems that can arise when local management and corporate executives operate out of the same location. Seemingly trivial issues, such as who presides at public functions and whose wife opens the flower show, can become a source of friction. Above all, I was concerned that my presence in Batawa might undermine the stature and authority of the person who was running the Canadian company.

Besides, it didn't seem practical for an organization whose executives spent most of their time traveling around the world to be located two and a half hours' drive from the nearest international airport. In the postwar period, when airline service was minimal and there was little or no chartering, we had a number of corporate aircraft for use by our executives. But once we had a choice of scheduled flights to most parts of the world and charters were available at a moment's notice, owning a corporate jet became an expensive status symbol rather than a necessity.

We found a suitable location for our headquarters on the northern outskirts of Toronto, near a main highway and, at that time, within twenty minutes' driving distance from the airport. It was sold to us by a small tile manufacturing company called Olympia & York, whose owners, the Reichmann brothers, were soon to become world-famous for their real estate developments in Canada, the United States and Britain. Sonja engaged the well-known Canadian architect John Parkin to design the building, and one foggy Saturday afternoon, while I was out playing tennis, the two of them huddled over some drawings in our temporary downtown Toronto office. When I returned, I was shown two sketches, one obviously far superior to the other. I have always suspected that the second sketch was a decoy, to make me believe that the final decision was mine.

One of the great features of the building is that it can't be expanded. Considering all the means of communication that now link various parts of our organization, I see no need for an army of experts to be stationed at headquarters. The function of a headquarters, in my opinion, isn't to dispense wisdom but rather to act as a kind of catalyst, to stimulate new approaches to marketing, product development and management. That was why, in outlining our specifications to the architect, we insisted that the building should be designed so that, if we were ever tempted to spawn a huge bureaucracy, we would be thwarted by lack of space and immovable walls.

Some of these ideas and management principles were the result of my own business experience. But for many others I owe a lasting debt of gratitude to organizations that provide the American business community with continuing education and opportunities to benefit from each other's know-how. My first exposure to this system dates back to 1940 when the faculty of the Harvard Business School invited me to a luncheon and a seminar with, I thought, a small group of students. Instead I found myself being led to the podium in Baker Hall, an enormous auditorium filled with what looked to me like hundreds of people. To put it bluntly, I was terrified. Here was I, a twenty-six-year-old with nothing but a high school diploma by way of formal education, addressing obviously mature students at one of the most famous universities in the world.

But there was no place to hide, so I gave my prepared speech and showed a film about Zlin, after which there was a forty-five-minute question and answer period. To my surprise, it turned out to be a thoroughly enjoyable experience. Years later, it stimulated my interest in adult education in general and business schools in particular.

During the war years, I had no time or opportunity to pursue this interest. But once the war was over I found that some of the American Management Association's conferences and seminars provided a marvelous opportunity to share information with people engaged in various types of business activity. Another interesting AMA feature was the creation of so-called councils whose members met periodically to review the quality of courses and suggest new topics of discussion. I was invited to join some of these councils, and I found the exchange of ideas with the chief executives of some of America's largest corporations a tremendous learning experience. The head of a large pharmaceutical company, for instance, described to us a technique for negotiating joint ventures. Apparently before signing an agreement, the company's senior executives made a point of spending three days away from their desks, envisaging all possible areas of conflict that might arise and rehearsing with their prospective partners ways in which they would deal with such situations. I was most impressed and, as a result, we introduced such brainstorming and role-playing techniques into many of our own company courses.

But much though I enjoyed attending AMA meetings and those of its Canadian counterpart, I was conscious of the age gap between myself and most of the other participants. Almost invariably I was at least ten years younger than anyone else. Then, one day in 1950 or thereabouts, I read a *Business Week* article about a chap named Ray Hickok, who had been sent home from the war to succeed his late father as head of the family-owned manufacturing company. To overcome his lack of business experience he had assembled a group of young chief executives who met once a month in New York to discuss their problems and benefit from one another's experiences. They called themselves the Young Presidents' Organization.

I was sufficiently intrigued to phone and make arrangements to attend the next meeting in a hotel on Fourteenth Street. There were about twenty people in the room, and we spent a thoroughly enjoyable, informative evening. A few months later at a convention in Boca Raton, Florida, I became one of the YPO's fifty founding members. The original rule was that, in order to join, you had to have become, before your fortieth birthday, head of a company with annual sales of at least one million dollars. The age limit is still the same, but the sales requirement has been gradually raised to five million dollars. The organization grew rapidly — today's membership is close to 8,000 — and we were able to invite top-notch guest speakers from all over the world to our sessions. Having never had the opportunity to attend a business school, I lapped up the management concepts to which they introduced me. The critical path method of planning, for instance, may seem old hat today, but to me it was a revelation when I first heard it described in the early 1950s, and I promptly engaged the speaker, a Harvard University professor named Paul Vatter, as a lecturer for our company management courses.

In 1961 I was asked if I could persuade Allen Dulles to address a YPO convention that was to be held in Puerto Rico. I had seen Allen only once since he had become head of the CIA, and considering that the relationship between the United States and the Soviet Union was particularly tense at the time, I assumed he would be too busy to accept our invitation. But to my pleasant surprise he said he would come. By the time he arrived in San Juan, the international situation had deteriorated into a crisis, but when Allen invited me to his hotel to discuss the program, he was calmness personified. Only the number of people coming and going suggested that anything unusual was in the air. Two days later he delivered an excellent speech, in spite of the fact that he had just heard about the disastrous Bay of Pigs landing in Cuba.

From the point of view of the shoe business, another invasion was beginning to loom on the horizon. Inexpensive footwear manufactured in the Orient was about to inundate the North American market and cause a fundamental restructuring of the shoe industry. The first challenge had occurred in the late fifties when low-priced, high-quality Japanese footwear had made its appearance in Canadian and U.S. stores. But at that time the North American industry had fought back with the help of its large North American customers. Partly out of patriotism, partly because they were afraid that tropical storms, transportation strikes or political upheaval in distant countries might disrupt their supply lines, these retailers were reluctant to become overly dependent on imports. Then Japanese costs began rising, and so the threat was contained.

But all the North American industry had achieved was a temporary reprieve rather than a victory. As their next move, the Japanese established manufacturing partnerships in Korea and Taiwan, and when their products invaded the North American market, the price differential overcame both patriotism and security of supply. Many companies folded while others responded to the challenge by phasing out or shrinking their domestic production and becoming importers rather than manufacturers. Shoes continued to be designed and marketed in the United States. But instead of having their designs produced in a local factory, company executives took them to Korea or Taiwan where the work could be done at a fraction of the cost. Today only about twenty percent of the footwear sold in Canada and the U.S. is manufactured in North America, and quite a few of the components that go into that domestic production are imported.

If we were somewhat late in accepting this reality, it was because of our traditional philosophy of lifetime employment. We were so intent on selling what we produced and thereby preventing layoffs in our North American plants, we failed to react to what was happening in the world marketplace. Take the sudden popularity of brand name athletic footwear that has swept North America and parts of Europe during the past few years. If some of our competitors stole the march on us, it wasn't because we failed to identify the emerging craze for aerobic dancing and the resulting need for a special type of shoe. Part of our problem was that our product development people treated aerobic dancing as a small part of their responsibility, whereas American companies such as Reebok and Nike took a leaf out of the book of Germany's Adidas and devoted their research and marketing skills exclusively to athletic footwear. But the determining factor was that these outfits had their shoes made in Korea by cheap labor, while we were trying to keep our plant busy in the high-wage environment of Maryland. It was a no-win situation. Though our athletic footwear continued to sell well in other parts of the world, we were badly mauled in the huge and lucrative U.S. market.

When the restructuring of our North American operations finally came, it hit us much harder than it would have done if we had accepted the inevitable a little earlier and joined our competitors on the Oriental bandwagon. We had to close our factories in Indiana and West Virginia, spin off the ones in Wisconsin and shrink our original plants in Maryland and Canada. What was equally serious, we had failed to build up the kind of marketing organization and relationships with Oriental producers that would have enabled us to derive some advantage from the new situation. It was a costly penalty to pay for clinging to a tradition that, no matter how worthy, had been overtaken by the force of events.

Setting up our own manufacturing facilities in Korea or Taiwan was out of the question for the simple reason that neither country would allow foreign-owned enterprises inside its doors. These countries are great believers in free trade as long as it means exporting their merchandise to Western countries rather than the other way round. In the rare case where they do permit foreigners to operate within their borders, they insist that all the production be earmarked for export. For reasons I shall describe later, that is something we refuse to do.

Our two-pronged strategy under the new circumstances was to concentrate on retailing and to confine our manufacturing to those products where we enjoyed a technological or geographic advantage. Our vulcanized footwear was an obvious example. This was a field where our highly efficient technology gave us a head start over our competitors. Furthermore, the technology was capital- rather than labor-intensive, which meant we were less likely to be outpriced by imports from low-wage countries. Finally, it was ideally suited to three products that were in great demand: industrial safety footwear throughout the United States, winter boots in Canada and the northern U.S. and, for a short while, jungle boots for American troops in Vietnam.

Over the past twenty years the only shoe manufacturers in North America who have survived are those who have either carved out a special niche for themselves, or who have close ties with merchants and are able to resupply them quickly when the need arises. Large department stores such as Sears in the United States or Eaton's in Canada like to have some domestic suppliers so that if sales of American cowboy boots suddenly take off, they can place repeat orders without waiting for shipments from overseas. Some American manufacturers have taken advantage of such fashion trends to boost their operations and actually export footwear for which there is a surge in demand. But, as a rule, all they do is use up their existing manufacturing capacity after which, if the demand is sufficient, they take off once again for Korea or Taiwan. We must be among the very few who, within the recent past, have built a new plant in the United States. The plant is in Ogdensburg, New York, and it owes its existence to the fact that the United States imposes a thirty-seven percent duty on Canadian-made slush-molded winter boots; if, on the other hand, we ship the plastic shells across the border and finish the boots there, the duty is only ten percent. At the moment we sell about one and a half million pairs a year of these boots in Canada, and we expect them to be equally popular in those parts of the U.S. where winters are just as frigid.

Up until now the only product sold in the United States that carries the Bata name has been our industrial safety footwear; and while we play an important role in that huge market, the average consumer isn't likely to be familiar with it. As for retail, we have recently acquired two chains of stores, one in North Carolina and the other in and around Texas. But neither operates under the Bata name, which is why Bata isn't as well-known in the United States as in most parts of the world. One of these days I expect that will change.

In Canada, on the other hand, we do have a countrywide retail network that serves as the backbone of our marketing organization. But with few exceptions the merchandise sold in those stores isn't made in our Canadian plant. Imports have hit the Canadian shoe industry every bit as hard as its neighbor to the south — the dozens of shoe manufacturers that used to operate in Quebec, Ontario and Manitoba have dwindled to a mere handful — and in spite of our dominant position in slush-molded footwear, our Batawa work force has shrunk to sixty percent of its former self.

A few years ago we sold our engineering division, though we could have kept it busy and profitable with military contracts for NATO. However, we had no wish to be picketed by peace activists, let alone subjected to the kind of violence experienced by at least one Canadian supplier to the military. Besides, the original, vertically integrated structure whereby Bata manufactured virtually everything from aircraft to shoelaces has long since become obsolete. That kind of production made sense in Zlin, partly because of the quantities of materials we used, partly because cartels pegged many prices artificially high. In those days we even made our own metal compounds for linotype material to be used in our printing presses because that was one of the commodities controlled by a cartel.

But, as I was to discover in later years, manufacturing everything internally can be dangerous to the health of an organization. Take shoelaces, a major item in a large footwear manufacturing company. Shortly after the war I found that shoelaces were costing us much more in Britain than anywhere else in Europe or North America. The reason, it turned out, was that the British company was manufacturing the laces internally on machinery that had been installed in the 1930s, whereas Holland, for instance, was importing high-quality laces from Hong Kong. But a lot depends, of course, on the availability of a given item. When we began using plastic soles, we couldn't buy them at a reasonable price, so we installed a polyurethane sole manufacturing operation that worked successfully for some twenty years. Today hundreds of manufacturers are producing those soles by the millions and you can buy them off the shelf for considerably less than it would cost us to make them.

In the case of shoemaking machinery, a major reason we had expanded our own production was our prewar feud with United Shoe Machinery Corporation, the industrial giant that had enjoyed a virtual monopoly in the shoe-machinery arena. Indeed it was USMC that spearheaded much of the opposition to our arrival in the United States. In all fairness I must admit that the company was tremendously inventive and spent huge amounts on research and development. During and particularly after the war, it dismantled most of the restrictive practices and policies to which my father had objected so strenuously. In due course, USMC, while still a dominant force in the United States, was overtaken in Europe by shoe-machinery manufacturers in Germany, France, Britain and particularly Italy.

Ironically, the United States antitrust people chose that particular time to launch a major attack against USMC. The company fought back, but the trust busters won, and USMC was divided up into a number of small, relatively insignificant components. And that, as far as I am concerned, was a great pity. With eyes fixed on their own backyard and with an outlook that was a decade or more behind the times, the authorities failed to realize that America needs strong companies in order to compete in a global marketplace. A few years later they tried to do the same thing to IBM, but, fortunately for the United States, the courts ruled in favor of sanity.

Rather than manufacturing our own machines, we now have technical services that develop ideas that we ask other manufacturers to implement. There is, for instance, a special type of machinery for making rubber footwear that we began thinking about before the war in Zlin and later in Batawa, without ever resolving all the technical problems. Then we took the idea to an Italian manufacturer whose experts, in cooperation with our own people, came up with a solution that is now being used all over the world. The manufacturer continues to pay us royalties for the idea and for our contribution to its development.

By adopting this approach, we have succeeded in establishing relationships with a number of manufacturers, none of whom enjoys a monopoly in the marketplace. So instead of relying for this type of research and development on small teams of our engineers in a couple of locations, we now have dozens of manufacturers in Italy, France, Germany and, most recently, Brazil, all competing for our business, and none holding a monopolistic position. As a result, I am convinced we pay less than we did when we were making our own.

All things considered, there came a point when we had to ask ourselves whether it made any sense to keep on manufacturing in Canada. One of the major justifications for the Canadian plant, namely its proximity to the United States, is no longer valid. True, the Americans are still and are likely to remain leaders in marketing expertise. But in manufacturing the epicenter has moved to the Orient, to Italy and, most recently, to Brazil. Nor do we need a Canadian plant to supply our retail stores. With the exception of slush-molded winter boots, there is nothing our Canadian stores need that we couldn't have made to our specifications elsewhere.

Nevertheless, we are determined to maintain our manufacturing presence in Canada. For one thing we do have in this country a technology that is unique and that may yet prove to be a jumping-off point for tackling the American market. But over and above that we want the Canadian plant to serve as a model and an experimental station as well as a training establishment for people from overseas.

If that isn't exactly the function I envisaged for Batawa in 1939, neither is the world what it was fifty years ago. I don't go along with people who moan about the shoe business being terrible. The shoe business has never been better than it is today. Millions of people are still barefoot, or in need of better shoes, and shoe sales in Canada and the United States have never been higher than they are now. What is not so great is the manufacturing arm of the shoe business in North America. For better or worse, the assembly line jobs have dwindled. On the other hand, there are unprecedented opportunities for planning, styling, designing, marketing, organizing.

I am sick and tired of people who have preached for the past twenty years that the shoe industry is dead. All they accomplish is to turn off potential recruits who have no wish to tie their talents to an industry that, according to its own spokesmen, suffers from a terminal disease. Shoe manufacturing is different from what it was and it has gone through some difficult times, but the only thing that is dead is the imagination of people who resent change and don't know how to cope with it.

PEOPLE, POWER AND POLITICS

IN 1986 I ATTENDED THE CELEBRATION of the thirty-fifth anniversary of our Faridabad plant in India. Its employees, mostly independent-minded refugees from northwestern Pakistan, had occasionally given management a rough time. On this particular occasion a fierce-looking, mustachioed union leader who had been particularly militant in the past made a speech in which he described all the fun he had had over the years, spearheading demonstrations, work stoppages and various attempts to intimidate management. Then, much to my surprise, he produced a beautiful gold-colored Pathan hat, plunked it on my head and said, "Now you're really one of us." It was one of the proudest moments of my life.

To me that incident, and the events that preceded it, epitomize our checkered relationship with trade unions. Over the years we have had our ups and downs; in an organization that operates in some eighty countries, that is probably inevitable. But I hate to see occasional problems blown up as though they represented an adversary relationship between management and labor. Because of all the elements that characterize our industrial organization, the one I value most and that is the most vital ingredient of our corporate culture is the loyalty and integrity of our people. Time and again when we ran into trouble, when floods threatened our plant in Bangladesh or when fire destroyed our factory in Kenya, our employees worked night and day to save equipment and minimize the damage. For all the changes that have transformed, within my lifetime, business and the environment in which it operates, these workers share the sense of common purpose that permeated the organization in its early days in Zlin, and that kept it alive throughout the war.

Oddly enough, it is a spirit that owes a great deal to an unfortunate encounter my father had, early in his career, with the trade union movement. As a boy growing up in Zlin, I often heard him tell how impressed he had been, during his trip to the United States in 1904, with the American unions' efforts to improve the living standards and working conditions of their members and how, upon his return home, he had encouraged his employees in Zlin to organize themselves into a union. What Father had failed to realize, and what many people don't fully understand to this day, is that trade unionism means different things to different people. In most Communist countries trade unions are part of the party apparatus and, as such, have nothing in common with their namesakes in Canada or the United States. In Poland a trade union has become a catalyst of political change; in Kenya it is closely affiliated with the government. In the Austro-Hungarian Empire and, after World War I, in Czechoslovakia, unions were ideological offshoots of rival political parties. In their efforts to attract recruits they were forever outbidding each other in demands for higher wages, more benefits or both. Father, who may have had a somewhat idealized view of industrial relations in the United States, labored under the illusion that unionization would imbue his Moravian employees with an American work ethic and a feeling of partnership with management. Instead, within two years of sponsoring the accreditation of the Social Democratic union in Zlin, he found himself faced with a bitter strike.

Though these events took place long before I was born, I was deeply conscious since early childhood of their impact on my father's thinking. As far back as I can remember, his goal was to create in Zlin an environment in which people would neither need nor want unions and, to the dismay of his critics, he succeeded. One aspect of that environment consisted of some of the highest industrial wages in Europe, along with modern housing, social services and recreational facilities. Another aspect was a profit-sharing scheme that was available to all employees, blue-collar workers as well as management. The idea was that, by age forty, employees should have sufficient savings to retire if they wished to do so. But to me the most important element of all was the sense of belonging, the enthusiasm that the company generated in its employees. People worked incredibly hard not just to earn a living but because they were proud of being part of a progressive organization.

That same relationship prevailed at our East Tilbury plant in England when I arrived there as a management trainee in 1935. Most of our British competitors were dismayed when we trans-planted from Zlin such supposedly revolutionary benefits as paid holidays and medical services. The Shoe Workers' Union, on the other hand, seemed relatively friendly, and though the docklands where East Tilbury is located was a union stronghold, they waited two years before attempting to organize our workers. Since there was very little the union could offer over and above what the workers already had, the response was minimal. And when the union followed up by calling a strike, it received a great deal of publicity but little support from the work force: only about five percent walked off their jobs.

After the strike petered out, we decided to create a so-called

management advisory committee consisting of worker representatives elected by secret ballot from different departments. This
committee met once a month with the chairman and company
executives and thrashed out with them any problems that had
arisen. A member of management was assigned to deal with each
issue, and those that hadn't been settled to the workers' satisfaction were brought up again at the following meeting. The system
worked extremely well and remained in operation until shortly
after the Second World War. At that time the British trade union
movement finally discarded its insistence on a collective agreement that would have imposed archaic and inefficient work practices on business and industry. Our British company responded
by signing a recognition agreement with the Shoe Workers'
Union, and their relationship has been harmonious ever since.

In the meantime, however, I had arrived in Canada and found
that some of the most vociferous opposition to our presence in
North America came from the trade union movement. At its
convention in June 1939 the Boot and Shoe Workers' Union
passed a resolution to fight the establishment of Bata in both
Canada and the United States on the grounds that the company's
practice of housing workers in dormitories and deducting room
and board from their wages amounted to "regimentation of the
worst kind." The union leadership didn't bother pointing out that,
in Zlin as in East Tilbury, only teenage apprentices were housed
in dormitories, that most employees were provided with comfortable, modern homes and that the cost to the workers was a fraction
of what they would have had to pay for equivalent accommodation.

This was particularly true in a poor country such as India, where
the living standard of the average villager or even an artisan is
often below subsistence level and where a dozen or more relatives
may depend for food and housing on the one member of the

family who has been fortunate enough to land a factory job. Indeed, in Batanagar in West Bengal, one of our major problems was trying to prevent the houses we had built for our employees from being turned into slum dwellings by twenty or more dependents living under the same roof.

These circumstances impose a moral responsibility on anyone doing business in the Third World. Employers there had better understand that job security is the one overriding industrial relations issue, infinitely more important than in Western countries; because if any one of these factory workers were to lose his job, it would be a real disaster not only for him and his immediate family, but for any number of other people, as well. These people have no safety net, no unemployment insurance or welfare payments to fall back on. For them, hanging on to their jobs can be, literally, a matter of life and death.

Security of employment is the main reason we never begin manufacturing anywhere in the world unless we are confident that we can sell eighty percent of our production on the domestic market. Governments that are short of foreign currency often try to persuade us to bend or abandon this self-imposed rule. But we know only too well that exports are subject to all kinds of disruptions, from transportation strikes to trade barriers. Australia, for instance, has changed its policy vis-à-vis imports three times since World War II. After being wide open, it turned protectionist and imposed both quotas and high duties on imported merchandise. Then, when wool prices soared and the country was flush with foreign currency, they went back to an open-door policy, only to slam the gate shut again a little while later. So any Indian enterprise that relied heavily on exports to Australia would have been in a bad way.

Fluctuations in currency rates present another danger to a business that is overly dependent on exports. The value of the

French franc, for instance, has changed repeatedly since World War II. When it is high, it is virtually impossible to export footwear from France. So our policy is that, as good corporate citizens, we will do our best to export up to twenty percent of our production and help earn foreign exchange in the countries where we operate. That way, even if there is a change in currency values or if trade barriers in a foreign country suddenly slam the door on imports, we can take measures to absorb the shock. With a loss of twenty percent you can maneuver; with 100 percent you face disaster.

Unfortunately our emphasis on security of employment isn't always compatible with efficiency and technological change. When my father planned our first plant in India, he gave instructions that as much as possible of the work should be done by hand rather than by machines. He clearly felt that generating employment was an important part of his mission. But as time went on, and as wages and costs kept increasing, it became impossible to follow that precept and still produce shoes that people could afford to buy. In order to provide our employees with decent housing and medical care, and in order to absorb the cost of all the statutory holidays and work restrictions dreamed up by the unions or imposed by the government, we had to modernize our production and distribution methods or risk pricing ourselves out of the market.

That is one reason why, whenever we started an enterprise in a low-wage country, I insisted that it be equipped with the most modern technology money could buy. Besides, it seemed nonsensical to provide African or Latin American workers with second-rate equipment and expect them to produce first-rate products. Unlike their North American or European counterparts, most of the people we employ in developing countries have, to begin with, no industrial skills or experience with which to overcome shortcomings in their equipment. Therefore we believe we must make their work as easy as possible.

Some of our friends and competitors used to shake their heads over what they considered our wasteful expenditures for modern equipment in our Third World plants, and the likely impact of those expenditures on the price of our products. In my view they were wrong. The determining factor isn't the cost of the machinery or its depreciation, but rather the ability of management to derive the maximum benefit from that machinery.

The validity of that theory was demonstrated, I believe, by the fate of a company called Diamante that was, during and immediately after the Second World War, our number one competitor in Peru. Originally owned by the president of Peru, it was sold to an American manufacturer called General Shoe Corporation, later renamed Genesco. While we were equipping our plant with the most modern machinery, Genesco opted for hand-me-downs sent to Peru from their U.S. factories or resold by other shoe manufacturers. This difference in environment and management outlook was, in my opinion, largely responsible for the decline of Genesco's fortunes in Peru. By the time the plant was finally sold, it had slid from its once dominant position to one-third the size of ours.

In some countries, unions understand that modern technology results in greater efficiency, which in turn means a more competitive plant and greater security of employment; in others they fight it tooth and nail. During my visits to our companies in various parts of the world, I always made a point of meeting with the union leaders and, in the vast majority of cases, found them cooperative and constructive. Normally we sat down over breakfast or lunch and, in the course of the conversation, I learned a great deal about them and their concerns. For my part, I tried to communicate to them some basic facts of life, such as the importance of delivering merchandise on time. If, for instance, they took advantage of the arrival of a major export order to make demands in defiance of a collective agreement, they might deprive a number of people of their jobs or prevent us from creating new jobs.

But that argument didn't carry any weight with highly politicized unions. In Batanagar in West Bengal, where the union leadership represents a spectrum of political parties including three shades of communism, one of the radical leaders told me point-blank that I was being naive if I thought he was interested in improving the work conditions of our employees. His only objective was to pave the way for a revolution, and to the extent that our workers were well paid and provided with generous benefits, we were thwarting his plans.

In highly volatile countries such as Bolivia, where inflation for a while reached astronomical proportions, labor strife was often an expression of dissatisfaction with the government rather than the employer. We had one strike because the airport wasn't built on time and another to protest against the failure by the department of public works to pave a road; we even had what we called "a retroactive strike" in support of municipal workers whose strike had been settled while our employees were on holidays.

Since these strikes had nothing to do with wages or working conditions, they didn't leave any aftermath of ill feeling. Indeed, when a military dictatorship in Bolivia outlawed trade unions and forbade any contact with their leaders, I continued to meet with worker representatives, not in their capacity as union leaders but as friends. Together we would drink a little chicha while we discussed employment conditions in the plant and the economy in general.

Halfway around the world our relationship with the union in Kenya has also been extremely amicable. At a meeting of the United Nations Commission on Transnational Corporations in

Manila, I shared a table at lunchtime with one of the expert advisers, a Kenyan trade union representative. This man had made an impassioned speech in the morning, charging transnational companies with all kinds of sins, so I braced myself for another tirade from an obviously hostile witness. To my pleasant surprise he turned to the other eight people at the table and said, "What I said this morning doesn't apply to the Bata Company. They're tough negotiators and they expect people to work hard, but they're fair."

But much more gratifying than occasional compliments from union leaders is my relationship with rank-and-file employees. Perhaps because people know that I once worked on the assembly line in Zlin, I have always enjoyed a feeling of kinship with our workers. Whenever I visit factories, especially in developing countries, it makes me feel good to be able to step up to a rubber mill and cut off some rubber compounds, or show people how lasting used to be done. I know perfectly well that there are times when employees place the equipment where they are sure I will see it and be tempted by it. Since they get a great kick out of watching me swallow the bait, I usually pretend I haven't noticed.

Respect for people and for their accomplishments, which has been an integral part of the company culture ever since my father's time, may well be the main reason why lifetime employment is still the rule rather than the exception within the Bata organization. Though our work force has shrunk from its postwar peak, the number of people who have been with us for twenty-five years or more continues to grow. This is particularly gratifying in view of the fact that, in most parts of the world, we now compete for capable people with many other progressive employers. At one time, in a country like Kenya, Bata was the only game in town. Today Kenya is bristling with industry, and when a newly arrived enterprise starts looking for experienced managers, the obvious companies to raid are the two most successful enterprises in the country: Unilever and Bata. But while some ambitious individuals have yielded to the inducements dangled before their eyes by these newcomers, the vast majority have chosen to stay.

Until a few years ago I made a point of personally presenting the longtime service awards, which included, among other things, a gold watch with my signature engraved on the back. A few months after officiating at such a ceremony in Pakistan, I got a letter from one of the recipients of the award. Apparently he had suffered an accident, and while he was recovering in hospital someone had lifted the watch from his bedside table. He wondered if I would consider replacing the watch. In spite of dire warnings that I would be unleashing a flood of "lost" watches from other employees, I decided to give the man the benefit of the doubt and sent him a new watch. I got a nice thank-you letter, and that was the end of the story. Six or seven years later I have yet to receive another request for the replacement of a lost or stolen watch.

On this and many other occasions my faith in the basic decency and integrity of people has been fully vindicated. Of course, we have had occasional instances of corruption or conflict of interest; but considering the size of the organization and the tens of thousands of people it employs, such incidents have been remarkably rare. And while I have been criticized at times, not without reason, for misplacing my confidence in people who didn't deserve to be trusted, I would rather err on that side than be overly suspicious.

One of the most distressing incidents in the realm of human relations occurred in England shortly after World War II. Though footwear was still rationed, the police in East Tilbury informed us that large quantities of our shoes were making their appearance on London's black market. So we launched an investigation and discovered that a small group of night shift workers were conveying shoes across the fence to accomplices who sold them to eager customers. The sad part of it was that the employees involved in this racket were people with over twenty-five years of service, but there was nothing we could do for them. They were charged by the police with illegally selling rationed goods, which was then a criminal offense in Britain, and they all went to jail.

But from a purely personal point of view, my most disappointing experience occurred in my own backyard in Batawa. The Boot and Shoe Workers' Union was certified in Batawa in 1940, and during almost forty years our relationship with the union was remarkably amicable. But the situation deteriorated abruptly when the union, after a couple of mergers, became part of the United Food and Commercial Workers International Union, an amalgam of militant groups that added up to the second largest union in North America. From then on all the issues revolved around power rather than wages or working conditions. We had our first run-in with the union in 1979 over the control of a proposed dental plan. We agreed to introduce the plan but insisted that it should be under our control. The issue was put to a vote and, to the union's dismay, the employees voted two to one in favor of the company. But the stage was set for a confrontation the following year.

Next time around the controversy concerned the terms and control of a proposed pension plan. The reason we didn't have such a plan was that our employees had decided to cash it in eleven years earlier when the Canada Pension Plan was introduced by the government and people thought it would take care of them in their old age. At any rate we were perfectly willing to launch a new plan and put an offer on the table that was actually more generous than the one proposed by the union. But from the point of view of the union leaders the problem was that we insisted on controlling the plan, and so, rather than let the workers vote on the company's offer, they called a strike.

It was a time when Canada's shoe industry was reeling under the impact of imports from the Orient, yet when we tried to deliver orders that had been promised to our customers, our trucks were attacked by picketing strikers, and there was a good deal of violence. But what hurt me most of all was the failure of the rank-and-file workers to stand up and be counted. Batawa up until then had occupied a special place in my heart. It was the first plant I had built, the place that had been my first home in North America, the launching pad, so to speak, for everything I had done in the past forty years. By the time the strike was settled those emotional ties had been stretched to the limit.

A few months later, at a Trent University function, a student asked me whether I intended to give up on Batawa in the wake of the strike. I said no, I wouldn't do that. But I added, "We will expect Batawa to justify its existence in the cold light of performance rather than any emotional involvement." While that may have been a bit of an overstatement, there is no doubt that my original enthusiasm and attachment to the place have suffered a lasting blow.

On balance my attitude toward trade unions is similar to my father's. Both of us have tried to provide people with wages and work conditions as good as or better than anything unionization could offer. But wherever our employees chose to cast their lot with unions, we worked with them toward what, I assumed, was our common purpose. Today ninety percent of our manufacturing operations are unionized. The only major exception is Belcamp in Maryland, where workers have voted repeatedly against joining a union.

As for the rest, the only times we have had problems were when union leaders abandoned the goal of providing better wages and working conditions for their membership and instead tried to pursue power. That, to me, is the most serious danger in the industrial relations arena, and it isn't confined to the Western world. The largest countries outside the Western orbit — the Soviet Union, China, India — all face the same problem. Creating a sense of common purpose between management and labor is one of the major issues facing all of us.

We have tried to tackle the issue by creating units of no more than 500 employees because most problems can be settled much more easily, with or without unions, in an environment where people know one another. Employee loyalty is already one of our greatest strengths. We hope to build on that strength and develop, in an increasingly automated environment, an even closer relationship with our people. I don't suppose we will ever achieve a utopian state of perfect harmony. But we certainly intend to give it a good try.

1 6

EASTERN APPROACHES

WHEN I WAS A LITTLE BOY, the mayor of Zlin was a prosperous manufacturer by the name of Stepanek. Strangely enough, Stepanek was also a rabid Communist who somehow managed to reconcile his status as an industrialist with the leadership of the Communist trade union. The Communists in those days were a powerful force in Czechoslovakia, clearly intent on undermining the stability of the newly independent country. I remember, as a child, listening to them as they spouted the party line at gatherings in Zlin's town square.

With the approach of the 1923 municipal election, my father decided it was time for Zlin to have a different kind of mayor. Since, under Czechoslovakian law, mayors were elected by councillors rather than by popular vote, Father formed a kind of citizens' forum, fielded a slate of candidates and ended up with a majority of seats on the town council. The new councillors elected Father as their mayor, and the people of Zlin voted for Bata candidates in ever-increasing numbers at two subsequent elections. The Communists were completely obliterated, and even after my father's death, when our general manager Dominik Cipera became mayor of Zlin, they never again managed to get more than a handful of votes. It was a humiliation they never forgot or forgave. After the war, when they came to power in Czechoslovakia, they singled out Zlin for special retribution. Most of our loyal managers were dismissed, a number were convicted and jailed for such offenses as "keeping in touch with the Bata family," and one of them, a Slovak by the name of Trojan who had distinguished himself in the anti-German Slovak uprising of 1944, was executed.

For my own part, I haven't forgotten that it was the USSR's friendship treaty with Germany that opened the door for Hitler to invade Poland in 1939, nor have I forgiven the Communists in Western countries for doing everything they could during the first two years of the war to sabotage the Allied war effort. As far as they were concerned, ours was an "imperialist war" and it wasn't until they themselves were invaded by the Nazis that they finally changed their tune.

After the Communist coup in February 1948, we adopted a policy of complete isolation from Czechoslovakia and, indeed, any country east of the Iron Curtain. For one thing we had no wish to trade with a government that had used devious means to usurp power in Prague, a government that had murdered my old friend Jan Masaryk, cruelly persecuted our employees in Zlin and expropriated, without a cent of compensation, the enterprise created by my father. Furthermore, I was determined to dispel any lingering doubts as to the identity of the Bata Shoe Organization. At a time when most of our senior executives were still people of Czechoslovakian origin, I wanted to make it absolutely clear that we were a Western enterprise with no ideological, emotional or financial strings to the regime that was in power in our native country.

Throughout the most frigid period of the Cold War, an additional concern was the danger that the Bata organization might be infiltrated by Communist agents, or that those of our people who had relatives behind the Iron Curtain might be subjected to blackmail. Indeed, in those days of constant tension and covert activities, we couldn't discount the possibility that I might be abducted during my frequent travels around the world. I therefore gave specific instructions that, should this happen, no ransom was to be paid. There was no way that I was going to be instrumental in adding to the Communists' illegal loot.

For close to twenty years our policy of total separation was in keeping with the East-West tensions generated by the Cold War. But with the advent of detente Western democracies became suddenly enthusiastic about trading with the Soviets. The theory promulgated by leaders such as General de Gaulle was that mutual trade would lead to greater understanding, which in turn would reduce the danger of war. The Soviets apparently agreed, and when they began shopping for consumer merchandise in Western Europe, we were reluctant to leave all that business to our competitors. So we decided that one of our French factories could allocate up to fifteen percent of its output to the Soviet market.

Then the British expelled a group of Soviet diplomats for spying and, in response, Soviet orders for British merchandise were promptly diverted to France. Our French company was overjoyed by this unexpected turn of events, all the more so since Western Europe was in the grips of a recession and business was decidedly slow. Moreover, the sheer size and nature of the Soviet orders enabled the factory to realize considerable economies of scale. Where France's domestic market might have been able to absorb 10,000 pairs of assorted winter boots, the Russians ordered 100,000 pairs, all in one style and color. It seemed like a manufacturer's dream come true and so, contrary to our rule never to become overly dependent on exports, let alone exports to one customer, our French company set out to take full advantage of this magnificent opportunity.

Before long I was horrified to discover that production for the Soviets had grown to thirty percent of the French plant's capacity. After what had happened in Britain, where fortunately we hadn't accepted any Soviet orders, I had hoped we wouldn't fall into a similar trap in France. As it turned out, the orders did peter out after De Gaulle made some critical remarks about the USSR; and though the break was more gradual than in Britain, it dealt a serious blow to our French company. With our French competitors, most of whom were in the same boat, scrambling for business and slashing prices, it took years to rebuild the markets we had lost.

In the long term, however, we had always planned to resume trading with Eastern Europe once political conditions had changed. In the late 1970s, during one of the periods of detente in East-West relations, the Polish government approached us with a suggestion that we help them operate a number of factories in the western part of the country. According to an agreement we negotiated with Poland's minister of industry, we were to assume responsibility for product development and help organize manufacturing procedures in these plants. While it was understood that most of the footwear produced under this agreement would be offered for sale in Poland, we undertook to export enough to the West to earn the foreign exchange we would need to pay for imported materials and machinery.

We sent over a team of production, design and marketing people headed by a man of Czech origin, who, presumably, would be able to learn Polish pretty quickly and, for a while, all went well. But it wasn't long before Poland's incredibly convoluted bureaucracy began to cause problems. Take, for instance, the case of an American customer who ordered shoes with a specific kind of buckle. Because buckles could, theoretically, be made in Poland, we were told that, rather than ask for an import permit, we should have the buckles manufactured locally. The problem was that footwear production was governed by the Ministry of Light Industry, whereas metal buckles came under the aegis of the ministry concerned with metalworking. Consequently our application had to make its way all the way up the hierarchy of one ministry and down the ladder of another, after which it was referred to a metalworking enterprise that, in due course, informed us that it would consider adding our buckles to its work schedule in two years.

Another problem concerned the setting of export prices for the Polish merchandise. The government officials whose approval was required insisted on setting these prices way above what the market would bear. Whether they did it because they were so hungry for foreign currency or because they were hoping to prove that Western capitalists didn't know how to sell shoes, I don't know. More than likely we just got caught between two rival factions, each determined to undermine the efforts of the other. To make matters worse, we discovered that the manager's secretary was a secret police agent. The final blow came when the minister of light industry, a progressive individual who seemed genuinely keen on establishing ties with the West, was killed in an automobile accident. His successor was far less interested in cooperating with Western capitalists and, given all the delays and bureaucratic bickering, we were rather relieved to shake hands and call it quits.

Around the same time the Canadian government was encouraging industry to make its technology available to the Soviets and help them modernize their economy. Accordingly we sent a team to the Soviet Union to tell the Russians about our technology for making slush-molded winter boots. When they indicated that they were interested in striking some sort of deal, negotiations got under way. Their idea was that we would provide them with machinery and know-how to run a factory capable of producing annually 600,000 pairs of boots. Since 600,000 pairs seemed like a drop in the huge Soviet bucket, we assumed they intended to use our plant as a prototype and reproduce it several times over. We therefore insisted that they also pay us for the reproduction rights.

Our Canadian officials had warned us, at the time of our first contact, that doing business with the Soviets was like making love to an elephant: all the activity was at a high level, much got trampled underfoot and it took two years for anything to emerge. Sure enough, two years later the elephant gave birth and a Soviet delegation arrived at our headquarters in Toronto to sign an agreement. After the ceremony, I invited the Russians back to our house, where we toasted one another with Canadian champagne. In this atmosphere of goodwill, I asked our visitors if there was anything we could do for them. To my surprise, they asked for an opportunity to see *Last Tango in Paris*. I wouldn't have thought that it was the kind of movie officials steeped in Marxist ideology would enjoy, but apparently I was wrong.

That summer a group of Soviet technicians arrived in Batawa to supervise the construction of their equipment and learn how to use it. They were a thoroughly nice, congenial bunch, and during the two months they were in Canada our employees took them fishing and boating, invited them to barbecues and generally made sure the visitors had a good time. Later that same year Canada's then minister of science and technology, Alastair Gillespie, led a group of government officials and business people on a goodwill trip to the Soviet Union. Since ours was one of the few Canadian companies that was actually building a plant for the Soviets, I was invited to come along. In Moscow we were quartered in the brand-new Intourist Hotel, where, our officials had warned us, stunningly beautiful KGB agents disguised as chambermaids were employed to pry secrets from high-ranking visitors. After one look at the chambermaids assigned to our floor, my colleagues and I concluded, sadly, that we weren't important enough to rate that kind of attention.

I asked for an opportunity to visit some shoe factories, but it took several days to make the arrangements, and when I was finally admitted to a shoe factory, I was steered straight toward a new assembly machine that had only just arrived from Leningrad. Obviously that was the reason for the delay: the Soviets were hoping we would buy their equipment. While the machine was impressive in many ways, it lacked the flexibility that would have made it suitable for our purposes. Essentially it was designed to assemble one kind of shoe, and major adjustments were required to switch to another style or even size. But as I was leaving, the manager of the plant said to me, "You see the tremendous effort the authorities are making to sell you that equipment, and yet we have been told we would have to wait four or five years to get it." There was a distinct note of bitterness in his voice.

The other plant I saw was the one where our new equipment was to be installed. It was a huge complex with some 20,000 employees, and the head of that enormous enterprise turned out to be one of the people who had helped negotiate the contract in Canada and who had been introduced to us as an engineer. While our equipment was to be housed in a new building that was still under construction, the existing plant apparently hadn't received a facelift since it was built around the turn of the century. Wet paint that had been hurriedly slapped on the walls in anticipation of our visit was already peeling and revealing generations of dirt. Furthermore, the lighting was terrible and the toilets indescribable. No one in Africa would have worked under such conditions.

From the plant we were taken to a beautiful dacha in a romantic, snow-covered forest outside Moscow. It looked like a scene out of

Doctor Zhivago. Our host was the deputy minister of light industry and the hospitality was sumptuous, with lots of caviar and vodka. In keeping with Russian custom a long string of toasts had to be drunk bottoms-up, and my neighbor, the head of the large enterprise we had visited, was supposed to make sure my glass was constantly refilled. Fortunately he was considerate enough to pour no more than a few drops each time, thereby enabling me to hang on to my wits and my sense of balance. At one point I asked the deputy minister how our slush-molded boots were going to be marketed. "Our job is to produce merchandise, not to sell it," he replied. "We're not responsible for what happens to the stuff once it leaves the plant."

In due course our plant was installed, and once our technicians made sure it was working properly, they returned home. We heard via the grapevine that the plant's output increased only marginally from year to year, presumably so that the people in charge could claim an annual improvement in productivity. Indeed, the managers and supervisors received some fancy decoration from the Soviet government for having done such a great job. But for ten years we never did hear whether or not they had taken advantage of their right to reproduce the plant. Then in 1987, while touring the Soviet Union with a group of North American executives, my son Tom visited the plant and saw our equipment in operation. "It is so successful," said the same manager whom I had met ten years before, "that we're thinking of replicating the machines and building several additional units." Tom pointed out that the technology was ten years old at the time they bought it and had been running for another ten years since then. "Would it not be better," he asked, "if we were to help you update your plant?" We have never heard from them again. For all I know they may be busy replicating that twenty-year-old technology.

What about Czechoslovakia, my native country and the original epicenter of the Bata Shoe Organization? Over the years Canada's Department of External Affairs made repeated attempts to remind the Communist government that it owed me both a moral and a material debt and to discuss with the authorities the question of compensation. But while all the other "socialist" governments had paid at least token amounts for the Bata enterprises they expropriated, Czechoslovakia refused to discuss the issue.

It wasn't until the mid-1980s that the Czechoslovakian government began to hint that some form of economic cooperation with the Bata Shoe Organization might be desirable. The virulent anti-Bata propaganda, which had been part of the party line during the postwar decades, gave way to favorable comments and even an almost friendly television documentary. The Canadian government interpreted these moves as a signal that an agreement might be possible, as long as the Communists could save face by calling it something other than compensation. Partly to show appreciation for the efforts of Canadian diplomats, we agreed to lift our ban on trade with Zlin — rechristened Gottwaldov in honor of Czechoslovakia's first Communist president and the man who, in 1948, spearheaded the putsch against the country's democratic government.

In the summer of 1986 I got a message from the Czechoslovakian embassy in Ottawa to the effect that a delegation led by Prime Minister Strougal and Foreign Trade Minister Urban was going to be in Ottawa following a visit to the Vancouver World's Fair. Would I be interested in meeting these gentlemen? I wasn't at all keen on being seen in the company of hard-line Communist leaders, so I replied that, unfortunately, I wouldn't be able to travel to Ottawa. They, in turn, suggested that Urban's deputy, Mr. Padevet, would be willing to come to see me in Toronto. So, along with a number of our executives, I met with him and with the newly appointed commercial counselor, Mr. Horak.

Padevet made it clear that the Czechs were looking for some sort of arrangement whereby we would provide them with our technology and know-how in product development so that their customers and, specifically, the Soviets would stop complaining about the quality of their footwear. They were also hoping we would help them purchase materials in the West and sell their products in óur stores. I, in turn, made it equally clear that any such arrangement was out of the question until such time as we had been compensated for the loss and the injustice we had suffered.

The next major event in this lengthy saga occurred in 1987 when I was invited to attend a meeting in Vienna with Svatopluk Potac, a man who had started his working life in 1940 as an apprentice in our factory in Zlin. He rose to become a foreman before transferring, after World War II, to the National Bank. By this time the Communist regime was in power in Czechoslovakia, and since anyone associated with Bata was considered politically suspect, most or our former employees had a hard time getting decent jobs. But, as a loyal party man, Mr. Potac apparently had no such problems. Indeed, he climbed the ladder to become governor of the bank and, at the time of our meeting, minister of planning.

We met in a private dining room at the Imperial Hotel. Potac had indicated that he would be accompanied by two other officials and, accordingly, I had invited my cousin Fred Mencik and Jerry Sedlacek, a senior executive in our organization, to join me. As it turned out, the only person who came with Potac was Padevet, who proceeded to place a big black box, presumably a recording device, on the sideboard. We kidded him that the box was the third man. The evening was pleasant enough, though the food was abominable. Potac started out by presenting me with two albums beautifully bound in hand-tooled leather and full of old photographs, including some pictures of the damage inflicted by American bombers during a raid in 1944. Apparently the people of Zlin had been warned about the forthcoming raid and had had time to take shelter so that there were hardly any casualties. The damage, however, was severe and concentrated almost entirely on the factories that produced footwear. This led the Communists to claim that the raid had been initiated by American shoe manufacturers eager to eliminate a competitor. That was ridiculous nonsense, and I told Potac as much. My own guess is that the navigators mistook the factory complex for a nearby power plant, presumably their real target.

Potac spoke about the tremendous advantages he foresaw from our cooperation in such areas as technology transfer, product development and marketing. Having asked me before dinner how many pairs of shoes we produced and how many people we employed, he had figured out that our productivity was approximately double theirs. But when I pointed out to him that our discussions were supposed to include the "old matters," namely compensation, he said that wasn't his understanding and that, in any case, the subject could only be dealt with within the framework of Czechoslovakian law. In the end, we simply agreed that there would be further discussions, and that he would mention my concern with regard to the compensation issue in his report on our meeting. He ended up by assuring me that I would be a welcome visitor in Prague, since my record was "spotless." Coming from a Communist, I wasn't sure if this was much of a compliment.

In March 1988 a team of our senior executives headed by Jerry Sedlacek visited Czechoslovakia, toured a number of shoe factories and was wined and dined by Potac. They had barely returned to Canada when Mr. Hegenbart, the deputy premier of the Czech lands (the western part of the federal republic of Czechoslovakia),

arrived with an invitation from Milos Jakes, the head of
Czechoslovakia's Communist Party, for me to come to Prague and
discuss the terms of an agreement. I accepted on the understanding that the compensation issue would be resolved. During a frank
and friendly meeting, which was also attended by Padevet and by
the Czechoslovakian ambassador to Canada as well as a number
of our executives, I made it clear that, if it weren't for our historical
ties to Czechoslovakia, we wouldn't even consider going into a
country where the market was small and the political situation, to
put it politely, uncertain. But given the emotional factor, we were
prepared to explore possibilities of cooperation.

The next thing I knew the date for my visit had been set for
June 15, 1988, and Bohumil Urban, formerly the minister of
foreign trade but currently yet another deputy premier, turned up
in Canada. A smartly dressed, obviously intelligent man, Urban
was a chemical engineer who had managed a government-owned
pulp and paper operation before being appointed cabinet minister.
While the official purpose of his visit was to meet the leaders of
Canada's Communist party, the truth was that he had come to see
me. When we met at our house, he explained that he was carrying
three messages. The first consisted of greetings "from your old
Bata friends in Czechoslovakia who are now the three most
important people in the government." This was a reminder that
Milos Jakes, like Potac and Lenart (a prominent Slovak party
member), had all at one time been employed by Bata. Jakes had
been a draftsman in our engineering department.

The second message was that I was to review and approve the
program they had drawn up for my visit to Prague. After my arrival
on Tuesday afternoon, I was to have dinner with Mr. Potac who,
since our meeting in Vienna, had been appointed deputy prime
minister. When I objected that the Canadian ambassador was
expecting me for dinner that evening, Urban assured me that the

ambassador, Barry Mawhinney, would be included among Mr. Potac's guests. The following day I was to meet the general secretary of the Communist party and "then we'll fly you to — " He hesitated for a moment between Zlin and Gottwaldov, then found a way out of the dilemma. "We'll fly you to see your old factory and, of course, to visit your father's grave." I told him that, under the circumstances, I would prefer to defer my visit to the factory until an agreement had been reached.

"Finally," he said, "I have come to tell you that we have concluded that we owe you not only a moral but also an economic debt. The leadership agrees with this principle." That, of course, was the crux of his mission; all the rest was window dressing.

Then he asked me what kind of amount I had in mind and I said, "You know very well what the enterprise was worth when you expropriated it in 1945. Index that for inflation, add forty-five years of interest, and you'll have the answer to your question."

He suggested that we agree on a reasonable figure and settle the issue then and there so that we could get on with the job of making decent shoes for the people of Czechoslovakia. I told him that was a bit too quick for my liking. However, I knew that he was flying home from Washington on Friday, while I was planning to spend the balance of the week in Zurich attending board meetings. "Why don't you stop off in Zurich on Saturday morning," I suggested, "so we can have another talk?" He said he'd think about it and, to my surprise, I got a message a couple of days later that he was coming. His plane landed in Zurich early on Saturday morning, he was met by the Czechoslovakian ambassador to Switzerland and the commercial counselor and after breakfast we sat down for a two-hour meeting. We parted on the understanding that we would see each other in two weeks in Prague.

Ten days later I was at home in Toronto when I got a long-distance call from Prague. At the other end of the line was Horak, the commercial counselor stationed at the consulate general in Montreal, whom I had met a couple of times during our discussions with the Czechoslovakian authorities. His voice sounded strange, almost as though he were reading a prepared text. The gist of his message was that the Czechoslovakian ambassador to Canada had been instructed to answer the questions I had put to Mr. Urban and, since the ambassador was currently traveling in the United States, Horak was calling to ask if he and the ambassador could come to see me on Saturday. I replied that, although I was leaving for Europe on Saturday night, I would be pleased to meet with the ambassador earlier in the day. We agreed that they would come for lunch on June 11, four days before my scheduled arrival in Prague.

Frankly I was puzzled. I couldn't recall having asked Urban any questions, and virtually all the details concerning my forthcoming trip had been settled, so there had to be some other reason for the ambassador's wish to see me. Then on Friday I got another call from Prague, this time from Urban's assistant, Padevet, to say that Mr. Zdenek Kovar was arriving in Toronto that afternoon. Apparently Kovar, who is a distinguished industrial designer, had been a classmate of mine during my childhood in Czechoslovakia and hoped I would find time to see him.

In my office the following morning, Kovar made an impassioned plea for me to abandon my claim for compensation and to help Czechoslovakia's government revive its shoe manufacturing industry. The nation, he assured me, would be forever grateful. "In fact," he added, "your gesture of goodwill would be published in the newspapers." I tried to acquaint him with some facts of life, but he had obviously been programmed to spout the sentimental line and refused to deviate from it.

By the time he had repeated his plea three or four times, and I had reminded him of Urban's admission that the government owed me a moral as well as a material debt, it was time for me to go home and meet Ambassador Janovic and Commercial Counselor Horak. They wasted no time informing me that the Communist party had decided that any payment of compensation was out of the question. They hoped, however, that this news wouldn't stop me from coming to Prague and discussing "things" at the highest governmental level. I, in turn, informed them that I had accepted Mr. Jakes's invitation on the understanding that compensation would be discussed. Under the circumstances I could see no point in going. I also made it clear that they were the ones who had slammed the door shut, not me. If at some future date they wanted to reopen it, I would give the matter some thought; but not by backing down on a matter of principle.

I was amazed. In anticipation of my meeting with the ambassador I had envisaged various reasons why he wanted to see me. I thought he might want to haggle about the size of our claim, possibly come up with a counteroffer or suggest that compensation should be paid in installments over several years. But though my opinion of Communist governments was never exactly flattering, I hadn't expected they would be so unprofessional as to renege, two and a half hours before my scheduled departure, on their own undertakings.

Was I disappointed? All along my attitude toward cooperation with Czechoslovakia had been somewhat ambivalent. On the one hand, I was far from enthusiastic about dealing with a Communist regime and being seen as helping it hang on to power. On the other hand, people kept assuring me that change was around the corner and that, by helping Czechoslovakia's economy emerge from the doldrums, I would be lending support to the advocates of change. That was certainly the attitude of the Canadian government and of Ambassador Barry Mawhinney, who worked hard to bring about an agreement. But after our painful experience in Poland, I was determined to be careful. Quite apart from the bureaucratic roadblocks that are endemic to all Communist countries, there is typically within these regimes a struggle between progressive factions that recognize the need for greater freedom and the hard-liners who are determined to discredit them. Had Bata come to an agreement in 1988, I have no doubt the orthodox faction would have done its utmost to sabotage our efforts and make us fall flat on our face.

A year after the aborted trip to Prague, a Czechoslovakian delegation was to come to Canada and present me with a face-saving maneuver. But once again the Communists changed their minds at the last moment, and after three years of on-again, off-again negotiations, not to mention a major investment of time and effort, my enthusiasm for any kind of deal was muted. Everything seemed in limbo — until the events of November and December 1989.

Now, as the saying goes, it's a new ball game.

RETURN OF THE
NATIVE

IN CZECHOSLOVAKIA THE STRAW that broke the Communist camel's back was the savage beating the police inflicted on unarmed student demonstrators on November 17, 1989. Appalled by the brutality of the attack, actors and musicians canceled all performances and proclaimed common cause with the students. Within days hundreds of thousands of rank-and-file citizens, previously cowed by fear of retribution, began staging massive antigovernment demonstrations in major cities throughout the country. Under the leadership of distinguished dissidents coalesced into a group called Civic Forum, the uprising quickly gathered momentum and forced the government to fall back from one rearguard position to another. For a while the Communists tried to prevent the inevitable by reshuffling the deck of party hacks within the cabinet and leavening the mix with a few new faces. But neither the people nor their newfound leaders were willing to settle for window dressing.

By the first week in December all Canadians with Czechoslovakian roots were throbbing with excitement at the turn of events in our native land. Over the years many of us had tried to distance ourselves, psychologically as well as physically, from a country whose rulers had transformed it from a model pre-World War II democracy into a hotbed of corruption, mismanagement and appalling disregard for the fundamentals of justice. For twenty, thirty or even forty years many of these expatriates had tried to forget the past — the false allegations, the ostracism inflicted on their children, the years served in jail for fictitious crimes, the dangerous escapes across closely guarded borders. Now all of a sudden these bitter memories gave way to euphoria and pride — pride in the integrity and intellectual honesty of the Civic Forum, pride above all in a generation of young people whom decades of indoctrination had failed to corrupt.

I was no exception. Having refused throughout my life to become involved in politics and having identified myself whole-heartedly with my adoptive Canada, I accepted within ten days two invitations to speak at rallies organized by Toronto's Czecho-slovakian community in support of the Civic Forum. On both occasions I sensed the electric mood of the audience and felt exhilarated by it. Somehow I hoped that my words would find their way to the airwaves of Czechoslovakia, and that they would provide encouragement to the country's champions of freedom.

But words weren't enough. In order to find out what I could actually do to help, I asked two of my most trusted and highly qualified associates, Jerry Sedlacek and Oto Daicar, to go to Prague on my behalf, speak to the leaders of the Civic Forum and ask them whether and when they would like me to visit Czecho-slovakia. Both these men speak Czech, both have spent most of their adult lives with the Bata organization and both have broad managerial experience in various parts of the world. Sedlacek, a youthful sexagenarian, was director of corporate planning at the time of his retirement; having accompanied me to Vienna for my meeting with representatives of the previous regime, he was thoroughly familiar with the history of those earlier negotiations.

Daicar, one of the pioneers who joined me in Canada in 1939, ended his official career as our regional coordinator for Latin America. Both men have remained active in their retirement and eager to volunteer for any special projects that happen to come along.

On December 9, the night my emissaries left for Prague, they carried with them a letter from me to Vaclav Havel, the brilliant playwright and courageous defender of human rights who had emerged as the dominant member of the Civic Forum. My message to him was brief and to the point: it congratulated Havel on his achievements to date and assured him of my support in his future endeavors. Just what form that support might take, and under what circumstances, were questions I hoped to discuss with him and his associates if and when I paid a visit to Czechoslovakia.

At the airport in Prague, Sedlacek and Daicar were met by Canadian Ambassador Barry Mawhinney, a fine diplomat who, over the years, had been repeatedly frustrated in his efforts to bring about a reconciliation between the Bata organization and the Communist government of Czechoslovakia. He explained that he was about to leave for Brussels, where Canadian diplomats were to be briefed about the Malta summit meeting between presidents Bush and Gorbachev. But while he wasn't going to be around to assist my emissaries in person, he assured them that members of the embassy staff would do whatever they could to be helpful. Meanwhile he set the wheels in motion to obtain for them an appointment with Vaclav Havel.

As it turned out, Sedlacek and Daicar had landed in Prague on a historic day. That very afternoon, in Wenceslas Square, Havel announced the appointment of a new government, which for the first time in almost forty-two years, wasn't dominated by Communists. To top off the good news, Gustav Husak capitulated to public demand and resigned from the presidency. Within hours signs reading Havel for President sprouted all over Prague.

That same Sunday evening I flew to Ottawa to attend a Monday meeting of the International Trade Advisory Committee under the chairmanship of John Crosbie, Canada's minister of international trade. That was a session during which the Pacific task force, of which I am the chairman, was scheduled to report on its findings, so I had to concentrate on our presentation and the discussion that followed. But in the back of my mind I couldn't help wondering why I hadn't heard from Sedlacek. We had agreed that he would call me at my hotel between seven and eight in the morning Ottawa time (1:00-2:00 p.m. Central European Time), unless there was an important reason to defer the call. Presumably something important had, in fact, caused a postponement.

Just before lunchtime my wife called to say that, since Sedlacek hadn't been able to reach me during the past few hours, he had called her in Toronto. He told her that he and Daicar had met with Havel earlier in the afternoon and that Havel had read my letter with obvious pleasure. When they asked him what would be a convenient time for my visit, he had replied, "The sooner the better." Sonja needed no prompting to know how I would react to this news. By the time she called me she had already telephoned our office in Zurich and asked the manager to charter an executive jet for our flight to Prague. Also, in response to a report that the Civic Forum was desperately short of all kinds of equipment and, specifically, fax machines, she had arranged for at least twenty machines to be purchased in Switzerland as quickly as possible so that we could take them along with us in the aircraft.

After further discussions and consultations, we decided to leave Toronto on Tuesday evening, get a good night's sleep in Zurich and take off on Thursday morning in time to arrive in Prague shortly before noon. Meanwhile, I invited two other individuals to join our party. One of them was Ernst Keller, a Swiss director of our organization whose extensive background in corporate restructuring, in Europe as well as Latin America, would be a valuable asset in our talks with Czechoslovakia's authorities. The other was Guido Zehnder, head of our Zurich office, who agreed to assume responsibility for logistics during our trip.

With four of us on board the Lear jet, along with our luggage, there was barely enough room for ten fax machines to be packed all around us. The rest would have to follow later. It wasn't a long flight. North Americans who lump Czechoslovakia in with Eastern Europe tend to forget that Prague is situated in the very heart of Europe, some 150 kilometers farther west than Vienna. Heading from Zurich across Bavaria, we had been airborne for less than an hour when the captain turned to face me and said, "Mr. Bata, I have a message for you from Czechoslovakian air traffic control. The message reads, 'Welcome back.'" That was when we knew we had crossed into a new, user-friendly Czechoslovakian airspace.

Though Sedlacek and Daicar had deliberately refrained from publicizing our forthcoming visit, the airport was teeming with thousands of people brandishing flags and homemade signs with all kinds of greetings and good wishes. As Sonja and I emerged from the aircraft, a youngish-looking man stepped forward to greet us. "I am Vladimir Dlouhy, the deputy prime minister," he said. "Welcome to Czechoslovakia." Making our way through the crowd was quite a challenge. It seemed as if everybody wanted to shake hands or add their own few words of welcome. Someone pushed a bunch of telegrams in my hand, while Sonja clutched several bouquets of flowers, using them almost as a shield against the surging multitude. Eventually we reached the VIP lounge where we were greeted by a veritable forest of microphones and video cameras. For close to half an hour we were bombarded with reporters' questions: "How does it feel to be home?" "How long will you be staying?" "Will you visit Zlin?" And, from the American press, "How much are you going to invest?"

A government car was waiting to drive us to the Canadian ambassador's beautiful, historic residence where Sonja and I had been invited to stay. Dlouhy sat in front beside the driver, Sonja and I in the back so that we could shake hands through the car's open windows with the thousands of well-wishers who lined the road for at least two kilometers from the airport. I was both thrilled and bewildered by the emotional outpouring we experienced from the moment we set foot on Czechoslovakian soil. It had never occurred to me that, after forty-two years of Communist rule, people would accord what amounted to a hero's welcome to a dyed-in-the-wool capitalist, even if he happened to be a native son. It was the sort of experience for which one gives thanks to the Almighty, without questioning the whys or wherefores.

After lunch and a briefing by the Canadian embassy staff, we were delighted to be joined by Ambassador Mawhinney, who, bless his heart, had left Brussels at four o'clock in the morning and driven some 600 kilometers back to Prague so that he could be on hand during our visit. By then we had been told that Havel was expecting us later in the afternoon, so Sonja and I joined the ambassador in his car and together we drove downtown, along the streets and across one of the bridges that I hadn't seen for more than forty years.

The Civic Forum had only just moved from the Magic Lantern Theater, where it had functioned during the initial stages of the popular uprising, into a big gray building near the foot of Wenceslas Square that had been hurriedly vacated by its previous tenants, the Czechoslovakian/Soviet Friendship Association. The ground floor was a beehive of activity: young people rushed in and out, painting or printing posters, producing Havel for President badges, operating copying machines for which they kept running out of paper. Their communications equipment was primitive, to say the least; there was only one telephone, which, the students said, was frequently interrupted, presumably by hard-line Communists who remained in some positions of authority. Yet among all this confusion the juices of creativity were flowing, new slogans were being coined, graphic artists were producing posters of excellent quality and eager teenagers were fanning out across the city, hand-delivering flyers with information about the latest developments or future demonstrations.

We were ushered upstairs to a room where Havel was officiating among bits and pieces of furniture, half-empty pop bottles and unfinished sandwiches, surrounded by some of those wonderful posters on the walls. He was shorter than I had imagined, a stocky figure with reddish, wavy hair, a small matching mustache and eyes that lit up whenever he smiled, which was often. Dressed in corduroy slacks, an open-necked shirt and a loose-fitting pullover, he somehow managed to radiate both warmth and authority. Knowing what I did about his courageous fight on behalf of human rights, his unconditional integrity and his brilliant intellect, I felt that I was in the presence of a great man.

Unfortunately the room was once again packed with cameramen and other representatives of the news media. I assumed they would take their pictures, record their thirty-second clips for the evening news and then leave us alone. Instead, they kept us under scrutiny throughout our meeting; it was like having one's in-laws as observers in the marital chamber. As a result we ended up mouthing generalities for public consumption, and the intimate talk I had hoped for never materialized. I asked Havel what we could do to help, and he replied that he would appreciate any advice or initiative that would make the country's economy and, specifically, the shoe industry more competitive in world markets.

"The quality is terrible," he said, pointing to his own shoes. "I am sure you could do a whole lot better than that."

But we didn't go into any details, nor did we touch on the future of Bata enterprises in Czechoslovakia. The only personal note was struck when Havel reached into his pocket for yet another of the cigarettes that he chain-smoked throughout our conversation. "I suppose your father would have fired me," he said with a smile. This reference to my father's ban on smoking in the workplace was the only indication of any past association between our two families. By tacit agreement, neither of us mentioned the fact that his maternal grandfather, Hugo Vavrecka, had been one of my father's closest associates and, for many years, the number one director of the Bata organization. Nor did I allude to the fact that, as a young bachelor, I had occasionally dated Havel's mother.

After the meeting the three of us — Barry Mawhinney, Sonja and I — decided to drive the short distance to Wenceslas Square, which isn't really a square at all, but rather a wide, tree-lined avenue dominated at its top by the national museum and, in front of it, the mounted statue of St. Wenceslas, the patron saint of Bohemia. When we emerged from the ambassador's car, we found a huge crowd listening to a speaker who was standing on the pedestal under the statue. He was discussing the forthcoming presidential election, which was a hot topic at the time and so, in an effort to hear what he was saying and to observe the reactions of the audience, we walked to the edge of the crowd, which filled the upper two-thirds of the square. Suddenly someone said, "There's Bata!" People began turning their heads our way, there were shouts of "Long live Bata," and before I knew what was happening, a group that had materialized out of nowhere took me by the arm and began shepherding me through the crowd. "Please make way for Mr. Bata," my escorts kept saying to the people

around us and, without any pushing or shoving, a corridor opened up all the way to the statue of St. Wenceslas. With Sonja and the ambassador in tow, we made our way to the foot of the statue, stopping every few seconds to shake hands with the friendly crowd. Once we got there we waited for a while until the speaker had finished explaining why the Communists' proposal to have the president elected by popular vote rather than by parliament was nothing but a delaying maneuver. The moment he finished the crowd shouted, "Now let's hear from Bata." Someone helped me climb across the chain that surrounds the statue and up the marble pedestal, and someone else thrust a bunch of microphones in front of me.

Never in my wildest dreams had I imagined myself standing between the hooves of St. Wenceslas's granite steed, addressing some 100,000 cheering people. To the best of my recollection, my speech consisted of variations on a single theme, namely that the world was watching with admiration the Czechoslovakian people's heroic march toward democracy. All I know for sure is that the words came naturally, and that people obviously liked what I was saying. I could barely utter a sentence without the crowd responding with "Right on," "Long live Bata," "Long live democracy." My guess is that I spoke no more than one-third of the time; the other two-thirds were taken up by cheers, hurrahs and rhythmic chants. I know now what people mean when they talk about being on cloud nine; that is exactly how I felt, and I loved every minute of it.

In the evening there was a concert in honor of the Civic Forum at Prague's historic Smetana Hall. I understand the auditorium holds about 1,200 people, and there wasn't an empty seat to be seen. Sonja and I were taken to the loges, where we joined Vaclav Havel, his wife, Olga, and most of those members of the new cabinet who were Civic Forum supporters. This was the first

performance by the Czech Philharmonic Orchestra since it withdrew its services in support of the "velvet revolution," as Czechoslovakia's bloodless, good-humored uprising has come to be called, and its rendition of Beethoven's Ninth Symphony, with its wonderful "Ode to Joy," expressed better than words the feelings of the newly liberated nation. At the end Havel went to the conductor's podium and thanked the audience and the musicians for their support. Then he introduced the new members of the cabinet and added, "We are also happy to have with us Mr. and Mrs. Bata." Everybody applauded. It was a truly joyous occasion.

After the concert we adjourned to a reception room, where we sipped local champagne and chatted with the invited guests. We met Dr. Valtr Komarek, the bearded first deputy prime minister and former head of the Prognostic Institute of the Czechoslovak Academy of Sciences, and Dr. Vaclav Klaus, the minister of finance, who studied economics in the United States and became an intellectual disciple of Milton Friedman. Also present was First Deputy Prime Minister Jan Carnogorsky, a brilliant Slovak lawyer who had been jailed by the Communists and released only a couple of weeks earlier. It was getting late and, under normal circumstances, we should have been exhausted at the end of such an eventful day. But the way the adrenaline was flowing, I, for one, didn't realize how tired I was until we got back to the ambassador's residence and fell into bed.

The following morning was devoted almost entirely to a three-hour meeting with the three cabinet ministers who were primarily responsible for the economy: Komarek, Dlouhy and Klaus. By then we had met all three of them — Dlouhy on our arrival at the airport, Komarek and Klaus at the reception following the concert at Smetana Hall. They struck me as impressive individuals whose grasp of the country's situation was all the more remarkable

considering that they had been catapulted into their cabinet jobs less than a week earlier. Dealing with them, one tended to forget that, theoretically at least, Komarek and Dlouhy were members of the Communist party. Even so, I was relieved to hear, a week or so later, that both of them had resigned from the party.

On our side of the table was the entire Bata contingent, plus Barry Mawhinney, Canada's ambassador, and two members of his diplomatic staff. The bulk of the meeting was devoted to a discussion of Czechoslovakia's economic problems. While the country's external debt (about seven billion dollars U.S.) is small compared to that of its neighbors, it is owed billions by Communist countries that are in no hurry to pay their debts. As the ministers pointed out, these "accounts receivable" were incurred because, for decades, Soviet governments had forced their satellites to subsidize politically compatible regimes around the world. Similarly the terrible pollution in parts of Bohemia is due to the Soviets' insistence that Czechoslovakia become, in effect, the forge for the whole of Eastern Europe.

We talked about the need for business education and for the creation of a climate conducive to entrepreneurship. The Czechoslovakian ministers made it clear that, though their objective was a market economy, they favored a gradual approach rather than shock tactics that might produce massive unemployment, or inflation, or both. As Klaus said, "We don't have the invisible hand of Adam Smith yet." Nevertheless they believed they could accomplish a turnaround in two to three years — a goal that seemed overly optimistic to me.

As for the Bata organization, Komarek emphasized that he and his colleagues were determined to remedy the grave injustice that had been done to my family's reputation by the previous regime, and he started dictating then and there an apology that, he said,

would be made public in January. I replied that, while I appreciated his intentions with regard to my family, I was more concerned with the persecutions that had been inflicted on many of our employees. Nothing could ever make up for the way these wonderful people had been hounded out of their jobs, humiliated, jailed and denied the right to have their children educated at institutions of higher learning, for no reason other than their loyalty to the Bata family. But, I said, "to the extent they or their children are alive, the government ought to make some sort of amends." Everybody agreed that this should and would be done.

As far as our enterprise was concerned, I made it clear that I was no longer interested in compensation. Now that Czechoslovakia was to become once again a democratic country, I assumed that our property would be restored to us so that we could do something constructive with it. As two initial steps in our forthcoming cooperation, our team proposed (a) that we would undertake an in-depth study of Czechoslovakia's footwear industry and of measures required to make it competitive in world markets and (b) that we would establish in the center of Prague a first-class retail store, a showplace for service and quality merchandise and a visible expression of the new economic climate. Both proposals met with enthusiastic acceptance by the three cabinet ministers.

After the meeting, Sonja and I drove with Komarek to the ten-story building at the foot of Wenceslas Square that housed the successor of our flagship store, formerly known as "House of Service." Though I had been warned about its condition, seeing it with my own eyes was a shock. Two out of three elevators were out of commission, the fixtures were hopelessly old-fashioned, the merchandise was shoddy, service virtually nonexistent. The manager told me that a firm that had been engaged to modernize the store had estimated the cost at the equivalent of five million

Canadian dollars. Considering that almost everything in the building — the plumbing, wiring, heating plant, elevators — needed replacing, the estimate seemed to me realistic.

After a sumptuous lunch for which Komarek had ordered every conceivable Czech delicacy, we were joined by the rest of the Bata team for a visit with Frantisek Cardinal Tomasek. He had been invited to a reception at the Canadian embassy later that day but had indicated that, at age ninety, he would prefer to have us call on him in his palace beside the presidential castle. We found the old gentleman remarkably chipper, and when he grasped my hand, he held it so firmly that there was no way I could have kissed the papal ring. We didn't discuss politics, though his courageous stand against the Communist regime was well-known. Instead he reminded me that he had known my parents and that, as a young priest attached to the church in Loucka, the site of our country home, he had provided me with some religious instruction. In parting he presented Sonja and me with ballpoint pens adorned with his portrait.

We went on to visit Foreign Minister Jiri Dienstbier, formerly a brilliant journalist who had been compelled, after the suppression of the "Prague Spring" of 1968, to earn his living as a stoker. In that capacity he had no need for a suit, and during the five days since his appointment to the cabinet, he had been too busy to shop for one. Fortunately Mrs. Mladkova, the widow of a Czech expatriate World Bank official in Washington, had arrived in Prague with some of her late husband's suits. She had given one of them to Dienstbier, and though it was a couple of sizes too large for him, it served the purpose for the time being.

The minister told us that he intended to undertake a complete overhaul of Czechoslovakia's foreign policy and that most of the ambassadors appointed by the previous regime would be replaced. Among the early moves on his agenda, he said, was the reestablishment of diplomatic relations with Israel, severed thirty-four years ago in the wake of the Suez War. What about economic problems? One of them, Dienstbier said, smiling, was the difficulty of filling the stoker's job he had vacated the previous Sunday.

I asked if he would take us on a tour of the Czernin Palace, which, throughout Czechoslovakia's brief existence, had housed both the offices and the home of the country's foreign ministers. We were amazed at the splendor of the building's interior — room after room of gorgeous tapestries, antique furniture, beautiful paintings: it was like Versailles, a world totally divorced from the drabness of most Czechoslovaks' everyday life. For me, the most moving sight was the apartment on the top floor of the palace where my old friend Jan Masaryk had lived, and the bathroom window through which he supposedly committed suicide. It was larger than I had imagined so that his murderers must have found it relatively easy to push him to his death.

Next on the agenda was a visit with the prime minister, Marian Calfa. A constitutional lawyer whose name was virtually unknown until his recent appointment, a Slovak who speaks flawless Czech, Calfa turned out to be a thoroughly charming man in his early forties. To me he neither looked nor sounded like a Communist and I was not surprised when, like Komarek and Dlouhy, he too resigned from the party.

By then it was time to go to the reception that was being given in our honor by Ambassador and Mrs. Mawhinney. The residence was packed with some 100 guests, although I understand only seventy had been invited: it was clearly the place to be. Among the guests I noticed a young man with sparkling eyes, dressed in dark pants and a blue sweater. To me he looked like a pleasant schoolteacher until Sedlacek introduced him as Father Vaclav Maly, the courageous dissident priest whose name had come to symbolize the Catholic Church's struggle against communism.

The following day, Saturday, had been set aside for a visit to Zlin, the hometown I had left almost exactly fifty years ago. Six of us — Ambassador and Mrs. Mawhinney, Deputy Prime Minister Valtr Komarek, Ernst Keller, Sonja and I — flew in our Lear jet to the Moravian capital of Brno. There we were met by the rest of the Bata team as well as Canadian Consul Bob McRae and Vice-Consul Pierre Dumont, and after a brief airport reception, we started driving toward Zlin. For me it was a sentimental journey, through villages and towns I had known so well as a boy and a young man. Some of them have been transformed almost beyond recognition. Uherske Hradiste, where my grandfather had boasted that his sons would someday own a factory with a chimney as high as those of the sugar refinery, now bristles with industrial chimneys that, presumably, spew noxious fumes into the atmosphere Monday to Friday. Even worse is Napajedla, a hornets' nest of hideous, huge factories that have more in common with Akron, Ohio, than with the small, charming Moravian town I remembered. On a more positive note I must admit that the highway was excellent and that the farmland we passed seemed in excellent condition.

Shortly after we turned off the highway on the road to Zlin, we encountered a cavalcade of cars that had come to meet us. We shook hands with the occupants, all of them members of the local branch of Civic Forum, who escorted us the rest of the way to Zlin. At the outskirts of town I was happy to see that the signpost with the name Gottwaldov had been pasted over with a streamer that said Zlin. The Civic Forum people had clearly decided to jump the gun on officialdom, which had decreed that the city would revert to its former name on New Year's Day.

Our first stop was at the cemetery, a beautiful piece of woodland that my father had donated to the city and where, by a strange stroke of fate, he was the first person to be buried. Standing beside his grave with a number of people around me, I found it difficult to concentrate on his memory. I would have preferred to go there alone in the evening but, given our tightly packed schedule, that simply wasn't possible.

From the cemetery we drove to the factory, where we were welcomed by members of the current management to the accompaniment of a brass band. After the obligatory introductions, we rode upstairs in the elevator Jan had furnished as an office so that he wouldn't waste any time between floors. Nowadays, I understand, it is used only as a tourist attraction. We took our places at a long table. On the far side were the managers, stiff in their business suits, all looking as though they had been cut from the same cloth; they reminded me of photographs of the Politburo taken at the Kremlin ten or fifteen years ago. On our side was our team of Bata executives and Canadian diplomats, along with the leaders of Zlin's Civic Forum. The general manager, Mr. Vodak, was so nervous that, in his opening remarks, he welcomed everybody — Sonja and me, the ambassador, our associates — but forgot to mention the Civic Forum. That may have been his undoing. A couple of weeks later I heard that he had been fired.

After more speeches, during which I was presented with a plaster bust of my father, presumably retrieved from some obscure storage room, we were given a quick tour of various parts of the factory. In the sample room we saw winter boots and industrial footwear of good quality, and while much of the machinery was old-fashioned, we were shown some brand-new German and American equipment that wouldn't have been out of place in a shoe factory anywhere in the world. My guess is that it represented an investment of at least half a million dollars.

After a light lunch at the local hotel, we attended a reception that the Civic Forum had organized for "old friends of Thomas Bata." In order to qualify guests had to prove they had either gone

318 • T H O M A S   B A T A

to school with me, or worked with me in the factory, or had been associated with me in the club of graduates of the Bata School of Young Men. Between 300 and 400 people fitted one of those descriptions, and though all of them were in their seventies or even eighties, their handshakes were firm and their memories clear. I enjoyed myself thoroughly, and so did Sonja, who was busy practicing the Czech she had been studying.

Later in the afternoon we drove to the city hall, where, I was told by the leader of the Civic Forum, I was expected to address the citizens of Zlin from the balcony overlooking the central square. Two days earlier I could have sworn that nothing could ever rival the euphoria I had felt standing on the pedestal that supports the statue of St. Wenceslas and being cheered by the crowd around me. Yet, standing on the balcony of the city hall where my father had been mayor, looking down on the square packed with thousands of people, speaking to the citizens of my hometown and hearing them respond with unrestrained enthusiasm to everything I said, all added up to an emotional experience every bit as overwhelming as the earlier one in Prague. Even though I realized that I was being cheered for what I symbolized rather than what I was, I felt overwhelmed by the emotional impact of it all. If I were to choose one highlight of my return to Czechoslovakia, one moment that overshadowed all others, I believe this would be it.

Before leaving Zlin I expressed a wish to see the house where I had grown up. It was smaller than I remembered it and its large, beautiful garden had fallen victim to road construction. Though the house had been converted into a center for "pioneers," that is to say junior Communists, the downstairs rooms were essentially unchanged, their wood paneling intact. But when I went upstairs to take a look at my former bedroom, now being used as an office, I was amused to see in a dark corner a bust of the late president

Klement Gottwald, architect of the 1948 Communist coup in Czechoslovakia. Obviously my wish to see that particular room had taken the staff by surprise and they hadn't had time to remove the bust to a suitable hiding place.

It was dark by the time we left Zlin for Bratislava, the capital of Slovakia. There we were met by Slovakia's minister of industry, who took us to meet the freshly minted Premier Milan Cic. After a discussion of Slovakia's economy, reinforced with *kolace* (pastries with jam in the center) and Slovak wine, we were treated to a delicious goose dinner in our hotel, appropriately called the Forum. Finally we retired to an oversize suite presumably built under the previous regime for the party faithful. The huge bedroom and bathroom, the private dining room with a table large enough to seat twenty guests, and the study all served as reminders of the privileges enjoyed by those Communists who had risen to the top of the power structure.

The next morning we drove two hours to what used to be one of our Slovak plants in a place called Partizanske, formerly Batovany. Though it was Sunday morning and our visit was the result of a last-minute decision, some 4,000 people turned out to welcome me. We were standing on a railway siding with cartons all around us when people started shouting, "Speech, speech!" So I climbed up on the cartons and gave my standard speech, which evoked the standard responses. One man got up and asked, "How come, every time a Communist party bigwig comes for a visit he is welcomed with banners and bands and a podium to speak from, and here Mr. Bata has to speak from the top of a carton? This is disgraceful." But I assured the audience that there was nothing I liked better than being surrounded by cartons full of shoes. What I didn't know at the time was that most of those cartons contained uppers that had been sewn in Vietnam from materials sent there from Slovakia, and then shipped back again to be converted into shoes. Apparently Slovakia suffered from such an acute labor shortage that the Partizanske factory used this circuitous route to produce four to five million pairs of canvas shoes every year.

In Partizanske, as in Zlin, it was wonderful to see a number of old-timers with whom I had grown up. One of them presented me with an original painting of my father, which he had kept all those years at considerable risk to himself and his family. Unfortunately quite a few others had been killed during an anti-German uprising in 1944, and many others were later liquidated by the Communists. It shouldn't be forgotten that, in defiance of their Nazi-subservient government, many Slovaks worked and, occasionally, died for the Allied cause.

Early in the afternoon we headed back to Bratislava, where our Lear jet was waiting to fly us to Paris. It had been a breathtaking three days and, come what may, I shall always remember them as one of the most wonderful, most heartwarming and most exhilarating experiences of my life. I have no way of knowing how long it will take for Czechoslovakia to become the model democracy it once was, for past wrongs to be righted, for the economy to recover from forty years of mismanagement and bureaucratic bungling. It won't be easy. But I came away confident that it will be done.

MY SECOND CAREER

A COUPLE OF YEARS AGO my son Tom attended a week-end seminar organized by the International Management Institute in Geneva. The topic of discussion was family businesses, and one of the areas of particular concern to the participants was the "father comes back" syndrome. In other words, the old man, having retired, can't stand having nothing to do, besides which he believes his successor is a fool. Result: he keeps turning up in the office and tries to start running the show all over again. The ideal remedy, the people at the seminar agreed, was to buy Father a small business to keep him occupied. One chap, for instance, had a father who loved horses, so the family bought him a stud farm and thereby got him off the son's back.

In my own case, I am happy to say, no such dramatic measures were required. When I decided, a few weeks before my seventieth birthday, that the time had come for me to vacate the chief executive's chair, I didn't have the slightest doubt about my son's ability to step into my shoes. Tom was by then a mature business executive with an excellent educational background and years of managerial experience, both within and outside our organization. The fact that he had recently gotten married was, in my opinion, an additional plus. While a person's ability obviously doesn't depend on his marital status, I know from personal experience, as well as from years of observation, that an understanding spouse and the stability of a family provide a chief executive with an invaluable emotional support system. I believe it is no accident that, in spite of the high U.S. divorce rate, the vast majority of *Fortune*'s 500 largest American companies are headed by men who are married to their original wives.

While I had always hoped, consciously or otherwise, that my son would someday succeed me, Sonja and I tried to make it clear to all our children that they were free to follow whatever calling they chose. Had Tom decided to be an antique dealer, that would have been fine with us as long as he worked hard to be a top-notch antique dealer. Our only stipulation was that our children use their talents to the best of their ability.

Tom graduated in science from the University of Toronto, spent two years working for one of our friendly competitors in Argentina and acquired an M.B.A. at Harvard before he decided to give the Bata organization a try. It was probably fortunate that he spent the following nine years in Switzerland and France, where he didn't feel I was looking over his shoulder to see how he was doing. When he returned to Toronto, I began delegating a number of my responsibilities to him. By then it must have been obvious that he was the heir apparent and, as far as I could tell, he was a popular choice. Had anyone else, particularly an outsider, stepped into my shoes, I have no doubt some of our senior executives would have resigned. As it was, not a single one left the organization after Tom's appointment as chief executive was announced. It was a remarkable vote of confidence.

As for my new role, I certainly didn't need a new hobby to keep myself occupied. Instead, retirement from the chief executive's job was for me a welcome opportunity to devote more time to a variety of other activities in which I had become involved over the years. One of these was the Business and Industry Advisory Committee, a body formed by the International Chamber of Commerce to advise the Organization for Economic Cooperation and Development. This committee, which was headed by the Swedish banker and industrialist Marcus Wallenberg, decided in 1962 that a group of "four wise men" should examine the potential for development in the Third World. Three of the wise men were prominent industrialists from the United States, Great Britain and West Germany. I was invited to become the fourth.

I had no sooner said yes than I was asked to go to Ottawa for discussions with Bob Bryce, Canada's deputy minister of finance, and Jake Warren, deputy minister of trade and commerce. As on a previous occasion when I put our Batawa enterprise at the disposal of Canada's war effort, I was pleasantly aware of the fact that I was talking to senior government officials not as a businessman looking for favors, but as a member of a team working toward a common objective. It took us only six months to complete our study and submit our recommendations to the OECD, but I have continued my association with the advisory committee ever since, first as an enthusiastic member, then as its chairman and, currently, as chairman of its committee on development.

In the latter capacity I launched studies of investment opportunities in a number of Third World countries, one of which was Colombia. When that study was completed, three of us made an appointment with the president and, in my badly broken Spanish, I presented him with the findings. The president thanked us in the same language, after which he turned to me and said in flawless Harvard-accented English, "Mr. Bata, you're a Canadian, are you not?" I replied proudly that indeed I was. "In that case," he continued, "there is something I should like to show you." He led me to his desk and from a drawer produced a report on the dangers of foreign investment signed by Canada's minister of national revenue, Herb Gray. "Here you are submitting to me suggestions about how we should encourage foreign investment," he said, "and yet your government is proposing to restrict that kind of investment in your own country. Isn't that rather strange?"

I must admit I was embarrassed. I couldn't very well tell him that, in this respect, I disagreed emphatically with the Canadian government. While there was no doubt that Canada was at that time being overrun by American investment and that some temporary countermeasures might be justified, I considered the government's Foreign Investment Review Agency a monstrous aberration. A country with a population of twenty-five million, next door to a neighbor twice its size, isn't that attractive a market to begin with. By imposing all kinds of conditions and by taking ages to arrive at a decision, FIRA sent most investors of any size into the open arms of the United States. We got the occasional pizzeria or dry cleaning establishment, while large- and medium-sized enterprises located south of the border.

Eventually even the Trudeau administration admitted that the economy was taking a beating and, as an outspoken critic of FIRA, I was invited to Ottawa to discuss possible changes. I told the government officials that, on the basis of my experience, what they should do was change not only the legislation but the trademark. As any businessman knows, when you have a product that customers don't like, you don't just improve the product, you give it a new name. I don't know whether they made a note of my advice. But a few years later, when the Mulroney government came to power, I was pleased to see that one of its early decisions was to jettison FIRA and create Investment Canada in its place.

But while there were times when I disagreed with specific Canadian policies, I never experienced anything but the greatest courtesy and cooperation on the part of cabinet ministers. As for the public service, I can't speak highly enough of the assistance I have received from our diplomats and trade representatives. Time and again they have provided me with valuable background information, and they have worked tirelessly in support of my claim for compensation from the now-defunct Communist government of Czechoslovakia. The relationship, I am happy to say, hasn't been completely one-sided. I, too, have been able to assist some of our newly appointed representatives by acting as door opener to heads of state or cabinet ministers in Third World countries, where my contacts may at times have been better than theirs. On balance it has been and continues to be an exceptionally happy relationship.

The only time I had even a mild problem with Canada's bureaucracy was shortly after the Suez crisis, when I inadvertently ran afoul of protocol. I had paid a brief and, on the whole, fruitless visit to Egypt before flying on to Lebanon where we had a small but successful enterprise. To my surprise I was whisked from the Beirut airport in a government limousine to the palace for lunch with President Kamil Shamoon. He questioned me about events in Egypt and about conditions that might induce organizations such as ours to move their Middle Eastern headquarters to Lebanon, which was, at the time, a haven of peace, prosperity and religious tolerance. Apparently pleased with what I told him, he announced that, in appreciation of what we had done in generating employment in his country, he was appointing me an officer of Lebanon's Order of Cedar.

But when the Canadian ambassador heard about my award, he got terribly upset. "You can't accept a foreign order without permission from Her Majesty," he informed me, "and such permission is never granted." In that case, I suggested, perhaps I ought to go back to the palace and return the order. The mere thought made him blanch with horror: we both knew that, in a

Middle Eastern country, such a gesture would be interpreted as a deadly insult. Instead, he said, I was to contact upon my return to Canada the secretary of state and report to him the grave breach of protocol that had been committed.

I did as I was told and thereby kept the bureaucratic channels buzzing with activity for a number of years. Sometime later, when President Zia of Pakistan bestowed without previous warning a similar award on me, I knew enough to keep the information to myself. Not that I ever looked for that kind of award. The only decoration that really matters to me, which I wear with pride, is the Order of Canada.

In spite of my interest in national and international affairs I have refused, without the slightest hesitation, repeated invitations to run for Parliament. It is not that I am squeamish about offering myself up for election. In a sense I feel I have been running for office most of my life. I ran for office every time I walked through a factory and shook hundreds of hands, every time I met with union leaders, every time I visited our large metropolitan customers or the small shopkeepers who sold our shoes in remote villages. I ran for office whenever I tried to persuade some president or prime minister that I was a good guy and that I headed a constructive and ethical organization.

But businessmen, I believe, should stick to their own field of expertise, and politics isn't one of them. I can think of very few business people who have gone into politics and made a success of it; I can think of quite a few who have been a dismal failure. The way I see it, business people can and should serve the community by volunteering their services in business-related areas. That, at any rate, is what I have tried to do. I joined the board of the National Ballet of Canada not because I was a ballet fan, but because I believed that by using my business expertise on behalf of a talented company, I was helping an institution that was destined to play an important part in Canada's cultural life.

Similarly I was delighted, in the early 1960s, when I was invited to join the board of governors of Trent University. Situated in Peterborough, a city 135 kilometers northeast of Toronto, Trent is a small educational institution based on the British system of tutorial instruction. It was a concept that appealed to me, and I have enjoyed being associated with Trent ever since.

One reason why I wanted to be involved not only in fundraising, but in the management of cultural, health and educational organizations was the underlying philosophy of citizen participation. This type of shared responsibility between the public and private sectors is confined almost exclusively to Britain, Canada and the United States. In continental Europe, for instance, hospitals, universities and cultural institutions are controlled exclusively by municipal or state governments; and while privatization is beginning to creep in, its progress is typically slow. The time, effort and money that British and North American business people, academics and professionals spend in support of our system are, in my opinion, a small price to pay for the financial health and efficient management of these institutions.

Company boards and, specifically, boards of chartered banks, are another matter. Considering how often they meet and the amount of homework that is required, I reluctantly concluded that my hectic travel schedule wouldn't allow me to make a meaningful contribution. Rather than be a director in name only I turned down almost all such invitations that came my way. The only two exceptions were IBM and CP Air. In the case of IBM I joined because of my tremendous admiration for technological excellence, and because I hoped that my own experience in running a global organization might prove useful to management.

In the case of CP Air, I was seduced by my love of aviation and by the company's romantic history. An additional inducement was the parent company's plan to spin off CP Air into a separate public company, which would have involved the interesting exercise of floating a share issue. The OPEC crisis put an end to that plan.

Another invitation I did accept was to join the international advisory board formed by the Canadian Imperial Bank of Commerce. Unlike the board of directors, this body met only two or three times a year, which I felt I could handle, and I was intrigued with the prospect of discussing bank policy with advisory board members from Europe, Latin America and Hong Kong. But while I believe we made some excellent recommendations, I also confess that, in those days of plentiful petrodollars, we tended to be more adventurous than the bank's own management. Indeed had CIBC adopted some of our recommendations, its Third World debt would be a great deal worse than it has turned out to be.

Eventually the advisory board was sacrificed on the altar of economy, while my association with CP Air and IBM came to an end when I reached the statutory retirement age of seventy. But rather than leaving me underemployed, the end of these activities provided me with an opportunity to step up my involvement on the international scene and, particularly, to participate in the fight against the vendetta that was being waged against multinational companies.

Spearheaded by left-wing politicians and backed by news media on both sides of the Atlantic, that vendetta degenerated into something approaching a witch hunt following the Pinochet coup in Chile and the death of President Allende. Allegations that these events had been supported by IT&T led to the formation of a United Nations body called the Commission on Transnational Corporations whose mandate included the drafting of a code of conduct for transnationals — the term used by the United Nations to describe companies operating in more than one country. About the same time, the International Chamber of Commerce formed a Commission on Multinational Enterprises to which I was appointed and that I have served ever since as a committed member and, currently, as chairman.

Yet another institution, unique in United Nations history, was a newly established panel of fifteen "expert advisers" with five members each from business, labor and academe. As the nominee of the International Chamber of Commerce, I was elected to the panel in 1983. The timing was perfect. For one thing, I was about to retire as chief executive officer, which meant I would have more time to devote to United Nations activities. Also, the antibusiness atmosphere that had prevailed for a number of years in and outside the U.N. was giving way to a more openminded attitude, particularly on the part of developing countries. At least some of them were beginning to realize that private enterprise and a market economy might not be all bad.

That is not to say that the transnationals' record of behavior is pure. There is no denying that past mistakes have led to tragic consequences and that safeguards are required to make sure such mistakes won't be repeated. It is also unquestionably true that, in an effort to extract the maximum amount of money in the form of royalties, some companies had engaged in questionable practices. Yet it is also true that many of the alleged sins were committed at a time when the world was largely unaware of the importance of environmental issues. When Rachel Carson published her book *Silent Spring*, she was widely branded as a crank. If in those days companies made no attempt in Africa to repair the gaping sores left behind by gravel pits or strip mines, chances are they were doing exactly the same thing in Europe or North

America. While that didn't make it right, it wasn't considered nearly as reprehensible as it would be today. Fortunately, if belatedly, we have all become environmentalists.

The Expert Advisers made a determined attempt to help the U.N. Commission on Transnational Corporations develop the code of ethics that, by then, had been in the works for ten years. But the obstacles were formidable. For instance, some countries refused point-blank to incorporate in the code a clause to the effect that governments had to observe international law, or that victims of nationalization were entitled to compensation. Another major obstacle was the Soviet bloc's insistence that state-owned enterprises in "socialist" countries were *not* transnationals and therefore must not be subject to the code. In other words, Swiss Air was a transnational because it had some private shareholders, but Aeroflot was not; Barclay's Bank would be considered a transnational but Moscow Narodny Bank wouldn't.

At one point the Expert Advisers decided to draft a code of their own, so we hunkered down to a weekend session — fifteen representatives of business, labor and academe from the United States, Canada, Germany, Tanzania, the Philippines and a number of other countries with a total population of billions of people — and we came up with a consensus. It was a compromise solution, and the International Chamber of Commerce wasn't happy with all its clauses, but we all felt we could live with it. However, when we presented our proposal to the Commission, the Latin Americans said that the clause about abiding by international law was unacceptable and they vetoed it. The U.N. code hasn't materialized to this day, and perhaps it never will.

In spite of all the frustrations, I found the U.N. experience extremely interesting. Gaining an insight into the functions and philosophy of the organization and participating in one aspect of its work left me convinced that, despite its shortcomings, the U.N.

could conceivably become the basis of a future world government.

A particularly fascinating development was the gradual change of attitude on the part of representatives of the Soviet bloc. In 1985, during my first year on the panel of expert advisers, it was obvious that, as far as the Soviets and their friends were concerned, the transnationals were bad guys, with no redeeming features whatsoever. The following year I was amazed to hear one of the Soviet delegates criticize transnationals for not investing enough in developing countries. For the first time there was a hint that an investment by a transnational might conceivably be beneficial. Toward the end of my four-year tenure, everybody agreed that we had to find ways of stimulating foreign investment. In fact, I was asked to chair a meeting of Soviet officials and Western businessmen on ways to stimulate joint ventures in the Soviet Union — something that would have seemed inconceivable when I first arrived at the U.N.

Another change occurred at the social level. In my capacity of chairman of the ICC Commission on Multinational Enterprises, I invited some of the U.N. delegates once a year to a reception at my hotel. The first year no Soviet bloc people were included in the guest list. The second year the Soviets were invited but hardly any of them turned up. The third year most of them came, and in my final year several of them approached me and asked if they could bring along some of their friends.

In view of the changing atmosphere, the expert advisers tried, in addition to struggling with the code of conduct, to come up with ways of persuading OECD enterprises to invest in developing countries. By then I was the veteran panel member, so I was asked to be the chairman and my main draftsman was a Finnish trade union leader. He was tremendously helpful, as indeed was a British Communist who, when he wasn't at the U.N., operated out of the World Trade Union Center in Prague. We worked in perfect harmony, and while our recommendations didn't bear fruit at the time, they did stimulate the interest of many U.N. delegates. Some asked me whether foreign investment would start flowing into their countries once they enacted an acceptable code of ethics. Frankly I had to admit that it wasn't quite that simple.

There are many reasons why, in the past, Western enterprises were reluctant, sometimes overly reluctant to take a chance on investing in the Third World. One was the woefully mismanaged economy in many of these countries; another was the fragmented market, particularly in Africa, where it was virtually impossible to achieve any economies of scale. Finally there was the "once burnt twice shy" factor, the reluctance on the part of enterprises to invest in countries from which they had previously been kicked out, with little or no compensation.

Working with the World Bank, business people including myself have been trying for years to set up some kind of guarantee scheme whereby investors would be compensated in case of expropriation or nationalization. After years of negotiation the Multinational Investment Guarantee Association (MIGA) officially came into being in Berlin at the World Bank meeting in September 1988, where I had the honor of being a speaker. To my mind, the birth of MIGA represents a milestone in the history of international investment. Under its auspices investors, who are assessed a premium in keeping with the magnitude of the risk, will collect compensation in the event their enterprise is expropriated.

The World Bank has also been enormously helpful in stimulating investment in developing countries by way of the International Finance Corporation, the bank's private-sector financing arm. Our tanning and shoe manufacturing expansion in Bangladesh is one of several projects we have undertaken in partnership with this dynamic institution. When the IFC established a Business Advisory Board, I was delighted to accept their invitation to become a member.

My involvement in these international organizations has turned out to be an ideal project for a company chairman who wants to remain active in the business without treading on the toes of the new chief executive. Since Tom can't possibly visit every year all the places where we have operations, and since my international activities require me to travel as much as ever, it is only logical that I should combine my attendance at conferences or committee meetings in distant parts of the world with visits to local Bata enterprises. This takes some of the load off Tom and gives me a great deal of pleasure.

Another way in which I feel I can continue contributing to the Bata organization is by maintaining my contacts with heads of state and other officials whom I have known for many years, and who may mistake my gray hair for a sign of wisdom. Seldom, however, do Tom and I call together on a minister or president. It is absolutely essential that he be seen as the head of the organization, not as my junior partner.

At home my main job, as I see it, is to do whatever I can to help Tom succeed, and that means making it perfectly clear that there is only one boss. For a year or so after he took over, I used to take his place at daily briefing sessions whenever he was out of town. Now I don't do that anymore, and I am careful about letting other executives know what I think they should or should not be doing. If occasionally I overstep the mark, I am sure to hear about it. But Tom and I do get together frequently, when both of us are in town, to review recent developments and discuss any suggestions I may have. Sometimes when I have a brain wave at night, I put it down on paper and make sure he gets it the following day. Sometimes he agrees with me and other times he doesn't, and occasionally we argue. But we have yet to have what I would call a flaming row.

People say Tom's management style is different, more analytical than mine. Personally I hope it is because, after being around for forty years, I am sure that change is overdue. On the other hand, I am delighted to see that he carries on the organization's tradition of getting to know the employees and letting them know he cares. Recently when we were visiting a Montreal shopping center, we were about to leave when he insisted on going back and saying goodbye to all the staff in our store. To me this gesture, this wish to make people feel appreciated, was a tangible sign that he is determined to perpetuate the Bata culture that was created by my father and that, I believe, has remained the foundation of our organization to this day.

It is a culture that is founded, above all, on service — a genuine concern for the well-being of our staff, our customers and the communities in which we operate. If many of our employees still think of themselves as members of a vast fraternity rather than an impersonal corporation, it is because they are proud of belonging to an organization that not only cares about people but believes in their creativity, their ability to overcome all obstacles. Time and again they have justified this faith.

All this was part of my inheritance, something to be cherished and nurtured. Yet I don't mind admitting that I look back with pride on the fact that I have succeeded in building, out of the bits and pieces of the enterprise that survived the war, a new, successful organization that has made an important contribution to the development of Third World countries. Not only have we provided jobs and a decent standard of living for thousands of our employees, but long before it became fashionable we opened up opportunities for education and advancement to people of all races and colors; we introduced them to modern technology and previously unknown standards of quality workmanship and we helped many of them establish businesses of their own. Above all else, this is the accomplishment I cherish.

To the extent I have been successful, I am happy to share the credit with dozens of dedicated colleagues. They are the people who backed me in good times and bad, who shared my vision and who spared no effort to translate that vision into reality. Throughout the desperately difficult postwar period, when many of our enterprises were short of everything including money, the word *impossible* wasn't part of our managers' vocabulary. No matter how insurmountable some obstacles seemed, they found ways to surmount them.

Another group of people to whom I am deeply indebted are our outside directors. More than once their expertise and their willingness to tell me the truth, pleasant or otherwise, have helped me make difficult decisions. On at least one occasion one of them also gave me a gentle lesson in humility. I had just come back from a tour of overseas factories, each of which had treated me to a reception fit for a king. When you are a young man in your thirties, that sort of thing is apt to go to your head. But Wilf Parry, our corporate counsel at the time and a member of our board of directors, was quick to bring me down to earth. "Tom," he said when he heard me describing the festivities staged in my honor, "you're beginning to sound like one of those Eastern potentates." He had a good point, and I have never forgotten it.

Last but by no means least, I have been fortunate enough to enjoy the unstinting support of my family. When Sonja and I were engaged to be married, Dominik Cipera, our general manager who had recently escaped from Czechoslovakia, warned her that I was married already, that the enterprise was and would always be my first love. In a sense, I suppose that is true. Yet during the forty-four years of our marriage I have never ceased to be grateful to her and, later, to our children for a relationship that combines affection, mutual respect and intellectual stimulation.

What about the future? The emergence of a unified Europe, the worldwide efforts to accomplish free trade and, above all, the triumph of democracy over Communist regimes in Central and Eastern Europe all signal the dawn of a new, fascinating era. At age seventy-five, some of my contemporaries may be content to sit in rocking chairs, watching all the excitement around them; personally, I have every intention of being part of it.

INDEX